THE SECOND CITY

THE SECOND CITY

A Backstage History
of Comedy's Hottest Troupe

Donna McCrohan

A Perigee Book

This book is dedicated to
anniversaries celebrated on 16 December—
The Boston Tea Party; Rasputin's murder;
the destruction of Wall Street by fire;
the eruption of Mt. Vesuvius;
the births of Ludwig van Beethoven, Jane Austen,
Margaret Mead, Noel Coward,
The Second City,
and my dad.

Perigee Books
are published by
The Putnam Publishing Group
200 Madison Avenue
New York, NY 10016

Library of Congress Cataloging-in-Publication Data

McCrohan, Donna.
The Second City.

1. Second City (Theater company)—History.
2. Comedians—United States. 3. Improvisation
(Acting) I. Title.
PN2277.C42S45   1987   792'.09773'11   86-30512
ISBN 0-399-51339-6

Book design by The Sarabande Press
Printed in the United States of America
1 2 3 4 5 6 7 8 9 10

Acknowledgments

Above all, very special thanks to Andrew Alexander, president and executive producer of Second City International; and to Joyce Sloane, Sally Cochrane, and Bernie Sahlins.

Special thanks, too, to Rick Alexander, Bill Alton, Dana Andersen, Alan Arkin, Ed Asner, Bob Bainborough, J. J. Barry, Shelley Berman, Eric Boardman, Roger Bowen, Peter Boyle, Jack Burns, Hamilton Camp, Dan Castellaneta, Del Close, Lenette Collias, Barbara Dana, Severn Darden, Don DePollo, Bob Derkach, Paul Dooley, Robin Duke, Andrew Duncan, Murphy Dunne, Ann Elder, James Fay, Jim Fisher, Joe Flaherty, Miriam Flynn, Josephine Raciti Forsberg, Alexander and Howard Frank, Jennifer Girard, Arlene Golonka, Ben Gordon, Laura Green, Rick Hall, Valerie Harper, Buck Henry, Burt Heyman, Sandra Holt, Bonnie Hunt, Tino Insana, Steven Kampmann, Linda Kash, Fred Kaz, Maureen Kelly, Richard Kind, Robert Klein, Eugene Levy, Richard Libertini, Mary Helen McMahon, David Mamet, Andrea Martin, Anne Meara, Ira Miller, Jan Morgan, Harry Murphy, Mike Myers, Paul Natkin, Sheldon Patinkin, Bruce Pirrie, Will Porter, David Rasche, Harold Ramis, Joan Rivers, Rich Rosen, Paul Sand, Avery Schreiber, Omar Shapli, David Shepherd, Martin Short, Paul Sills, Cheryl Sloane, Wendy Slutsky, Lauren Spencer, Viola Spolin, Jim Staahl, David Steinberg, Jerry Stiller, Deborah Theaker, Betty Thomas, Dave Thomas, Robert Townsend, George Wendt, Hugh Wesley, Patrick Whitley, Fred Willard, Mark Wilson, and Sam Woodruff.

Finally, my sincere appreciation to Roger Scholl, my editor, and Chris Pepe, his assistant, for their tireless energies above and beyond the call of duty.

CONTENTS

Cast reunion at the twenty-fifth anniversary celebration. (Photo courtesy of Paul Natkin/Photo Reserve, Inc.)

Introduction: "The Oldest Brat Pack"

"By now, virtually anyone who likes to laugh knows about Chicago's Second City, the comedy troupe that primed such humor hotshots as Dan Aykroyd, John Belushi, Bill Murray and Gilda Radner before they were 'discovered' by 'Saturday Night Live.' "

So *Newsweek* reported several years ago. (Actually, Aykroyd and Radner are from Toronto's branch of Second City.) Over its twenty-five-plus–year history, a combined total of nearly three hundred different Second City players from resident and touring companies has been turned loose on society, and we have only begun to reel from the impact.

When you go to Second City, you expect to laugh. Yet its members resist being labeled joke-tellers. They consider themselves observers. The laughter they're after is the laughter of recognition. Recognition, with a jigger of wry. Among the notions they've offered are:

- The increasing popularity of postmarital sex;
- The Dyslexic Theatre's production of *Annie Get Your Nug;*
- An airline reservations clerk booking a seat: "Smoking or no smoking? Movie or no movie? Are you a pragmatist, idealist, or humanist? Are you a tit man or an ass man?"

The Second City has stood at the vanguard of intelligent humor throughout a history that spans over a quarter of a century. It has featured the brightest talents and latest developments in comedy, beginning with its earliest days when a handful of inspired players transformed "Golden Age" funny into early "New Wave." Thanks to them, you suddenly couldn't sit on a kitchen stool without feeling you had to do a monologue. The germ of Second City gave rise to The Premise, The Committee, The Third Ear, Third City, the Pitschel Players, the Pentagon Players, the Ace Trucking Company, the Graduates, and the entire tradition of comedy clubs.

Mike Nichols, Elaine May, Shelley Berman, and Barbara Harris paved the way for Second City. Dan Aykroyd, Alan Arkin, Jim and John Belushi, Jack Burns and Avery Schreiber, John Candy, Robin Duke, Valerie Harper, Eugene Levy, Shelley Long, Andrea Martin, Bill Murray and Brian Doyle-Murray, Catherine O'Hara, Gilda Radner, Harold Ramis, David Rasche, Paul Sand, Martin Short, Dave Thomas, Betty Thomas, and George Wendt all brought down the house there. David Mamet spruced it up, as a busboy. Robert Klein and David Steinberg honed their skills at Second City—sometimes on each other. Joan Rivers got her first taste of celebrity there—often from the depths of disenchantment. Robin Williams has become a sort of honorary member. The list goes on. And on.

Now, as the *Chicago Tribune* observed, "There are few things we find funny that can't be traced back to some Second City source." Second City alumni are everywhere—frequently in tandem and even en masse—writing, directing, producing, and starring in the top TV shows, blockbuster movies, Broadway plays, nightclub acts, and award-winning commercials.

On one television show alone—*Saturday Night Live*—a succession of Second City players was seen by as many as twenty-five million people in a night. At one time, Second City graduates John Belushi and Dan Aykroyd were on the number one TV show (*SNL*) and had the number one record, *Briefcase Full of Blues* (which sold over two million copies and went double platinum), while Belushi simultaneously starred in the number one movie, *Animal House*. A recent videotape, *The Best of John Belushi*, is one of the most successful original-programming video products in the history of that industry.

Animal House (1978), cowritten by Harold Ramis, grossed eighty-seven million dollars by the end of its first year. At the time, it was the biggest-grossing comedy ever, inciting a nationwide frenzy of toga parties, inspiring all three major networks to produce TV ripoffs, and ushering in a new wave of youth comedies that continues to generate box-office magic.

In the wake of *Animal House*, the comedy *Meatballs*, cowritten by Harold

Dan Aykroyd (center) and Bill Murray (right) with producer-director Ivan Reitman (left) in Ghostbusters, *the top-grossing comedy of all time. (Photo copyright 1984 Columbia Industries, Inc.)*

Ramis, Brian Doyle-Murray, and Ivan Reitman (coproducer of *Animal House* and a school chum of some of the Toronto Second City crowd), starred Bill Murray and became the surprise hit of 1979.

    Ghostbusters (1984)—the top-grossing movie of all time—was cowritten by Harold Ramis and Dan Aykroyd, and starred Dan Aykroyd, Harold Ramis, and Bill Murray (in the role originally intended for John Belushi, who died while the script was being written). *SCTV* graduate Rick Moranis played a strong supporting role. In its first six months alone, *Ghostbusters* grossed $202,000,000.

    Bill Murray, who in addition to *Meatballs* and *Ghostbusters* played Dustin Hoffman's roommate in *Tootsie* (without screen credit, in a part written anonymously by Elaine May), was voted one of *People* magazine's "Twenty-five Most Intriguing People of 1984" and was named the number one male star by U. S. theater owners.

    In the 1986 hit *Nothing in Common*, half of the cast then appearing on Second City's Chicago stage portrayed the ad agency's creative staff, and won sweeping praise.

Nor is Second City's film influence a recent phenomenon. Elaine May has been writing major (fifteen million dollar) scripts in Hollywood for years, often pseudonymously. Mike Nichols has directed such classics as *Who's Afraid of Virginia Wolf* (1966), *The Graduate* (1967—which secured his Academy Award for best director), *Catch-22* (1970—with Second City alumni Alan Arkin, Richard Libertini, and John Brent), and *Carnal Knowledge* (1971). Alan Arkin (*The Russians Are Coming, the Russians Are Coming, The Heart Is a Lonely Hunter, Catch-22, The In-Laws*) has twice been nominated for the Oscar, while *The Russians Are Coming* . . . enjoyed the unique honor of being favorably cited by both the *Congressional Record* and *Pravda*.

On the Broadway stage, *An Evening With Mike Nichols and Elaine May* (1960) made theatrical history, and was soon followed by Mike Nichols's directorial triumphs with *Luv, Barefoot in the Park, The Odd Couple, Lunch Hour* (with Gilda Radner and David Rasche in the cast), *Gilda Radner—Live From New York*, and *The Real Thing*. To date, Nichols holds no fewer than six Tony Awards. Alan Arkin, called by Nichols "the best actor in America," won the 1963 Tony Award for best dramatic actor, the Theatre World Award, and the *Variety* New York Drama Critics Poll for his Broadway appearance in *Enter Laughing*, before going on to direct *Eh?, Little Murders, The White House Murder Case*, and the original Broadway production of *The Sunshine Boys*.

Second City's Barbara Harris won the 1967 Tony Award as best female star of a musical play for her role in *The Apple Tree* (directed by Mike Nichols, with Robert Klein in the supporting cast). In 1966, the editors of *Cue* magazine declared her Entertainer of the Year.

Playwright David Mamet, former Second City busboy, won the 1984 Pulitzer Prize for his *Glengarry Glen Ross*.

On television, Second City graduate Valerie Harper (*The Mary Tyler Moore Show, Rhoda, Valerie*) has won four Emmys for acting. The actor who has won the most Emmys (seven) is Second City affiliate Ed Asner (*The Mary Tyler Moore Show, Lou Grant*). Second City's multi-Emmy winning Alan Alda (*M*A*S*H*), has been one of TV's top-paid writer/director/actors. He was voted best all-time actor in the 1985 *People* magazine poll.

Second City faces have consistently pervaded TV's hottest shows—Betty Thomas on *Hill Street Blues*, David Rasche on *Sledge Hammer* (among its writers are Second City alumni Mert Rich, Tino Insana, Jim Fisher, and Jim Staahl, with Ann Ryerson starring in a recent episode), Linda Lavin on *Alice*, Shelley Long and George Wendt on *Cheers*, Richard Libertini on *Taxi*, Ann

Counterclockwise from top: David Rasche in the title role of ABC's comedy satire Sledge Hammer *(copyright 1986 Capitol Cities/ABC, Inc.); Betty Thomas as Officer Lucille Bates on NBC's* Hill Street Blues *(National Broadcasting Co., Inc.); Shelley Long and Derek McGrath, seated, with Ted Danson, in NBC's* Cheers *(National Broadcasting Co., Inc.)*

Elder on *Laugh-In*, Derek McGrath on *Dallas*, Andrea Martin on *Kate & Allie*, Jim Staahl on *Mork & Mindy*, Steve Kampmann on *Newhart*, Bob Dishy, Robert Klein, and Avery Schreiber on *The Twilight Zone*, and Joan Rivers on *The Tonight Show*. Some Second City grads have headlined their own shows—Joan Rivers on *The Late Show Starring Joan Rivers*, Jack Burns and Avery Schreiber on *The Burns and Schreiber Comedy Hour*, Robert Klein on *Robert Klein Time* and *Comedy Tonight* (which featured fellow Second City players Peter Boyle, Macintyre Dixon, Judy Graubart, and Lynne Lipton), David Steinberg on *The Music Scene* and *The David Steinberg Show*, and the dozen-plus veterans of the Second City stage who wrote and performed, often simultaneously, on *SCTV* (*Second City TV*).

Second City talents are also found behind the scenes in prominent positions—Theodore J. Flicker (writer/director on *The Dick Van Dyke Show*, *The Andy Griffith Show*, co-creator of *Barney Miller*), Eugenie Ross-Leming (writer of *Mary Hartman, Mary Hartman*), Ann Elder (writing for *The Carol Burnett Show*, *Mama's Family*, Lily Tomlin's specials), Valri Bromfield (creative consultant of *Head of the Class*), Jack Burns (*Fridays, The Muppet Show*), Steve Kampmann and Peter Torokvei (writing for *WKRP in Cincinnati*, of which Kampmann later became producer), and Brandon Tartikoff (president, NBC Entertainment), who was active in the Second City workshop program under Jo Raciti Forsberg.

Second City players have dazzled the nightclub and campus circuits everywhere—from the days of Mike Nichols and Elaine May, whose *Improvisations With Music* became the first bestselling spoken comedy record. From that tradition have come Jerry Stiller and Anne Meara, Jack Burns and Avery Schreiber, Shelley Berman, Robert Klein, David Steinberg, Joan Rivers, John Monteith and Suzanne Rand. Some Second City players have provided cartoon voices—John Belushi and Bill Murray (*Shame of the Jungle*, a parody of Tarzan), Gilda Radner (*Witch's Night Out*), Hamilton Camp (*The Smurfs*). *Ghostbusters* inspired its own cartoon series. In addition, Second City players are omnipresent writing, directing, and performing in, a staggering number of award-winning commercials. Martin Short, whose Ed Grimley character began on the Second City stage, was offered a million dollars to play him in a soft drink commercial (he turned it down).

Robert Klein—a participant in the HBO look at *Humor and the Presidency*—was earlier offered a teaching fellowship in stand-up political satire by the dean of the School of Drama at Yale University (he turned it down).

On an earthier note, Second City player John Candy was named one of the Ten Sexiest Men by *Playgirl* magazine in 1985. . . .

Each Second City company consists of a bunch of smart young men and women in their twenties, hanging around with each other to learn the ropes of improvisation and ensemble acting. "Each few years," says Avery Schreiber, "brings a new brat pack. We of Second City are the oldest brat pack." The faces change while the process of infusion goes on. Second City regularly replenishes itself, while turning out a constant stream of talent from its ongoing pool. As more experienced players depart the troupe for greener pastures, usually after three or four years (just like college), new talents replace them. Accordingly, competition is not unknown within the ranks of Second City. Neither is creative angst. Neither are frustration and rage. Workaholism is common. Insane momentum is the norm. Yet close friendships consistently emerge, and one's days with Second City—before the agents and later success, when the only tension was the furor to create—are regularly remembered as the happiest in a player's life.

What follows is not a linear history. It's a matter of spirals, not straight lines. Textbooks are linear. Ideas ricochet. People work with people, then with other people, go in different directions, only to have their paths cross again. In an atomic reaction, each bounding particle slams into another one; each has an impact on the other; each goes off impacting and being impacted upon. There's no tracing the course of each particle, only the aggregate effect. That's what the Second City is. An atomic reaction.

Today, performers come to Second City with precisely this expectation. The atomic reaction. The pipeline. The Second City connection. Second City has a track record. They come to get on the track.

But in the beginning, Second City meant a paying job, an opportunity to mouth off, and a place to drink coffee with friends. . . .

1
Beginnings:
A Theater of Us

The scene: Chicago in the fifties. The city that gave us Al Capone and Mrs. O'Leary's cow, meat packing moguls Armour and Swift, a superior kind of silent movie and the first great movie palaces, Hugh Hefner and Kukla, Fran and Ollie.

The fifties: When the Depression had finally faded into memory, and World War II was a closed chapter in history books. People were buying houses for the first time, in rural areas that were about to become the suburbs. They purchased cars, and drove them to shopping centers. They welcomed TV as the newest member of the family. They were giving birth to postwar babies, and starting savings plans that would send those babies to college, where hardships would be a thing of the past. Members of the counterculture were known as beatniks, for whom caffeine was the drug of choice. New technology was embraced as a pal: from radium dials in watches to x-ray machines in shoestores to ensure that Junior's shoes fit. . . .

In Chicago in the fifties, the University of Chicago, a unique and uniquely bohemian institution of higher learning, held intellectual prominence. Class attendance wasn't mandatory but performing brilliantly on final exams was. Mathematicians mingled with Thomist Marxists. Students laughed quietly to themselves about Rabelais and Kant. The typical student was an idea junkie, but one not too sure about the implications of technology, which, rumor had it, gave people numbers in place of their names.

Setting a pattern that would later become a Second City hallmark, a group of University of Chicago students and sojourners found in each other much more than friends and colleagues. They found soul mates. Drawn together by an affinity for theater on a campus that had no formal drama department, future Fulbright scholars Paul Sills and David Shepherd met Mike Nichols, Ed Asner, Eugene Troobnick, Zohra Lambert, Bill Alton, Andrew Duncan, Barbara Harris, Elaine May, Anthony Holland, Sheldon Patinkin, Bernie Sahlins, and others. "I think when we started," says Sahlins, "the actors were children of the Depression. There was a lot of intellectualization going on in the Depression. There was not much else to do. I know I grew up thinking that if you didn't play the violin or write, you were guilty."

Their shared passion gave them not just something to talk about, but an actual common cause. Chicago's theater at the time centered primarily around traveling companies of New York shows, a few amateur theatricals, and some college repertory offerings. At the Univesity of Chicago was the University Theatre, along with a less formal group called "Tonight at 8:30."

A tall, blond, blue-eyed lad named Mike Nichols fell in with the group. Nichols (born Michael Igor Peschowsky) was the son of a Russian-Jewish physician, Dr. Paul Peschowsky. His grandmother, Hedwig Lachmann, wrote the German libretto of the Richard Strauss opera *Salome.* His grandfather, Gustav Landauer, had been head of the German Social Democratic party and one of the first victims of Nazi anti-Semitism. Dr. Peschowsky fled Germany, set up a medical practice in New York, and took the name Nichols.

Nichols was a premed student before turning to acting and, later, directing. His debut as a director was Yeats's *Purgatory,* starring Ed Asner. It was presented by "Tonight at 8:30" as a curtain-raiser to *Androcles and the Lion,* in which Nichols played Caesar. The piece, only eight minutes long, was performed in the corner of a room. Among those who saw it was Paul Sills, who experienced the "shock of recognition" at Nichols's directorial finesse.

Paul Sills had a special affinity for the theater through his mother, Viola Spolin. "When I was a girl," says Spolin, "we didn't have television or radio. We read a lot, and we played games. All the families were large, there was no traffic on the streets, so we were always playing. Of course, games are dramatic in structure. And we had our own theater. We charged an admission of ten pins or a penny." As she grew older, Viola Spolin continued to play—charades, for instance—introducing her son to spontaneous drama as a way of life. For them, "Give me a Where, a Who, and a What" was a source of family fun long before it became a cornerstone of The Second City improvisational approach.

When Spolin took a position as supervisor of drama projects for the WPA, she found herself working with neighborhood groups, nonactors, often immigrants who didn't speak the language. They were self-conscious and inhibited on stage—hesitant in responding to each other and "the moment." Realizing from her own experience that children at play are spontaneous, creative, and completely immersed in the moment, Viola Spolin began experimenting with improvisational games. These games bypassed the intellect, releasing the players' spontaneous emotions through play. The games worked, have been refined over the years, and today are at the core of the entire improvisational theater movement. Inseparable from the games has been, and is, Paul Sills, who had, says Viola, a "vision of where it could go." Sills—attractive, charismatic, enigmatic—remains their foremost spokesman to this day.

Though he went to the University of Chicago without any intention of breaking into the theater, soon he was directing a massive body of works on

Omar Shapli (left) and David Shepherd (right) set the stage for a revolutionary new form of theater. (Photo courtesy of David Shepherd)

campus and, inevitably, off. The latter took some doing, but the time was very right.

The time proved right, too, for David Shepherd, who had come to Chicago with a Harvard B.A., a Columbia M.A. in history of the theater, and a devout belief in theater for the masses. He had left the East Coast for the U of C's fertile ground because "things could grow there." Once in Chicago, says Shepherd, "I became aware of the energy of 'Tonight at 8:30.' I decided to work with them, make my money available to them, and do whatever they wanted me to do. I figured that once I had demonstrated to them that I could be of use, then I could ask them to do my popular theater, which is what happened."

David Shepherd and Paul Sills joined forces with Eugene Troobnick, a writer as well as a theater enthusiast, and a staunch supporter of "Tonight at 8:30." The three took over and rebuilt a second-floor Chinese restaurant, launching Playwrights Theatre Club, a professional repertory company. Beginning with Bertolt Brecht's *The Caucasian Chalk Circle* in 1953—followed by the Hindu *Shakuntala,* Jean-Paul Sartre's *Dirty Hands* (translated as *Red Gloves* to emphasize its Communist theme), and twenty-one more plays over the next two years—they achieved an astounding output. Not every offering was a masterpiece. But to people starved for theater, they filled a genuine need.

Omar Shapli—initially drawn to the University of Chicago by its Egyptology program—soon became a major figure on the Playwrights scene. Prior to that, he'd been active with "Tonight at 8:30." As Shapli recalls, "I presented myself to them one day announcing that I wanted to direct George Bernard Shaw's *Man of Destiny.* I wanted someone who looked like Napoleon for the lead, because that was the only way I knew how to cast people." Shapli was put in touch with a young man—a beefy former all-city tackle in high school—who worked the swing shift at the Ford assembly plant. The auto worker, already a fairly experienced actor, was Ed Asner. On seeing him, Shapli instantly proclaimed, "That man is Napoleon!" The resulting production, Shapli continues, "was widely praised, far beyond any contributions of mine as a director. I don't claim to have introduced Ed Asner to the mysteries of the art. In a way, he introduced me into the mysteries of the art, because he was marvelous."

Of his own involvement in both "Tonight at 8:30" and Playwrights Theatre Club, Ed Asner reflects, "I wanted to be an adventurer, to lay a pipeline in South America, but I didn't have the guts. And I never got a lead as to how you worked in South America, but I heard you're supposed to bring your own gun, to cut off the blow-dart natives. I thought that sounded very intriguing. In those days, I was looking forward to what I referred to as safe adventure. Amazingly, I found it—in the theater.

"The world was in ferment. Ferment was taking place everywhere. It was taking place off-Broadway, as opposed to stodgy old Broadway. We were merely the Chicago version of off-Broadway. The revolution was going on in New York, with us in Chicago, in England in a different way.

Ed Asner in a Playwrights production. (Photo courtesy of The Second City)

John Osborne's play, *Look Back in Anger,* was a breakthrough in 1956. The move was away from classical situations and drawing rooms. The masses were being heard from. There was a tremendous energy."

Performing with Playwrights represented, for Asner, an adventure of high energy and high ideals, complete with its own risks. The audience hailed from the university, everyone a critic. Of this species of blow-dart native, Asner recalls, "Even when I'd get good mentions in the two daily newspapers that monitored us, the damned campus paper, the *Maroon,* would come out and they'd pan me. It was tough, but the anger kept us going. 'We'll show them. We'll show them.' "

He played Thomas à Becket in T. S. Eliot's *Murder in the Cathedral.* University of Chicago denizen Elaine May was among those in the supporting cast. For another Playwrights effort, *Miss Julie,* future Second City Member Zohra Lampert played the manhating title role. Elaine May directed. An actor was flow in from New York to play Jean, but May and Lampert preferred Ed Asner. "Very flatteringly," he remembers, "they fought for me. I got the

Elaine May and Mark Gordon at The Compass. (Photo courtesy of David Shepherd)

part, and I did my damnedest to slim down as much as I could, failing as always. I played Jean. A chubby Jean. The play was a disaster. I don't know why in terms of Zohra and Elaine, but in my case, maybe I didn't believe in it. I think we were dedicated to life. It's a play of the dead."

Elaine May, daughter of Yiddish actor Jack Berlin, came as no stranger to the stage. As a child, she'd toured with several shows, including one drama in which she appeared as a boy named Bennie. She gave up the role on reaching eleven because: "I had developed breasts, and our people do not believe in breast binding." She left school at fourteen. "I really didn't like it. The truancy people came around and threatened to take me to court, but I called their bluff. I sat around the house reading mostly fairy tales and mythology." She re-entered academic turf when it occurred to her that she might enjoy taking classes at the University of Chicago. She never officially enrolled, but she would sit in on sessions and join—sometimes dominate—discussions. On a campus distinguished by its concentrated "gray matter," she was widely considered to be exceptionally bright. Though she was pretty—slender, with black hair and brown eyes—her most noticeable feature was her quick, cutting wit. She'd come by way of the West Coast, as had another recent arrival, a friend of Paul Sills's, Alex Horn. Asner's reaction was, "What is this? Are we going to become a California clique?"

In the course of people meeting people, it was inevitable that Elaine May and Mike Nichols should collide because, recalls Nichols, "It was said that she and I had the cruelest tongues on campus." Their first meeting was less than propitious. He was appearing in a "Tonight at 8:30" production of *Miss Julie*. May, in the audience, glared and thought it was garbage. Her scorn for the effort colored her view of him. But one night at the train station, waiting to go home, they fell into an improvised secret agent dialogue with each other. Fast minds, fast mouths, and half-fast public transportation paved the way to rapport. At least it was a beginning, and a taste of what was ahead.

Tom O'Horgan joined Playwrights as a harpist and composer, showing some of the promise that led to his later nightclub routine—an improvisational humor act on the harp. In the next decade, he would go on to stun Broadway as the director of *Lenny, Jesus Christ Superstar* and *Hair*.

In 1954, Bernard Sahlins—part hobbit, part Dutch uncle, part urbane tale-spinning shmoozer—became a co-producer of Playwrights. He, too, was a University of Chicago graduate. "I owned my own tape recorder manufacturing business while helping to produce the first Playwrights Theatre Club. The talent was terrific. It was marvelous theater. . . .

"That's when Paul Sills and I and David Shepherd and many of the people who would be in the first Second City company and in the Compass Players really started to work together. All of the ideas that resulted in Second City were inseminated at that time."

The same year, Playwrights moved to larger quarters. Then, in 1955, the fire department slapped them with a laundry list of violations (which may have had more to do with politics than fire hazards). Lacking funds for major renovations, Playwrights Theatre Club was forced to close.

Following Playwrights's demise, David Shepherd returned in earnest to dreaming his fondest dream—a theater of immediacy and palpable engagement. Playwrights, in his eyes, fell short of the mark, serving perhaps not so much plain people, but more its own pretensions. What he wanted was a reborn commedia dell'arte—a theater of the people that, like it's sixteenth-century predecessor, would draw on common themes, farcical content, and improvised dialogue. With University of Chicago law student Roger Bowen (a reviewer for the *Maroon*), he mounted a few experiments for "Tonight at

8:30." The scenarios of Shepherd and Bowen intrigued Paul Sills and Viola Spolin, and led to what would become Second City's immediate forerunner, The Compass Players.

Andrew Duncan, a key witness to the proceedings and about to be a founding member of both The Compass and The Second City, was at the University of Chicago "when the whole improv thing" started.

"I saw a notice in the paper about a theater and I went and auditioned. It was for *The Wild Duck*. I got the part, Hjalmar Ekdal. And while I was doing it, Paul Sills came. He always went to the theater. And he came back after the show, just happened to be walking by me. I didn't know who he was, but he said, 'I'm going to have a workshop. Would you like to drop in on it?' And he explained what he was doing. So I went to this workshop and there was an enormous number of people there, at least sixty. Out of that they chose the group."

Ed Asner, while admiring the process, chose not to take the leap: "I was interested, but distrusted myself and it. Particularly with foreign-born parents, I'd say that my quest for satisfying them as well as the world tilted more toward establishment models. I felt I was on tricky enough ground being an actor without going off to have fun improvising. My guilt rose too high for that."

In 1955, professional improvisational theatre, as we know it today, was born. The Compass Players nurtured their improvisational talents in workshops conducted by Paul Sills and Viola Spolin. The Compass Players had no prepared scripts, only brief scenarios (each a page or less) outlining general action. The scenarios dealt with first dates, parents and offspring, folks on the job. Dialogue was improvised. The group hired a piano player when they could afford one—which was intermittently. The stage was bare, except for a few chairs—bare of objects, but full of potential, of space, with which the improvisational actor can pantomime anything until it all but materializes: a phone, a Fuller brush, a Greek vase, an automobile, a camel. The players focused on acting, not comedy. These were witty, fun-loving people, who had nothing against humor but considerable contempt for onstage "jokes." Stand-up comedy in this context was anathema. Humor would arise from the way characters related to one another in a performance, from the moment, from the improv. Humor was permissible, even desirable, but never the ultimate goal.

As a job, being a Compass Player had its drawbacks, such as a low paycheck, or no paycheck whatsoever. It is a lucky trailblazer who can also pay the rent. "To those of us who founded The Compass Players and the Second City Theatre," says Roger Bowen, "improvisation was a medium of expression. The thought of what it might do for our 'careers' was extremely remote. We were outsiders, misfits, pioneers."

The house was small—a storefront attached to a bar not owned by The Compass. The atmosphere evoked the cabaret scene of Germany between the wars. Compass quickly became a student hangout for the University of Chicago crowd. For the price of a beer, patrons could sit through a show, or two, in a night. A beer cost about sixty cents. Food was served at the bar and by performers on their breaks. If the audience eats and drinks, it was reasoned, can merry be far behind?

"The idea of Compass and later Second City," says Andrew Duncan, "was a theater of *us*. We wouldn't be foreigners—Ibsen or Chekhov or whatever—and we'd be in a theater that was concerned with the community. The issues of the community, the politics, the social issues."

"My notion in The Compass," adds David Shepherd, "was that the stage was a mirror. So much so that it was almost called 'The Mirror.' I wanted to present on the stage a dramatization of whatever the audience was reading, present it not as a burlesque but as an analysis. I was striving for constant response to the topic of the day, whatever that topic might be."

To the extent possible, it was not "we the actors, them the audience," but "we together, mutually involved." When The Compass staged *How to Catch a Tax Evader,* a real lawyer filled the lawyer role. And Monday night—usually a night off in the world of the theater—was designated as amateur night at The Compass. On these nights, audience members took to the stage, as actors, folksingers, whatever. Some Mondays were understandably better than others.

In its first ten weeks Compass created ten separate two-hour shows. Each opened in front of the audience. No previews. Cold. Toward the end of each evening, to develop a fresh source for their improvisations, the cast attempted a radical departure from formal theatre. They turned the audience, in a sense, into playwrights, by inviting suggestions for brief sketches which members of the cast then performed. Cold.

"It soon became apparent," concedes Andrew Duncan, "that actors are limited. That is, if you're short-circuiting writers by using actors who write in their heads while on stage, that's fine. You can look at it from a certain point of view and say they were trying to save money, or they didn't have the people to write for this theater. Let's train actors to be writers. Whatever.

Some people could do it, and some couldn't, more or less. But it soon became apparent that *anybody* would dry up. You just can't keep going. So the scenario form was started as a way to get around that. Then *that* dried up. So a new source became the audience, which is another aspect of involving the community. The original was very crude. We'd come out and say, 'What's on your minds?' "

Elaine May, another of the original Compass members, directed, improvised, and wrote scenarios for the group. Many reflected her concern with feminist issues that later became prominent. For example, in *Georgina's First Date*, a dumpy high school girl was pressured to become popular at all costs.

Mike Nichols, who had briefly moved to New York, studied acting with Lee Strasberg, and worked at Howard Johnson's ("I was fired when somebody asked me the ice cream flavor of the week and I said chicken"), had returned to Chicago, where he teamed up with Elaine May in The Compass. He remained with The Compass for the better part of three years, though tearing himself away for occasional stints on a local FM station and a radio soap opera in Philadelphia. At The Compass, May improvised gamely with several different actors, while Nichols was comfortable improvising only with her.

David Shepherd attributes the flawless chemistry between them at least in part to their basic difference as performers: "Elaine was very big on people scenes. Mike went for more pointed scenes. In working with Elaine May, his function was to sharpen her wit, and her function was to explore. The reason they were so great together is the constant tension between her desire to explore and his desire to sharpen." Together, the two created scenes of deliciously observant humor, drawn from the convolutions that arise when people are forced to relate to one another on various emotional levels. A mother and son. A husband and wife. A girl and a boy—

One night they tried a scene as two teenagers in the back seat of a car. They had no props other than the chairs they were sitting on, but the space around them was pregnant with possibilities. Steering wheel, windows, doors. They had no particular dialogue in mind. But what they said worked. Their awkwardness, their nervousness, was right on target. They kissed and groped, fumbling to keep their pantomimed cigarettes lit throughout the encounter. The audience thought them fabulous—primarily because each audience member saw himself or herself on stage. This was the comedy of The Compass. Mike Nichols: "When you see someone making a fool of himself, it's the easiest thing in the world to identify yourself as the same sort of fool. The role of the writer or the artist is to be the competent observer."

Mike Nichols and Elaine May. (Photo courtesy of Pictorial Parade, Inc.)

Later, when Mike Nichols and Elaine May skyrocketed to fame with their own nightclub act, this sketch was included. In fact, most of their nightclub material was first conceived on The Compass stage.

Severn Darden, a flamboyant young man given to sporting a cape and cane, was a paragon of eclectic thought and weird pranks. He left the University of Chicago for New York, where he ran into David Shepherd who was there recruiting for Compass. Darden returned to Chicago, joining the group just after it began. Creator of some of the most popular characters ever seen on the Compass and later Second City stage, he is most identified with the role of Professor Valter von der Voegelweide. He is not the result of an improv suggestion. Nor is von der Voegelweide. The professor is the ultimate philosopher academician: "Who are we? Are we just a bunch of me or shall I include them?" Darden was doing him before he ever started acting: "I used to lecture at the Art Institute of Chicago. I discovered anyone could lecture there if you were connected with the University. That's when I began doing him. But I don't think he was German then."

Darden improvised with Elaine May, often and successfully, but the process could be painful. Part and parcel of her wit and intellect was a keenly developed sense of what made her skin crawl. She could be forcefully single-minded in conveying it. "Working with me on stage she was wonderful. She was always good. But she had this fierce competitiveness. We argued. She terrified me. . . ."

When Darden left for the summer to appear at the Barter Theatre, Shelley Berman came in to replace him. Berman wasn't the typical Compass player. For one thing, he wasn't from the University of Chicago. For another, though he'd appeared impressively as a straight actor, he was associated with commercial comedy, a notion entirely alien to Compass players.

Says Berman, "Mark and Bobbi Gordon, who were already with The Compass, had met me in New York. Mark, who knew me as a kind of humorous individual, brought me in. I was just cracking the ice writing, as a free-lance comedy writer, and my only market was the Steve Allen *Tonight Show*. This was 1955. I didn't know where I was going to go anyway. The Compass sounded like good work, even though it was fifty bucks a week. No. Less. I joined this group. They were on the South Side, a place called the Dock or the Deck. I never did learn which. I think it was called the Dock but the sign said the Deck. It was in the Hyde Park area, near the University, but we moved from there almost immediately. As soon as I joined, I guess they got kicked out of the Dock or the Deck. Actually, they moved to a larger room.

"Mark and Bobbi Gordon were not University of Chicago people either. So I felt at home at least. But I wished, oh God how I wished I were a University of Chicago person, because I've always envied the student mentality and I've envied their knowledge. They had enormous knowledge. Staggering. Like nothing I'd ever experienced."

Berman, working from his background, had visions of distinguishing himself by standing out from the others. He was getting laughs, but at the expense of his teammates. "I was sort of verging on thirty, a bit older than the rest of them, and I was getting scared that nothing was ever going to happen to me as a comedian. My predisposition at that time was to be a comedian, to get out there and be funny. And I would hog the laughs where I could. I would hog the scenes where I could. I would be on that stage every possible minute. I wanted to be in everything, and I wanted to get all the laughs. I really wanted to do it all, and I was pretty much of an irritant to some of the others."

He violated the unwritten, ultimate Compass (and later, Second City) taboo—don't just go for the joke, and don't ignore the other people on stage when you should be relating to them in character. One example sharply etched in Shelley Berman's mind is a scene called "The Father and Son":

"Mark had a marvelous idea. I played his Jewish father. He was my son, who was coming to me to say he wanted to be an actor. We did the scene, and I made one joke after another. After the scene, he said to me, 'Why does it have to be that way always, Shelley? Why do you have to reach? Why does it *always* have to be funny?'

"But for me it felt right, I felt it was working. One more time we tried it, as an improv. And he came on as the son, and as the father I started giving him static. Told him he was ridiculous. Frankly speaking, I thought he would keep fighting me and wherever the comedy would lead, it would lead eventually to a conclusion. But I was going for laughs again, by denying him and just making a fool of him. So he said, 'All right, pop,' and turned around and stomped out. The scene was over. *That* scene was over. I was taught a lesson, which is that when you're going to just go for the laughs, you're sealing off all possibilities for exploring anything richer."

Along with this ultimate infraction in the eyes of The Compass itself there were taboos imposed by the owners of the bars where The Compass played. As Andrew Duncan remembers them, "Early on, we were in bars which were not owned by us. Some of these owners were fairly rigid in their sensibilities. One of us came out in underwear once. The owner had a fit. Elaine had a way of sitting, folding her legs, that could have been construed as flashing. I don't know if she did it on purpose or didn't know or didn't care. But it upset them. And David Shepherd—I remember I was in a scene about gift-giving once. Intellectuals, in Greenwich Village or Hyde Park, exchanging gifts. Somebody had decided that a poor struggling student really needs an omelette pan. The most useful thing in the world if you're starving, right? So I said, 'And when you're not using it for cooking, you can always use it to keep your diaphragm in.' David Shepherd was furious. He didn't want that kind of humor."

When The Compass was about a year old, Bernie Sahlins founded the Studebaker Theater Company in a twelve hundred–seat house in downtown Chicago. An offshoot of the Playwrights concepts, it brought in guest stars like E. G. Marshall and Geraldine Page, while giving Compass regulars a supplemental source of income.

In the second year of The Compass Players, there were rumblings within the ranks. The theater had been started to involve the community. But the participating community consisted essentially of amateur actors. Their free time was limited. They had jobs. They had families. Those willing to invest enough energy and dedication in the workshops were few and far between. And the most supportive amateurs were least like the proletariat community David Shepherd had in mind. The group, as he saw it, had become the province of professional actors. Since he considered actors to be insular—cut off from the proletariat pulse of the slaughterhouses and stockyards—Shepherd wasn't happy. "We were never able to address that much. What we were able to address was the tyranny of the middle-class Jewish family. That's what Compass was all about."

In April 1957, Theodore J. Flicker, in partnership with David Shepherd, opened a Compass in the Crystal Palace in St. Louis. The neighborhood was relatively avant-garde, with "Let's hang out" and "Come to my pad" in the common parlance at a time when the rest of the country still thought hanging out was what clothes did and pad was how a cheat inflated a bill. The original St. Louis company consisted of Flicker, Del Close, Jo Henderson, and Nancy Ponder.

Meanwhile, in Chicago, morale was low. The Compass, now moved from the Dock to a larger house on Chicago's Far North Side, no longer nestled in the Hyde Park bosom of its loyal supporters. In view of the weakened lifeline and low morale, The Compass in Chicago ceased operation in 1957. The Studebaker Theater didn't last either. Shelley Berman started a group called the Commedia Players, which fared badly and ended fast. Severn Darden, Elaine May, and Mike Nichols joined Flicker's company in St. Louis. It lasted a few months longer before closing its doors in late 1957.

When Compass disbanded, Mike Nichols and Elaine May pulled their material together into a nightclub act. They took it around the country—from the Village Vanguard, the Blue Angel, and Down in the Depths in New York to Mister Kelly's in Chicago to the Mocambo in Hollywood. They presented a concert-length version at New York's prestigious Town Hall in 1959. The exposure led to television—*The Steve Allen Show* and *Omnibus*—and nationwide acclaim. Their albums became sensations. On Broadway, *An Evening With Mike Nichols and Elaine May* opened October 8, 1960. Hailed by critic Walter Kerr as a triumph of "genuine, jaundiced, festering observation," it included such scenes as these:

Elaine May, comforting the bereaved in a mortuary: "Hello, I'm your grief lady."

Mike Nichols as effete Southern playwright Alabama Glass, addressing the PTA with his languid high-pitched voice. He reveals the plot of his new play, about a young man who has been unjustly accused of not being a homosexual, and the man's wife, who is in love with a young basketball team.

Elaine May as a brainless movie star promoting her new "pitcha," in which she'll portray Gertrude Stein.

Elaine May as a telephone operator, supervisor, and managing supervisor, who will not grant Nichols a free call though a pay phone has stolen his last dime.

Mike Nichols as the brilliant rock scientist telling his mother how wretched he feels for not writing and calling more often. Elaine May, as his mother, hasn't eaten in three days for fear of having food in her mouth when he rings. Nichols moans, "I feel awful." She rallies. "Oh, God, sonny, if I could only believe that, I'd be the happiest mother in the world."

Each night on Broadway, Nichols and May performed set pieces—of which they never wrote down a word. These were followed by improvisations. The audience was asked for a first line and a last line of dialogue, and an author whose style they should emulate. Though the lines could be anything and the authors ranged from Plato to Batman and Robin, Nichols and May always took the first suggestion they heard. It was more of a challenge that way. They then improvised an appropriately styled scene to take them from the first line to the last. Broadway gaped in awe.

On television—sitting on their stools, creating and developing relationships out of dialogue and objects out of space—they were like nothing viewers had ever seen. So far-ranging was their influence that it seemed as though they invented satire. In short order, the team of Mike Nichols and Elaine May revolutionized comedy.

Suddenly very public figures, they both preferred to keep their private lives to themselves, foiling interviewers' questions by answering them preposterously. Once, May gave her vital statistics to columnist Earl Wilson as 24-35-127½. Another time, Mike Nichols concocted the rumor that he was representing the United States in the 1958 Olympics, as a member of the equestrian team.

Shelley Berman was off like wildfire, too, with his first two records, *Inside Shelley Berman* and *Outside Shelley Berman* on the Top Pop charts for 134 weeks and 73 weeks respectively. Berman based his act on the material and techniques he'd developed through improvisation. "The Father and Son," one of his most successful routines, evolved from the improvisation he'd done with Mark Gordon. What Nichols and May did for team comedy, Berman proceeded to do for single acts. In the days when comedy monologues were traditionally stand-up—Henny Youngman, Jack Carter, Myron Cohen—he started a trend by using a stool. "I was really not a comedian. I guess I could act in a funny way, or find funny things to say, but I was an actor. I needed to relate to somebody else. I was able to create a situation in which I could talk to somebody who didn't exist on that stage. It didn't make sense to pretend somebody was there. But I could certainly pretend I was holding a phone. I could pantomime a phone, which we all had done in improvisation. Now, if you're going to talk on the phone, it seems kind of ridiculous that you'd be standing up for a long time. So I sat on a chair. When I went to nightclubs, if I sat on a chair, I disappeared, because the stages were too low. So I asked if I could borrow a barstool, wherever I went to work. So there was the phone and the stool, which became highly identified with me."

By now, Berman was so thoroughly a convert to improv methodology that it led to complications in the outside world. "At The Compass, we never memorized a line. For my first three LPs, nothing was written down. It had to be transcribed by someone so that I could publish it and copyright it.

"And when I'd go on television shows, they'd say 'We need your copy for continuity acceptance.' I said, 'I don't know the words I'll say. It's improv.' 'You mean it's different every time?' 'Well, not exactly. But if I write something down, you'll want to confine me to it.' And im-

Shelley Berman on Dinah Shore's show. (Photo courtesy of Pictorial Parade, Inc.)

provisations always sounded awful when they were written down. One time, for Steve Allen's show, they made me write down what I was going to say. I didn't know what to write. I didn't know how to write down coughs. A cough used to get so much laughter. When I was coughing into the phone, and apologizing for coughing into the phone, it worked. No question about it. But there's no way to write that down. They made me audition the routine and it died in the audition."

He also discovered a whole new world of taboos. The taboos which prevailed at The Compass were minuscule compared to television. "I did a *Dinah Shore Show*. I had a scene where I'm on a date, and I say to the girl, 'When two people are holding hands, can anyone ever be really sure whose hand is doing the sweating? And that's one thing a guy can't fight, sweat.' That line always got a laugh. People identified with it. When I did it at rehearsal, I was advised to change it because 'sweat is an unpleasant word for a Sunday night family show.' I didn't know what to do with the line. Perspiration doesn't do it. They didn't want it anyhow, because it was too close to sweat. They came up with a word—moist. So I was saying, 'That's one thing a guy can't fight, moisture.' The audience screamed. The double entendre got way out of hand and the audience went crazy. At least sweat is sweat.''

In 1959, David Shepherd opened a new St. Louis Compass, this time with Nancy Ponder, Alan Arkin, and Jerry Stiller. When Stiller first joined the group, it was without his wife, Anne Meara. As he explains his interest in the troupe, "Anne and I lived in a tenement on West Eightieth Street. One day a dope addict was found on our doorstep. He was dead. The dog that I'd used in Shakespeare in the Park came up the steps and ran the other way while they examined this guy. We said, 'We've got to get out of this thing.' That's when we were doing Shakespeare in the Park and making just enough money to survive. When we looked across the hall from our window one day, across to the other side, maybe twenty feet away, we saw two guys grabbing each other and beating the hell out of each other, because one of them was holding out on money for dope. And we could feel them coming into our apartment, even though there was a yard between us. And we're looking at them. And they're looking at us. They could kill us. I felt those guys could come right across, or come downstairs, and say, 'What are you looking at?' And we're actors. And I said, 'This is acting? This is show-business?' And this was at the time in our life where we said, 'Oh my God, gotta do something else.' "

Jerry Stiller was hired. A break for The Compass seemed inevitable when the company was invited to appear on Jack Paar's show. "We figured, well, this is going to be it. We went on Paar. He introduced us. They went to a commercial. So they never announced one word of who we were, what we did, or anything. It was if we had done three minutes and they had forgotten us. It was as if we had not been on the air. I'll never forget that. Got on an airplane back, I was praying the plane would crash. That's how disastrous it was." That's also how new improvisation still was.

David Shepherd booked the company into the Crystal Palace in St. Louis. They needed another girl. Stiller got wife Anne the audition. "I told David that I couldn't go to St. Louis unless he hired my wife." Anne Meara was hired. Though fresh out of Bertolt Brecht's *Puntila and His Servants*, she took immediately to demolishing that invisible "fourth wall" between an actress and her audience. Stiller was relieved: "The rest of us were not very good at taking suggestions. One of us would step out and say to the audience, 'We'd like to take suggestions.' Because most of us were very new at this thing. Shy. Anne was the one who had the courage and the nerve to ask for suggestions, so after a while, the taking of the suggestions became as much a part of the evening as the stuff itself. She got to bantering with them and talking back and forth and made it funny.''

Beyond the success of the banter, the improvs, and the moment—in fact, underlying them—was the effect of the improvisational process on its practitioners. "In addition to the fact that you were just an actor up until that time, having done Shakespeare in the Park, and Chekhov, and everything else," Stiller reflects, "we now were discovering that we could write. It was the beginning of it. We didn't call it writing. We called it improvising. But essentially you were writing your own people, you were becoming these characters. It was a big discovery. For us, it was the beginning of what later became our act."

Later, their act became one of the most sought-after in clubs and on television. They also cut a record with Shelley Berman, called *Sex Life of the Primate*. "Ostensibly," wrote Berman on the record jacket, "I am the writer of the material on this recorded revue. The writing process however, is not quite what is generally envisioned. Much of this material came about as a result of organized and planned 'improvisations' . . . many of the lines which elicited considerable laughter from our studio audience were in fact created by the actors themselves. Jerry Stiller and Anne Meara, as a fine comedy team in their own right, created invaluable character and line contributions. . . .''

Score an early victory for what would become the Second City connection. Yet soon this avatar of The Compass too was unable to stay in business, and closed its doors.

In 1959, Paul Sills was employed as the house manager at the Gate of Horn, an adventurous Chicago nightclub. The club had its moments. But the moments Sills leaned toward were of the old Compass variety—the improvisation, the group, the transcendence. He talked about it with Bernie Sahlins and Howard Alk. They were ready to join forces and start a new theater.

In 1959, Sahlins sold his tape recorder factory to raise capital for the new venture. "I retired on enough money to be very poor. So we all had nothing to do and decided we'd start this little coffee shop so we could have a place to sit. The show was almost an afterthought. When we started doing the show, we didn't even know quite what form it was going to take, really. Whether we should have a continuous scenario with a single plotline, or just do the scenes we had come up with. Right up to two or three weeks before opening, maybe a month before opening, the idea of disparate scenes and a nonunified show was up for debate. Mike Nichols was in New York. He and Elaine had already made it. We called him, 'Come on in, we want to sit and talk about this.' He came in for a few days. He and Paul and Howard and I sat down and agonized again over the whole thing. We finally came to the conclusion that we'd just do scenes."

On Chicago's Near North Side, they leased a defunct Chinese laundry and the adjoining hat shop on the fringe of an up-and-coming—some called it seedy—residential area off Lincoln Park known as Old Town. Both stores had been abandoned by their former owners in a hurry. "Angry customers continued to call for months after we were ensconced, brandishing their laundry tickets and demanding their linen." The partners put the two buildings together, creating a theater and a coffee shop. They paneled the interior with discarded phone booth doors, painted black. The stage was framed by red velvet opera drapes. The stage itself remained bare, except for chairs the actors would sit on, a door for exits and entrances, and the piano for musical accompaniment. The piano was placed on stage because the room was too small to put it anywhere else. The atmosphere, as at The Compass, was reminiscent of the world of Bertolt Brecht, Kurt Weill, and 1930s German cabaret.

The new troupe took its name from a caustic *New Yorker* magazine piece, "Chicago, the Second City," written by A. J. Liebling in 1951. Liebling had suggested that when it came to culture, Chicago ran a poor second to New York City. The team seized the enemy's banner and planted it as their own—a polite way of telling the enemy where he himself might plant it.

The room seated one hundred and twenty, and admission was set at one dollar. As at The Compass, smoking and drinking were permitted during the show. The menu offered hamburgers on black bread, espresso at thirty-five cents a cup, and similar fare.

Howard Alk, Roger Bowen, Severn Darden, Andrew Duncan, Barbara Harris, Mina Kolb, and Eugene Troobnick comprised Second City's first cast. By design, The Second City was more a revue than The Compass had been—slicker and more commercial. The men wore three-piece suits, and the women, stylish black dresses and pearls. Paul Sills directed. Bill Mathieu played the piano. They all wondered how long the company would last, and how long they'd be getting paid.

"We worked organically," explains Barbara Harris. "That's a way of saying there was no money. Actually, there was a little salary, just enough to live on. But the main thing is that we were working with people who were interesting and nourishing, people who had something to offer each other."

The Second City opened for business on 16 December, 1959. Earlier in the year, Fidel Castro had assumed power in Cuba, and Nikita Khrushchev had toured the United States. Dwight Eisenhower commenced his final year as president. The hit stage shows in Chicago were *The Music Man* and *West Side Story*. Three Westerns—*Gunsmoke*, *Wagon Train*, and *Have Gun Will Travel*—dominated the TV ratings. Chicago, as depicted by a new series, evoked the image of Eliot Ness gunning down felons in *The Untouchables*.

As the first Second City customers arrived, the carpenter was still nailing down the carpet.

Bernie Sahlins outside Second City's first building, on opening night. (Photo courtesy of The Second City)

2
Creating Second City Humor

John Belushi called Second City the "Oxford of Comedy." This implies all sorts of attributes. It suggests, for instance, an institution of higher learning. That, like a school, it has classes, graduates, and reunions. And that, like Oxford, it's the best there is.

All this is true of Second City. Like a top university, Second City is greater than the sum of its parts; has a special knack for finding gifted talents early in their careers; and graduates committed alumni—once with Second City, always with Second City. The Oxford of Comedy revels in its old school ties.

Second City's fundamental concepts over the years have been few and consistent. Work at the top of your intelligence, and let the humor come from relationships, not shtick. Specific references change from one decade to the next, but not the need for substance. Substance is forever. Roger Bowen's scenario "Businessman," a highlight of Second City's opening night in 1959, is a good example:

Big business is on the ropes. The Japanese have perfected a bargain sports car, the Hicoupet Mark III. It will sell in the U.S. for $49.95.

Who can save American free enterprise? This is a job for—*Businessman.* Off with his Ivy-League suit and into his crime-fighting garb, Bermuda shorts. "Faster than a speeding ticker tape, more powerful than a goon squad, able to leap loopholes in a single bound," he springs into action by totalling the car against a tariff wall. Next, he dukes it out with Collective Man, matching slogan for slogan. Collective Man hits him with "the irresistible historical momentum of the worker's movement." Pow! Zowie! Shmek! Businessman counters with everything from the eight-hour day to the thinking man's filter.

The substance is timeless. When Businessman heads South to lick the plight of blacks in segregated lunch rooms (by replacing the lunch rooms with vending machines so people can eat in the great, free outdoors), the specific reference may seem dated. But not the substance. And when Businessman heads off to help another "oppressed" minority—the Boers in South Africa— it's hard to think of the line as being almost thirty years old.

Also nailed that first night were doctors, President Eisenhower, FM radio and opera (with "A Posthumous Work of Verdi"). Later there followed a Freudian Western, a quasi-Roman drama entitled "Insipidus," and an adult evening class in "Great Books" (in which one woman's insightful interpretation of the marriage of Jocasta and Oedipus who don't know they're mother and son in *Oedipus Rex* is "I think he knew it all the time"). Silent movies were parodied in the Chaplinesque "City Blights," and Ingmar Bergman's films in "Seven Sealed Strawberries."

More recently sketches have hinged on such weighty concerns as the trained amoeba, which tap dances and jumps through hoops. "But it doesn't pay to be nice to amoebas. They kind of take advantage of your friendship, milk you for all you're worth, and then split."

Not surprisingly, Second City from the beginning has had a reputation for being "smart." (Show titles, heavy on literate puns, have included "Justice Is Done, or Oh, Cal Coolidge," "Tippecanoe or Déja Vu," "Freud Slipped Here," "I Remember Dada," and "Orwell That Ends Well.") The players have known a few things. The audiences have known what the players were talking about. This kind of smart humor generally invites the label "satire," a commodity of which The Second City is reputed to be a temple.

Satire is a word taught in school in connection with something like *Gulliver's Travels*, which can, if you're not paying attention, be a story about little guys tying down a big guy with string. Students draw goofy pictures of their teacher on the blackboard and call it satire. Their teacher can be the most beautiful woman in the world, but they'll draw her with a knobby nose and a hairy mole on her chin and they think they've deftly satirized her.

But true satire is more far-reaching than simple ridicule or humor. If the teacher has a mole and a strange nose and someone draws these in an exaggerated manner, the caricature may qualify as parody but it's not satire. It's only satire if it targets a defect that's hurting someone else. Satire ridicules to expose, with the idea that awareness is a step toward remedy.

As a rule, Second City abhors the cheap shot and cheap laugh. Bernie Sahlins, the only Second City member who's been there since day one—most of the time as its owner and guiding force—distrusts cheap. "It's true there are more taboos at some times than others, but to violate the taboo is the simple thing to do, and the easy thing, and has nothing to do with satire. I think the more taboos there are, the easier and cheaper it is to do the work, but the ideas when the easy targets aren't out there and you turn to the proper targets—your own shibboleths and icons, your personal taboos—that's when you're really doing good work."

Harold Ramis joined Second City in the late sixties with a group that saw many a taboo hit the dirt, yet, he recalls, "We still had our internal censors working. We respected the Second City rule of always working from the top of our intelligence. Bernie would help weed out some of the really cheap laughs. Del Close, when he directed us, was very good at encouraging people to go for the better jokes, not the easy jokes."

"I don't object to laughs," Bernie Sahlins adds, "but I have vetoed things that would work. It works to pull your pants down. That it works is not what we're about. Satire doesn't consist of violating taboos. It's true when we started that there was a period of oppression, that political humor was not being done, and you just said Eisenhower on stage and it was orgasmic. People seemed to think it was political if we said 'Marshall Field.' That came from violating a taboo. But that isn't the function of satire, or its definition. Rather, what we have is bringing to bear an ironic point of view on the difference between what people profess and what they do, what ought to be and what is. If Reagan calls a missile a peacekeeper, that in itself is an irony. It has to do with the fact that we consider the world without heroes."

"Businessman" is satire. Splitting amoebas isn't. Second City does satire brilliantly, but not exclusively. The common denominator lies elsewhere. Says Sahlins, "The key to what it is comes from an analysis of who the audience is and who the actors are. They're the same age, and have been throughout the history of the Second City. They are eighteen to thirty-five, and basically, the fact is that if you're a young person wandering around the world being bombarded by all these phenomena, the newspaper headlines, war, love, all that, you're not always aware that these are also the concerns of others like yourself. You're not aware that these random phenomena can be isolated, can be discussed, and that doing this will annihilate their randomness. When they come here, they're addressed by their peers about these things, with an attitude of irony and iconoclasm. They form a community with the people on stage.

"But I don't consider us topical humorists or even satirists. I think that what we do essentially is kind of social commentary about longer-term ideas, which are even more profound than just the newspaper headlines."

"What we go for," says Harry Murphy, "is the oh-wow laugh. The laugh of recognition that says 'I never really looked at it that way.' That's the most satisfying."

Recently, the Chicago company of The Second City was going to do something on the situation in Ireland. They could have improvised a scene about the Catholics and the Protestants, the Irish and the British. That might have been very funny. But what they came up with was an Irish bar in Chicago, where a Protestant Irishman is exhorting his countrymen to be terrorists and die. At the same time, he's decrying the terrorists in the Middle East. While this is going on, he's being hit on by a Catholic prostitute. The scene was funny while being *more* than just funny. By presenting the issues on a human scale, and bringing them into our own hometowns, it transformed the phenomenon of the Irish situation into our own lives and the lives of people around us.

David Steinberg and Burt Heyman had a similar impulse twenty years earlier, playing two men reminiscing in an Irish pub. "They just don't write old songs like that any more. . . . You'll never see those days again unless something terrible happens."

Before them, likewise, as two Irishmen, Alan Arkin and Severn Darden waxed nostalgic about wakes, mothers, and old flames.

"Do you remember Mollie?"
"Ah yes, she was a beautiful girl."
"Yes, with the green gums."
"Yes, with one foot bigger than the other."
"Yes, with the receding hairline."
"And the hump on her back."
"Ah, she was a beautiful girl. They don't make girls like that any more."
"No. If they did, it wouldn't be the same."

The specific references change. There are always new world leaders, new weapons, new slogans. But the human element remains immutable.

However, Second City is not always about the world situation, either. A scene might pit a guitar-playing beatnik against an up-tight square, or it may focus on two socially awkward misfits, Mildred and Morris, thrown together by the dimensions of a hallway.

In one memorable scene, a shy nebbish gets sand kicked in his face. The weakling goes home, takes the bodybuilding course, and returns to the scene of the crime. When the bully comes back, the weakling confronts him. The weakling's girlfriend laughs her fool head off at the sight of him. But the weakling has muscles now, and he uses them. Bop! Right on her chin. That'll teach her not to laugh.

Of course, it's possible to be smart and human and not be funny. Albert Einstein, a smart human, was not in and of himself funny. But history records that Marilyn Monroe had his autographed picture, leading Second City to speculate that the two had dated. In the scene, Einstein's mind isn't on sexual arousal. He can't get his thoughts together on the subject of matter and energy. Suddenly, Marilyn blurts out the theory of relativity, which just sort of popped into her head. A breakthrough for science—and good news for Einstein. Now he can concentrate on converting his energy to what matters, Marilyn Monroe.

Einstein, being one of us, can be funny. As H. Allen Smith once observed, a humorist is "a fellow who realizes, first, that he is no better than anybody else and, second, that nobody else is either."

Or, as Gilda Radner once commented, "I often think of myself as a court jester. It's as though the United States were a kingdom, and my job was to relieve the kingdom of its tensions by reflecting life comedically."

Generally, though not always, a Second City player takes workshops during the day. Generally, though not always—and more in Second City's early years—the workshops rely heavily on the games originated by Viola Spolin during the Depression as an outgrowth of her work with Chicago's community groups. Spolin, who relocated to Los Angeles in the late fifties, returned to Chicago when Second City began in 1959. In Los Angeles, her classes at the Young Actors Company—ten- and twelve-year-olds—improvised inspired comedy through the games, long before improvisation was being publicized as a new movement in theater. In Chicago, Spolin instructed Second City actors, while son Paul Sills directed them, in the use of her exercises and techniques. In the process, she was able to codify the games, ultimately writing her landmark book, *Improvisation for the Theater*,* considered to be the bible

*Her latest book, *Theatre Games For Rehearsal*, expands on the theme. Together, the books are followed throughout the world—from England to Brazil (where the techniques are called "The Viola").

of the improv movement. Concurrently, Paul Sills became its godfather.

The games develop acting ability, intuitive agility, and ensemble skills. They enable the actor to focus on where, who, and what—where you are, who you are, and what you do. They lead to the development of character and space. They teach movement and the handling of space to suggest a picture. They bring the actors to a stage, chairs, lighting, and one another. They center around actors relating to other actors through contact—eye contact, physical contact, use of the environment. They teach awareness, enabling actors to experience the full depths of the senses. When a Spolin-trained player touches hand to cheek, it's not enough that the hand feels the cheek. The cheek also has to feel the hand. The games emphasize nonverbal communication. If you have to cogitate while you're doing them, you're missing the point.

Says Spolin, "The idea is to hurtle you into the present time, which is something other than clock time. You are not waiting for. You are in waiting. The ball player stands there waiting for the ball exactly the same as the audience waits. For what? You don't know the answer. The outcome of the present time is as yet unknown, as yet an undiscovered probability."

Hamilton Camp, who has worked with Spolin, Sills, and the games for at least twenty years, explains that you can't explain it. "It's only been in the last two years that I really started to understand—no, understand is the wrong word. It implies that you've hammered it out intellectually. Eventually, you divine, you intuit."

Valerie Harper, already a Broadway dancer and actress when she began studying the games—and now their obedient disciple—compares them to Baryshnikov and ballet. "Baryshnikov once said he works not so much to be a dancer as to transform himself into the space in which dance can occur. The games have that effect. Viola considered herself a ballet mistress. You can dance all you want to at night, but you should be preparing yourself each day at the barre. I remember once when we were doing *Story Theatre*. Paul Sills decided we were too terrible and that nothing could be done for us, so he walked out. For the next four days, Viola worked with us, doing the games. When Paul came back, it was a whole new situation. We were on a whole new level.

"I began taking the games in the workshops because I wanted to be in Second City. But they're so much more than that. They teach connectiveness. They permeate everything. I've even used them to work through headaches. As a rule, actors take classes, and if they can't get work acting, the classes have no application at all. But Viola's classes really carry over into life." Indeed, psychologists, social workers, and speech therapists have long employed the techniques in their work.

"It's always easier onstage to improvise talking than it is to improvise doing something," adds Peter Boyle. "What you're doing is one of the things the games are about."

Paul Sand caught the bug at a tender age. "My parents were great. I'd wake up in the middle of the night and I'd go to their room and I'd say, 'Can I study piano?' They'd say 'Yes.' Then I'd go back to bed. 'Tap dancer?' 'Yes.' That didn't last long. 'Can I study to be an actor?' 'Yes.' I hung on to that one, and mom found Viola Spolin through UCLA. Mom said, 'I don't want my kid to be a Hollywood actor.' We made a deal. I could study but I wasn't allowed to be a professional until I was an adult. I couldn't take kid actor jobs.

"So I started with Viola when I was eleven. She was a very wonderful teacher, and she insisted you drop your mood the minute you stepped off stage, as a safeguard. Otherwise, you'd carry it home and be a crazy person. I used to go to class every day after school. Every day, I did some new game. I think Paul Sills and Elaine May came out to Los Angeles to visit his mom, and I was in the class. That's how he knew me, and then he asked me to join Second City when it got underway.

"But she was doing all these games with us. We were like the guinea pigs. Now it's all ingrained. I pick up her book and say, 'Oh, that! That's what I was doing?' I still don't understand it intellectually. I couldn't explain a game if I had to. It's like having been bilingual since childhood, like switching from one language to another without going through the process of saying 'this equals that.' "

Depending on who you talk to, the games can be everything from a mystical transmutation to a pain in the kinesis. They can fine-tune genius. They can leave people cold. Joan Rivers "wasn't going to be told that I had to go to class during the day. I couldn't bear passing space objects and have them change."

The games have inflicted misery, as when Ann Elder, brand new at Second City, longed for nothing more urgently than a place to sit. "I had never improvised. I had never taken a class. I had never *stood* on stage. And there I was in improv classes in the afternoon, absolutely baffled. I heard, 'Find your atmosphere. Where's your where?' I can remember Viola saying,

'Ann, you're not in your where,' and me saying, 'I don't know where my where is. I don't even know what my what is. What is my where, and where is my what?' All around me are the brilliant guys in my company, like Avery Schreiber and Dick Schaal, miming and pulling. And I'm drowning in my where."

The games have drawn blood. Jack Burns wasn't quite sure how they should be attacked. "I think Viola was probably a little disappointed in me. Some days I'd call in sick. I remember one time I thought I was doing great. I was standing on a chair. All our bodies were supposed to intertwine, finding our space and our where and all that. I stood on this chair. The chair broke. I went down. I knocked myself out. Viola thought that was great because I really put myself into it. I said, 'Great? This is killing me.' "

The games have made bold men humble. David Steinberg concedes, "In proportion to how I was on stage, I was probably the worst person in the workshops. I don't think they even wanted me in the workshops, I was so bad. Viola and I didn't get along in the workshop situation. We liked each other, and she was funny, she was great fun. I liked her and I always admired her as a person, but I wasn't a workshop kind of guy, you might say. It wasn't intellectual condescension on my part because when you saw Dick Schaal take the workshop stuff and be the funniest human you'd ever seen on stage, or Paul Sand, or any of them, you had to be somewhat in awe.

"On stage, I was notorious for walking through everybody's where. They'd create a table and I would stand right in the middle of it. We're in a room, I wouldn't see the room.

"The workshops were there to make you present on stage. They enhanced the degree to which you could be in that moment when you were on stage. In my day, if you weren't good at the workshop, you weren't considered good. But fortunately, once I was on the stage, I was very much present, very much in the moment. I lived for it and loved it. And Paul Sills just encouraged me to come at it in my own way."

The games are powerful stuff. Alan Arkin clearly remembers many times "running off stage after a scene, and finding myself putting down imaginary props that I had just used. I noticed other people doing the same thing." Dick Schaal is widely considered the mahatma of making the invisible visible. When he works, his objects are so real to him that he gets in a state where it's all there. One evening when the show was over, he went down to the bar. He sat down at the bar, took an invisible bottle of beer, and poured it into an invisible glass. It wasn't until he couldn't taste the beer that he realized what he'd done. He wasn't kidding. His two worlds had merged. The guy is *good*.

The games have even driven actors to gibberish, but that's deliberate.

Dick Schaal, master gamesman, excels at "making the invisible visible." (Photo courtesy of Howard Frank Archives/Personality Photos, Inc.)

Gibberish is one of the exercises. It forces actors to communicate by showing rather than saying. Properly done, gibberish relays meanings though the syllables themselves are meaningless. It strengthens a company's group ESP, a fundamental ingredient of ensemble improv. It also provides the basis of a popular Second City improvisation, the translation sketch. In this, one player speaks English and "translates" for the second, who speaks only gibberish. Questions are taken from the audience. The gibberer answers the questions in meaningless syllables. The "translator" listens carefully, then gives an answer to the question. It would seem that the burden to be clever falls on the one speaking English. In practice, this may be the case. In theory, it's not supposed to be.

Says Paul Sand: "It's a give and take exercise. If you really want to get your point across in gibberish, the other person will hear you. What it takes is openness, an amazing openness to be a listener. Otherwise, you're pretending to be listener, you're pretending to be empathetic, and what you're giving off is someone who's pretending. So you really have to listen to the person who's throwing the gibberish at you, and then you really can get it. Then the other thing is that if you're throwing the gibberish, you have to know what you mean to say. You can't just make strange noises and leave it to the interpreter to bail you out."

Funny people have come to the workshops expecting to do comedy. They were in for rude awakenings. Mary Gross saw an ad for a workshop. She went, but she didn't want to go on stage. She offered to pay her fee and observe. Nothing doing. She had to get up there and struggle. "At the time, I didn't know that what we were trying to do was just create a reality and the humor came out of the reality. So I got up and made some ill attempt to be funny. I went home humiliated and wept. And then I thought I'd go back. I felt I had to go back to save my dignity."

Shelley Berman never studied with Viola Spolin. Yet, since his Compass days, he's taught improv in colleges. "The students are always disappointed in the first class. The second class they love. But the first class is where I won't let them do anything. And oh God, they get upset, because they want to be funny right away. I won't let them do that. I make them listen to each other. I make them work on the most basic level of responding to what is available. Not bringing in something from left field."

This ties in with Second City's aversion to a cheap joke, except that in terms of the workshop, any joke is cheap. Plotting the next joke may lead to another joke, but it blocks spontaneity. It also cuts off the other players. While they've invested their full energy in relating to the character you're playing, you're ignoring them to whip up a snappy ad-lib.

"Improvisation is play," explains Paul Sills. "Play brings an immediate response, which is not gasps of horror, but identification with the actor's play, which is naturally laughter—not necessarily laughter at a joke, but laughter with the playing. What it's not is laugh-factory stuff. That's different. That's stand-up. This cult of so-called comedy just to make joke-joke-joke isn't meaningful. It's just nothing. And I'm not interested in having influenced joke-making. When you have dialogue, improvisational dialogue, you're going to get your humor."

"Paul Sills," says Paul Sand, "is a true gentleman. He's almost aristocratic in his gentlemanliness. He's a very fine, considerate man. But I've seen him like knock people down and strangle them on the floor whenever they told a joke."

The games teach actors to get out of the way and let *it* happen. "Trust the POC" (point of concentration—a key concept in Spolin workshops). Working from the POC engenders relationships. Once this occurs, if humor arises, it's okay to laugh. When Viola Spolin laughs in workshops, it's a genuine, gutsy laugh of recognition and appreciation. It's an encouraging thing to have happen.

Josephine Raciti (Jo) Forsberg was a classical Shakespearean actress with Playwrights background when she came to Second City. She took Spolin's classes, became an understudy for the women in the cast, and threw herself wholeheartedly into the workshop program. Within a few years, Spolin left Second City to pursue a project called Game Theatre—which involved the theater audience personally in theater games. Jo Forsberg assumed directorship of the workshops, and of the Children's Theatre of Second City, which had been originated by Viola Spolin. Forsberg would cast some of the better workshop players in Children's Theatre productions, as a step in their training. In addition to the Spolin techniques, she developed her own series of exercises designed to place performers in contact with every inner resource. As long as a performer has untapped potential, says Forsberg, "It's raw chicken. And who can eat raw chicken? Without the skills, it's like a musician going to a concert and playing an instrument that's out of tune. When you are an improvising player, you are your instrument. *You're* the instrument. You don't have to walk around with a cello in order to express yourself."

Jo Forsberg (with notebook), Bill Murray (seated to her left), and other students evaluate scenes during a workshop. (Photo courtesy of Josephine Raciti Forsberg)

Like Viola Spolin, Jo Forsberg instructs through play. "In order to do anything creative, you have to be playful. You have to be able to take the responsibilities of the skill, the goals, and combine them with playfulness. Whether you're sad or glad, mad or bad, get out on the field and play the game. In playing the game, you see the irony of some of the truths. This is the basis of satire."

Like all Second City training, Forsberg's methods break down the inhibitions that hamper ensemble performance. "She has helped many people discover for the first time in their lives the meaning of working together," says Brian Doyle-Murray, who went on to join, as both writer and player, that mighty ensemble effort known as *Saturday Night Live*. "When I started in her workshop, it was the turning point in my life."

Since the inception of Second City, workshops have been conducted by a distinguished list of mentors and Second City grads—among them Spolin and Forsberg, Sheldon Patinkin (whose association with Second City dates back to Playwrights), Del Close (a veteran of the original St. Louis Compass Players), John Candy, Martin DeMaat, Robin Duke, Michael Gellman, Linda Kash, Catherine O'Hara, Peter Torokvei, Don DePollo, and Jeff Michalski (sages of more recent Second City vintage), and, according to Bernie Sahlins, "If everybody's very, very sick, I can be beaten into teaching a workshop."

3

A Funny Thing
Happened on the Way
to the Seventies
(1959–1964)

*T*he Second City opened two weeks shy of the sixties. It was life before Dylan and the Beatles. Before the pill and the sexual revolution. Before the moon walk. Before the Berlin Wall. Before photocopying and color television became as commonplace as breathing pollution. The big news in Canberra, Australia, focused on a delegation of aborigines seeking government aid to stop the import of plastic Japanese-made boomerangs that were cutting off their business. It was the same planet as the one we now occupy, but not quite the same world—with the same aspirations, seen through different eyes.

At The Second City, every performance voiced concerns that presaged the sixties, verbatim. Richard Libertini, who would soon belong to the Second City cast, remembers the first time he saw a Second City revue. "I can't even explain the impression it made, except as a sort of hipness. It was much hipper than anything else going on, because of the people involved, and the fact that they were using improvisations."

The improvs were as current as the headlines—if not ahead of them. They were as fresh as each night's suggestions, which came from what people were thinking at the moment. When a piece worked, it was brought back later in the week as part of a revue that preceded the evening's improvisations.

This combination of revue followed by improv sets has remained Second City's format ever since.

The cast—Howard Alk, Roger Bowen, Andrew Duncan, Eugene Troobnick, Barbara Harris, Mina Kolb, and Severn Darden—was sharp, aware, fully informed, spilling over with social conscience. Howard Alk, coproducer and player, had the reputation of knowing everything that was happening on any given day. Roger Bowen had a background in debating, law, and literary criticism, wrote extensively and spoke fluent Japanese. He created "Businessman" for Second City's opening night. Andrew Duncan and Eugene Troobnick, each with impressive theatrical credits, were each exceptionally well-read. Duncan, as Paul Sand remembers him, "was like Kennedy. He read everything. I bet he even had a rocking chair." He had also served as staff psychologist in Illinois's Cook County prison. Eugene Troobnick, assistant editor of *Playboy*, later claimed credit for Nixon's defeat in the 1960 election. (Nixon lost Illinois by 0.1 percent of the vote. Losing Illinois cost him the election. At Second City, Troobnick had been performing anti-Nixon satires. "Must have convinced at least one-tenth of one percent of the voters not to vote for him. Right?")

Barbara Harris, who started acting professionally when she appeared as a flaxen-haired baby in a Betty Crocker ad, stood 5'4" and retained her button face. Yet her looks belied her mental prowess. Harris was an expert in psychology, equally conversant with the works of Freud or Fromm. On stage, she combined sexiness, brains, and vulnerability to create a new kind of comedienne—a nubile Kewpie doll—for a world used to its funny women presented as zany klutzes.

Mina Kolb, radiating a comedically appealing world-weariness, gave fresh meaning to off-the-wall humor. A miraculous improviser, she is frequently referred to by admirers as "one of the funniest women ever seen on stage." To Paul Sand, she was "so hip, we didn't know what hip was. She'd show up in suburban drag. She had her hair done. This was, to us, I mean, she had her *hair* done . . . and wore expensive dresses, and shoes that must have cost her three hundred dollars. She'd get in a car and go home to her husband and her cats. But then she'd show up and you could not shock her, because she knew everything already. You couldn't even goose her. She'd just look through you. She was deep. She could have played Lady Macbeth."

According to an early program note, "A great deal of thought has gone into Severn Darden." A great deal of thought has likewise poured forth from him, whether answering questions taken from the floor, or wanting to have an elephant on stage, fed and watered just before showtime to produce the desired effect—a spontaneous performance by the elephant. Darden has been compared to Orson Welles and an emu. "His ability to close the gap between psychotic and genius," says Avery Schreiber, "was amazing, for the intellectual aspect of it, and the truth and reality of what he was doing, and his total involvement in it." As Bernie Sahlins describes Darden: "There have been, in various companies, seminal figures. Severn gave the work a whole kind of important intellectual flavor that has remained, and the necessity for a ref-

The players of The Second City: Background, left to right—Eugene Troobnick, Alan Arkin, Bill Mathieu (pianist/composer), Mina Kolb, Severn Darden. Foreground, left to right—Barbara Harris, Paul Sand, Andrew Duncan. (Photo courtesy of The Second City)

erence level. Our whole first company was intelligent but Severn was especially true to a very high intellectual standard and we have remained that way. People who come in with something else are still tempered by those residual attitudes, and their own work is modified by them."

Howard Alk once explained Severn Darden in terms of the theory of recognizable forms: "The audience should have a sense of what the people in the troupe are. Thus, Gene Troobnick is the schlemiel, Andy Duncan is the All-American boy, and Severn Darden is the madman. We used to say that we have eight people onstage and the function of seven of them is to protect the audience from Severn."

Not long after the opening, sleepy-eyed Paul Sand joined the company, bringing with him the years of experience he acquired studying with Viola Spolin and, in France, with Marcel Marceau. Shortly after, Alan Arkin came aboard, a young, macho, guitar-playing folksinger whose other claim to fame was singing with the Tarriers and coauthorship of "The Banana Boat Song," which at one time was number one on the hit parade. As a child, he used to perform at family gatherings. An aunt remembers him saying to playmates, "Let's play circus. I'll be everything." In high school, friends nicknamed him Twitch. "I was constantly banging something. I couldn't sit down for two minutes without playing drums on something. I had more energy than I knew what to do with." He attended Vermont's Bennington College, a women's school that accepted men on scholarship for their drama department. "I went kind of wild at Bennington. I didn't shave. I wore black boots, no socks, no underwear. I played the guitar and made a general nuisance of myself." At various times, he also repaired vacuum cleaners professionally and wrote science fiction for *Galaxy* magazine.

Arkin did not approach Second City with great hopes for the future. "I went because I couldn't get work anywhere else. That's exactly the truth. I was starving in New York, absolutely nothing was happening. Sills had seen me in David Shepherd's group in St. Louis, which I just did for a summer thinking I'd go back and have a career in New York again. But nothing materialized. I was deeply in debt, and Sills had offered me a job at Second City if I wanted to come to Chicago. My first reaction was Fat Chance. Then, when nothing materialized for about a year, I called Sills thinking I'd give up everything and go to work in Chicago for a hundred and a quarter a week. I went there in a state of despair, thinking I'd be in Chicago for the rest of my life. I was very grateful to have the job. I just didn't expect much to come of it."

Instead of closing the door on Arkin's future, it thrust him into the spotlight. As Second City's fame rose, so did Arkin's, dramatically—with a range of roles from Nikita Khrushchev to folksinger parodies, from a fifteen-year-old delinquent to an eighty-seven-year-old pretzel vendor inspired by his own grandfather.

As would prove true throughout the history of The Second City, all these people did not remain in the company simultaneously. A player would leave for another project, then come back. Others departed permanently. When a person left, a replacement would be arranged. Roger Bowen's sabbatical, for example, created the opening filled by Paul Sand. When Severn Darden took time off to be in *Hamlet*, Tony Holland (magical mind and literary whiz, who, Joan Rivers says, "has never, ever owned a book that had an illustration in it") stepped in. The net result is that the company has right along stayed pretty much the same size. Five or six men. Two or one women.

The Second City opened its doors with an admission of one dollar, offering a bohemian cabaret ambiance, permission to smoke and drink, seemingly just right for the proletarian masses. The crowd that arrived smacked more of university than slaughteryard. Within the first year, according to *Playboy*, the club had "gained a national reputation for presenting the best satire to be seen in the U.S.A. today." "When the limousines started pulling up," says Andrew Duncan, "the word *surprised* doesn't cover it. We didn't see how it could be happening."

We forget today what effect satire had then. We've been exposed to Norman Lear and a hundred other lampooning influences. In 1959, an actor couldn't even say *sweat* on television. Satire was "serious business. Conventional society was the enemy," according to Roger Bowen, "a force hostile to our values and our individual quirks, and our satire was a counterattack, a relief from the oppression we felt.

"We never planned for Compass or Second City to be satirical theatres. Neither David Shepherd nor Paul Sills really liked satire and they were always dissatisfied, but when you deal seriously with an H-bomb society, it either comes out satire or it comes out tragedy, and you can't hold a nightclub audience with tragedy."

An early taste of The Second City came in the form of the Kennedy-Khrushchev debates. Roger Bowen recalls "always trying to think of new ways to involve the audience, and one of the things I came up with was having them play the Washington Press Corps and ask questions of President Kennedy and Premier Khrushchev. Alan Arkin played Khrushchev and answered

questions in Russian gibberish after they had been translated by his interpreter, Tony Holland, who then translated the answers into English. I played
Kennedy. A few of the questions and answers I remember were:

Q: Mr. President, do you favor the use of poison gas and germ
    warfare?

A: Yes, and anything else that will help us avert the horrors
    of nuclear war.

Q: Mr. President, don't you believe in disarmament?

A: Of course I do, but you have to remember that if we give
    up our armaments, some other means must be found to fight
    our future wars.

"Khrushchev liked to use old proverbs, so Tony asked me to cook one
up for him. I gave him, 'When the hunter pisses on his foot, the owl screams.'
Tony got a pretty good laugh with this line and an even better one when he
transposed the phrases, although it wasn't quite as good that way. We'd get
the same questions over and over, so we had a chance to perfect our answers."

A scene called "The Nightmare of John Kennedy" found JFK ready to
address the Democratic National Convention when, to his chagrin, he realized
he had no clothes on. But brother Bobby urged him on: "Never mind. Go
out there and show them your boyish charm."

The questions were tied to the headlines. When something was hot,
timely, and terrifying, it was certain to be on someone's lips, addressed somehow on the Second City stage. "Extraordinary things were happening at that
time," says Andrew Duncan. "I remember the Bay of Pigs happening, and
there was a meeting to decide whether that night we would do the press
conference with that in it. It was agreed that it would be an escape valve. We
did the press conference and the audience screamed with laughter, just releasing their fear."

In another scene, Alan Arkin was a Puerto Rican sitting in the park,
wanting nothing more than to sing, enjoy the fresh air, and play the guitar.
Along came Andrew Duncan, as a social worker. "Juan, don't you want to
have some of the good things in life?"

"Oh, sure."

"I mean, wouldn't you want to buy a car?"

"Yeah."

"Wouldn't you like to have a house?"

"Yeah, yeah, yeah."

"You know, Juan, you have to work to have those things."

"Do you have those things?"

The scene ends with the Puerto Rican teaching the social worker about parks, fresh air, and singing.

Duncan remembers scenes that met with violent reactions. "We did some political spots on the local politics of Chicago, and we were stink-bombed at Second City. They threw lead shot through the window, and it was some sort of device that when it went through the window and hit the floor, it broke and released a stink that made the place uninhabitable for a couple of days."

The Second City offered satire with a biting edge. It assumed the intel-

Andrew Duncan on the stage of the first Second City. (Photo courtesy of The Second City)

Left to right: Ed Asner, Fred Willard (crouching), Shelley Berman, George Wendt
recreate "Football Comes to the University of Chicago" for the twenty-fifth anniversary
reunion. (Photo courtesy of Paul Natkin/Photo Reserve, Inc.)

ligence of its audience. It addressed people who laughed at references to Dada
and Wittgenstein's Vienna. It took on local issues and personalities, such as
Loyal Davis, father of future first lady Nancy Reagan. Says Darden, "He was
a brilliant surgeon. That's why his reputation was so powerful. He would
purposely humiliate not students but doctors who were training with him, in
public, frequently. Davis is a fairly common name, so one thing we repeated
quite a bit, Barbara would say to me, 'You can't get along with anybody.'
And I would answer, 'I can get along with Dr. Davis, and nobody can get
along with him, he's such a nut.' Invariably, five or six doctors in the audience
would know exactly who I was talking about. And University of Chicago
students were in the audience. When they laughed, the whole audience would
laugh with them. They probably thought people were laughing at the way I
said *nut*."

The Second City targeted social foibles from folk singers to intellectuals.
In "Football Comes to the Univesity of Chicago," Coach Hardin (Duncan)
tries to explain football symbols on a blackboard to students who question

the religious implications of the crosses, his use of geometric terms like *line*, and the relevance of Kierkegaard. (Coach: "There's a left guard and a right guard. No Kierkegaard"):

Morgenstern: Oh, sir.

Hardin: Yes.

Morgenstern: I hate to interrupt, but those things you call lines?

Hardin: Yard lines. Yes?

Morgenstern: If those were really lines, they'd be infinite and go all the way out to the end of the universe and make the game very long and tedious.

Hardin: Really? Well, what do you call them then?

Morgenstern: Those are line segments.

Hardin: I can accept that. Now, let's say we have the ball on the forty-seven yard line segment. Now, the circles here have the ball.

Morgenstern: I beg your pardon, sir. Those are not circles. They're ellipsoids. But let it pass.

Hardin: All right, ellipsoids.

There were wonderful scenes about people finding their places in one another's lives. In *Museum Piece*, Alan Arkin plays a beatnik. Barbara Harris is an up-tight, neurotic young woman: "I have numerous problems in the area of the spontaneous." They meet in an art museum. Not without difficulty, he wears her down, getting her to emote spontaneously to his accompaniment on the guitar. He makes his move, telling her he has no place to live. She panics and beats a retreat.

In "First Affair," Barbara Harris portrays a teenager home from a date, and Severn Darden is her father. He demands to know what she's been up to. She has no intention of telling him, and makes it quite clear that his old-fashioned morality has no value in her world view. What's a parent to do? Her father asserts, "I know as much as the next man about marijuana. I have read 'Reader's Digest.' "

In another scene, Paul Sand and Barbara Harris are alone in the woods as youngsters, boy scout and girl scout. They're talking about how to survive if they really get lost. Romance, unspoken, is in the air. Then a horn blasts, and they troop back to the bus to go home. "But," says Paul Sand, "it's a metaphor really. Spending a long time with somebody avoiding the romance part, and the bus horn honks, and you walk away before you had a chance to start."

Paul Sand, alone in "Phono Pal," learns to get along with a record. "I'd just come from France, where I sort of hung around Marcel Marceau's company. I didn't want to be a mime, but I wanted to go to France, and get away from home, and things like that, so I found him and auditioned and got into his company. When I came back to the United States, I hadn't talked in about a year, because I didn't know French in France and I'd been in a mime company. Then Sills called me and I went to Chicago, to Second City, and I was afraid to talk. Especially when I walked in and saw Severn Darden, who's the most luscious performer in the world, being so erudite, and all of them so knowledgeable. They knew all about politics and who's the bad guy and who's the good guy. I was ashamed of my ignorance, so I just kept quiet.

"Until I was on a bus one day, and I saw a man reading *How to Win Friends and Influence People.* So that night, one of the suggestions from the audience was 'phonograph record.' That's when I thought of a guy buying a "How to Win a Friend" record. Eugene Troobnick said, 'I'll be the guy on the record.' We did this thing about a man buying a record with instructions on how to win a friend, and that's the first time I talked."

In a metaphorical Mephisthophelean piece, Severn Darden, as a magnate of towering wealth, sits in his study as a storm brews outside. Enter the devil, Eugene Troobnick, offering the world in exchange for a little obeisance. Booms Darden, "Young man, do you know what a holding company is?" By the end of the scene, the devil is doing office work for the magnate, having gleaned which forces really rule the world.

For sheer silliness, consider the legendary mountain climbing scene. Picture Paul Sand and Andrew Duncan pantomiming the arduous trek up a Himalayan mountain. They're pantomiming hanging onto the rope for dear life. Whoosh. Whoosh. It's windy up there. Another man is offstage—a clumsy character allowed to tag along because he financed the expedition: Severn Darden. He's hanging from, swinging from, and ultimately sailing through space on, the end of a rope. All offstage.

"Watson?"

"Yes?"

"Catch this Leica camera. It's expensive. Be careful."

"Whaaaat?"

Eventually, Watson's companions lose all patience with him. They cut the rope.

As conceived on the Compass stage, this scene dramatized the racial issue—whether Edmund Hillary was going to reach the peak of Everest alone, or whether he was going to permit Tenzing Norkay, of Nepal, to conquer the summit with him. By the time Second City presented the vignette, only the hilarity remained.

"One time," Darden remembers, "Hillary was in the audience when we did it, accompanied by Khumjo Chumbi, who was a Sherpa. Chumbi didn't speak English, and he didn't realize that the different sketches were unrelated. He put them all together in his mind and decided I was a king who had been deposed, because at one point I was wearing a helmet, then I wasn't. Hillary's publicity men wanted me to go with Hillary to their base camp in Nepal, which would have been fun, but I couldn't make it."

The Second City was politics, parodies, people scenes, and more. One thing it was not was like television. To begin with, says Paul Sand, "We were sleeping half the day, at the movies the second half, and we were working at night. We never had time to watch television." Severn Darden "didn't own a television set until 1963. That's how little interest I had in it." Roger Bowen sees the difference between Second City and TV as no accident: "To re-state the difference between Compass and the original Second City group on one hand and the comedy one sees on television on the other, I would say that we did what we wanted to do and hoped there would be an audience for it. Television writers and performers do the opposite. They begin with what the audience wants and build everything on that. This seems to me to be the difference between artists (even bad ones) and entertainers (even good ones). . . .

"If we had ever got on television it would have been on some educational channel as a curiosity, something of interest to the intelligentsia, not for the mass audience of *That Was the Week That Was* or *Saturday Night Live*."

"We treated it," says Andrew Duncan, "in a kind of snobbish way, looking down on television. We had a game called 'Hurt,' a University of

Chicago game, in which you sat around in a very civilized way trying to hurt somebody with statements about them, like, if you were crude, you might say, 'It's much nicer being around you since you started bathing.' That would be on the lowest level. One of the more sophisticated levels would be to say, 'Secretly, you enjoy watching television.' "

In the beginning, they did not parody television, did not spoof commercials, did not "do" TV personalities. Essentially, they were well aware the television machine had been invented, yet were not among those who had wished it into being. That notion began eroding in a very small way with the broadcast of the Army-McCarthy hearings in the early fifties. Slightly more, it dispersed with the first televised presidential debates between Richard M. Nixon and John F. Kennedy in the fall of 1960. Then too, as cast members would be invited to guest on TV programs like *The Sid Caesar Show* and *The Jack Paar Show*, it became clear that this device was not without its uses.

Another interesting use of television is retrospective. By looking back at the programs of earlier generations, we can freeze-frame popular attitudes and see what could and could not be broadcast on the air. On February 22, 1960, Jack Paar walked off his show because NBC had forbidden him to tell a joke about a W. C. The joke, even by the standards of 1960, was quite tame. But the general public was perceived to be sensitive to tales about toilets.

On the Second City stage, players went much farther. In one scene, a young innocent enters a drugstore. He has a date for the first time. He wants to be prepared. He gets in line. The drug store is full of people. Though the waiting seems interminable to him, he eventually reaches the head of the line. The clerk asks, "Can I help you?" Embarrassed, the young man goes to great lengths to describe what he wants without naming it. At last, he gets his point across. Without having said the word. "Oh," says the clerk, whose voice carries, "You want a *contraceptive*."

That scene could not have appeared on TV in 1960. What's most significant, however, is that the scene was not concocted by an actor dying to shatter a taboo by uttering "contraceptive" in public. In fact, it was about exactly the opposite—dying not to say it. It was a human scene, a people scene, about fears and foibles and human beings as they are.

The day had not yet dawned when "shit" could be said on The Second City stage without earning the strongest reprimand—even though, in scatologically modest 1960, the word would have gotten a five-minute laugh. A five-minute laugh, but not a Second City laugh. A cheap laugh. Very lowbrow.

Andrew Duncan (left) and Paul Sand (right) in the lobby of the first Second City.
(Photo courtesy of The Second City)

Besides, the actors would look so awful if it backfired. Shelley Berman, for one, "never got the laughs saying shit. I've seen actors who just were so good at getting a laugh saying shit. Just the right way, the right time, and have the right kind of character to say it in just the right place. I never could do that. When I said it, it was just somebody saying shit."

No sooner had The Second City completed its first landmark year when another landmark presented itself to the waiting world. April 1961 saw the release of the company's first record album, a Mercury LP called *Comedy From the Second City*. Recorded live on the premises in January, the scenes included "Emma," "Great Books," "Cultural FM," "Businessman," "Caesar's Wife," "No George, Don't," and "Man in the Nightclub." Credits for the cast read: "Howard Alk, Alan Arkin, (Roger Bowen on sabbatical), Severn Darden, Andrew Duncan, Barbara Harris, Mina Kolb, Paul Sand, Eugene Troobnick. Composer-Pianist, William Mathieu. Director, Paul Sills. Produced by Howard Alk, Bernard Sahlins, Paul Sills." The album is a collector's item now, and still extremely funny. Age has not staled, nor custom withered, its infinite impiety.

As the LP spun on discriminating turntables across the land, Playwrights charter member Sheldon Patinkin became Second City's general manager, and Second City was making the acquaintance of a woman whose only enemy, apparently, was the number of hours in a day. Joyce Sloane was, and is, a dynamo, a house mother, a miracle worker. Tino Insana sees her as "the spirit of Second City." To Bernie Sahlins, she's "an island of calm in the midst of all this turbulence, with a quality of serenity and unflappability only saints can maintain that long." "She's a lovely person, a radiant person," says David Rasche. "She's a real behind-the-scenes person, a very, very, very important part of making Second City go, because whenever there was something that Bernie couldn't do or didn't do, she would do it. You need a mink coat for a scene. 'I can't get a mink coat.' The next day, there's a mink coat, or something that looks like a mink coat. Joyce got it. You have trouble with an apartment, she finds you an apartment. You got trouble and need bail, she's your bail. She'll stay up, she'll talk to you. You have something to celebrate, she'll throw you a party. She was a very important influence on everybody. She's a very caring person."

She is, particularly when all around her is insanity, the voice of reason— as when tension mounts and players insist, "I'm not talking to anyone about this except the Voice of Reason."

Joyce Sloane arrived during the construction at 1846 North Wells Street, next door to The Second City, of an edifice that would house a new experiment supplementing the output of Second City proper. Called Playwrights at Second City, it embraced the goal, not surprisingly, of enriching the fare of Chicago's theater-going public by presenting the sort of quality plays that might not otherwise be offered. Its producer was Bernie Sahlins. Its artistic director, Paul Sills. Its production manager, Sheldon Patinkin.

Joyce Sloane was hired to sell out the house. "I had experience in public relations and ticket sales. My family had been involved in theater, and my former husband was a circus producer. A man who was like a Dutch uncle to me taught me the business, because that's how the show traveled. When The Second City opened, I was home getting ready to have a baby. After Cheryl was born, this Dutch uncle said to me, 'What you ought to do is sell theater parties. There's nobody doing it in Chicago. It will keep you busy. It's interesting for you. You'll like doing it.'"

"A friend of mine sent me to Irving Seidner, who was then the public relations person, and I set up an appointment. The first person I met was Sheldon Patinkin, who was very nice. Then I met Bernie, and we climbed in and out of this structure that was being built. He gave me an assignment. He wanted me to sell out the whole week, the opening week. I didn't know that it's unheard of for a theater to open with eight sold-out performances. What did I know? I was young and stupid and someone told me what to do so I did it. I sold all eight performances of Jules Feiffer's *The Explainers*.

"In fact, I sold two opening nights, so I made one a preview. So actually, I sold nine performances. And—here we go again—on opening night, they were tacking down the carpeting. The bar, which was a few steps down, was piled high with glasses. We had a garden where we served hamburgers, and we had a grill for making the hamburgers. We'd forgotten to connect the flue. In walked all these lovely ladies in their pretty summer dresses, and the smoke backed up into the theater. That was opening night."

The Playwrights at Second City debut of *The Explainers,* on 9 May, 1961, marked the begining of *Village Voice* cartoonist Jules Feiffer's career as a dramatist. He was already an established cartoonist, with his weekly strips syndicated in some fifty newspapers internationally, and his cartoon book, *Sick Sick Sick,* an acclaimed bestseller. British critic Kenneth Tynan considered him "the best writer now cartooning."

The combination of Feiffer and the Second City mentality could not have been more natural. Both targeted sexual paranoia, political hypocrisy, and people who would give anything to be nonconformists like everyone else. His characters, explains Feiffer, "are on the periphery of the in-group—which means they've never quite made contact, but they're aware that contact has been made somewhere."

Derived from Feiffer's cartoon strips and devised in collaboration with Paul Sills, *The Explainers* gave Chicago something innovative in the way of theater, and gave Second City players a new outlet for their energies. Paul Sand "segued into that because I was tired of the format, on the Second City stage, of the lights going out every three seconds when the stage manager thought you had ended an improvisation, or having to wait for a laugh or the lights to go out when you were dying. I was real glad when Feiffer started working with us and we started doing longer pieces."

In the years to come and in various ways, the relationship between Feiffer and Second City players would continue, both in Chicago, and in New York with plays such as *Little Murders* and *The White House Murder Case*.

In the next few years, Playwrights at Second City would continue bringing quality theater to Chicago, introducing Edward Albee to Chicago with *The Zoo Story*, staging the first professional Harold Pinter production in Chicago with *The Caretaker*, premiering Bernie Sahlins' *The Puppet* and, in August 1961, presenting Playwrights' own set-in-Chicago, full-length, improvised version of *The Threepenny Opera*. Called *The Big Deal*, it starred Win Stracke and Alan Arkin and featured original music by Bill Mathieu.

And in July of 1961, The Second City sent its first company to New York City, by way of Los Angeles. Andrew Duncan recalls the chain of events. "Once Second City started and the momentum was building and people were coming in limousines, the Chicago papers loved us but also, people would come from New York and say, 'This should come to New York. This would be great in New York.' We say, 'No, you don't understand.' It really got to a point where we took a vote whether we were going to go. When we were offered the Broadway deal, I think the vote fell five to four.

"First we went to California, all the original people except Arkin, because of course we still needed some sort of nucleus to stay in Chicago. Then Paul Sills came to us in California and asked whether we needed anyone else. We said, well, Arkin would be a great addition. So Arkin was moved in."

Arkin, appearing in *The Big Deal*, associates that moment with "one of the anecdotes of my life. I had to leave *The Big Deal*. Sills, the maniac genius, rehearsed my understudy to take my place. During rehearsal, he decided that he didn't like the show, and rewrote it during rehearsal that afternoon. I came on stage that night, and I was playing the performance I'd been playing for six weeks, and it's a different play. I'm in one play and the entire rest of the cast is doing another play. I staggered through the act in terror, and then called a company meeting to find out what the hell was going on. They told me, and I suggested that we should go back to the version I knew. Otherwise, it would have been a total catastrophe. They did, so we got through the performance. That evening was one of those classic actors' nightmares."

From The Second City ran eight weeks in Los Angeles's Ivar Theatre. Workshops, held during the day, attracted new faces and new talents that might, conceivably, form a West Coast Second City when the Broadway-bound contingent headed east. Paul Mazursky and Larry Tucker were recruited locally to head the fledgling group. When the New York band departed, this group stepped in, using material created in Chicago while developing some of their own. What they produced was a good show that never took hold. It closed, but was followed shortly by Mazursky and Tucker's Third City—a show with a Second City flavor and a brief but rewarding success.

Meanwhile, Chicago's pilgrims were invading New York. Preceding them improvisationally in the Big Apple was Theodore J. Flicker's The Premise, which had opened in 1960 and would remain in business until 1964. Over those four years, Premise players would include, among others, Godfrey Cambridge, Gene Hackman, Buck Henry, Diana Sands, and George Segal. Dustin Hoffman, on The Premise kitchen staff, had been working at odd jobs ranging from waiter to typist for the yellow pages. ("I slept on Gene Hackman's kitchen floor, and every morning at three A.M. the refrigerator would have a heart attack and wake me up.")

From the Second City opened at New York's Royale Theater on 26 September, 1961. The cast was Howard Alk, Alan Arkin, Severn Darden, Andrew Duncan, Barbara Harris, Mina Kolb, Paul Sand, and Eugene Troobnick, with music by William Mathieu, and staged by Paul Sills. Producers were Howard Alk, Bernard Sahlins, and Paul Sills together with Broadway/TV biggie Max Liebman (formerly producer of Sid Caesar's *Your Show Of Shows*). Among the sketches were "Football Comes to the University of Chicago," "Museum Piece," "First Affair," and "Phono Pal," along with forays into West Germany, Laos, and New Jersey ("Hoboken Story"—a sort of *Julius Caesar* à la *West Side Story*, with waterfront union honcho Julio Squeezer, his pal Brute, his gal Cal, and "Mrs. Stickles from the National Labor Relations Board").

Critic Walter Kerr raved: "People are always asking where the new comedians are coming from. They're coming from Chicago. Coming? They're here. There are no fewer than eight brand new, bright new, bubbling new entertainers capering all over the stage of the Royale as though they'd been born to Broadway, or better. In at least two instances we are presented with what are really miniature plays, and quite perfect ones." Critic Robert Coleman wrote a dump that amounted to high praise: "There may be a limited audience for 'From the Second City,' but we doubt that it will prove to be Mr. and Mrs. Average American Playgoer's dish of tea. Ordinary ticket buyers are getting more than a little fed up with beatniks and avant-garde-ism."

It was The Second City's first brush with people who drank tea from a dish. The experience also found Second City working in a large theater instead of a comfy cabaret, and shorn of improvisations, because producer Max Liebman didn't want them in the show. In November, the troupe kissed Broadway good-bye to take root in a setting more its style. They re-opened almost immediately at Square East in Greenwich Village, six blocks from The Premise on Bleecker Street.

Square East was a coffeehouse-cabaret (the building was formerly a dye-sponging plant). It stood plunk in the middle of a college crowd, that of New York University. There were two shows nightly, Tuesday through Friday and Sunday, three shows on Saturday, plus improvs. Acoustics weren't great and not every seat was perfect, but The Second City had found its own kind and was packing the seats once again.

Their first revue at Square East was *Seacoast of Bohemia*, with "additional material by David Shepherd, Roger Bowen and the audience." Lynda Segal had joined the group. Paul Sand and Mina Kolb were temporarily on sabbatical (she had a role in the 1961–62 season of TV's *Pete and Gladys*, among other acting engagements). In due course came new revues, among them *To The Water Tower* (Tom O'Horgan composed and played the music) and *A View From Under the Bridge* (its title, in typical Second City fashion, spoofing a nearby off-Broadway event—Arthur Miller's *A View From The Bridge*).

What helped the Square East gig immeasurably was the sudden appearance of David Susskind, camera crew in tow. Andrew Duncan remembers: "Second City was, in a sense, getting too big. It was in Chicago and it was in New York and it was trying to be centrally located in Chicago and run by one man. My theory is that they more or less wrote off the New York group to function however it could. By some fluke, David Susskind saw us on a local Channel 2 Sunday morning program that used us to illustrate some little thing on political satire. Susskind had missed us on Broadway and missed us off-Broadway, but when he saw this, he came to Square East and did a whole two hours of us on his show, which put us on the map. Then people were lining up for—years."

"Up to that point," says Alan Arkin, "we had been playing to a fairly elitist audience, the college crowds, the intellectuals, professional people. After the Susskind show, all of a sudden, we became the 'in' thing to go see. We were getting the mink coat crowd. And we were getting all kinds of referential laughs, that had nothing to do with the humor. That's the kind of laugh I've always hated, where people laugh because they understand your reference and are letting you know that they know what you're talking about, and how smart they are, which has nothing to do with their having been shocked or pleased or delighted.

"There was one night when people were going crazy, much more so than we deserved. They weren't really appreciating us as much as they were showing each other how much they were appreciating us. I was furious, and I went backstage and said to Severn, 'Damn this audience. I hate this crowd. You mention Thomas Mann, you get a laugh.' So Severn was in the next scene with me. We went onstage. I had a scene where I was putting on a suit of clothes, and I turned to him and said, 'How does it look?' He answered, 'You look just like Thomas Mann.'

"It had absolutely nothing to do with anything, and it brought the house down. What's funny is that I was furious for days because, by proving my theory, he went and got one of the biggest laughs of the evening."

In a sense, The Second City's biggest problem in Greenwich Village was that it became so successful. Its players were forever being drafted for Broadway, movies, television (an industry still largely based in New York*), and commercials. By 1962, four Broadway shows were using Second City alumni. Alan Arkin, in *Enter Laughing,* won raves. Tony Holland in *My Mother, My Father,* and Barbara Harris and Zohra Lampert in *Mother Courage and Her Children,* were likewise acclaimed. Second City director Larry Arrick handsomely staged *The Heroine.*

As alumni left, new players and directors filled their shoes—some from

---

*The police drama *Naked City,* famous for its Big Apple location shots, featured Alan Alda and Barbara Dana in a scene about improvising in a Greenwich Village coffeeshop. Alda, looking driven, played a cranky young poet.

Chicago, some through local contacts, and some through workshops run by Paul Sills in New York. Joan Rivers, who had joined the Chicago company, left to find other things in New York, then fell in with Square East briefly. Pierre Epstein was snatched off the street by Alan Arkin. "We'd worked together and become friendly during *Enter Laughing*," Epstein remembers. "I was walking along Forty-seventh street and Times Square and Alan and his wife, Barbara Dana, drove by in a yellow Volkswagen. He said, 'Get in. What are you doing?'

"I said, 'This, that, and the other thing.'

"He said, 'Why don't you do some Second City?' So I did."

Arlene Golonka took the workshop route. "I came from Chicago, but I lived in New York. In Chicago, I went to the Goodman Theatre with Barbara Harris and knew that whole bunch, but I never belonged to it until New York, where I went to Paul Sills's classes. Jo Anne Worley was in the workshops with me. When Barbara Harris left Second City, Jo Anne and I split her routines and took her place."

Alan Alda came to the New York workshops by way of a Compass arm in Hyannisport, where his JFK press conference improvisation often found him taking questions from reporters in the audience who had put the same questions to the real Kennedy earlier in the day. (After a while, Alda shifted from Kennedy impersonations to doing William Buckley. He discovered that the answers he'd used as Kennedy worked just as well coming from Buckley's right-wing lips.)

Paul Dooley—whose background included a club act of Shakespearean dou-

Alan Alda as TV's Hawkeye Pierce on M★A★S★H. (Photo courtesy of Howard Frank Archives/Personality Photos, Inc.)

bletalk with characters named Scenario, Portfolio, and Fellatio—came in and understudied "*everyone*. It's funny being an understudy when there's no script to learn. I had to learn everyone's part and I'd go on for everyone as they went on vacation. By the time the whole cast got back, I was indispensable. I knew everyone's role, and could fill in anywhere."

Barbara Dana, who met Alan Arkin while both were in *Enter Laughing*, became Mrs. Alan Arkin about the time that a new New York team was required. To this day, she's not exactly sure what happened, but thinks "it was a kind of quick thing. It almost seems Alan and I were on our honeymoon when Sheldon Patinkin called and said they needed something at Square East and Severn was available. I had no improvisational training, and the three of us went into the show with one week's rehearsal. They of course were old hands at it. We worked most of that one week on a scene that never went into the show. It was called 'Circus,' and I was the great and famous Wanda who could hang by my armpits. We didn't fall back on any of the old scenarios. Everything was from scratch." The results were very favorably reviewed.

Alan Myerson, who directed The Second City in both Chicago and New York, went west in 1963 and founded San Francisco's The Committee. It would welcome to its bosom, over the next ten years, such Second City alumni as Roger Bowen, John Brent, Hamilton Camp, Del Close, Severn Darden, Bill Mathieu, Dick Schaal, and Avery Schreiber.

As The Second City rolled on at Square East, old alumni who had left would drop by for guest improvs, while new alumni were being turned out hand over fist. Bernie Sahlins finally decided it was "too much. Every week I had to fly in to replace all the people who had been discovered and pulled out. You can't have this kind of theater in New York because everyone is so career oriented. Where you're *going* becomes more important than what you're doing. The work at hand becomes a stepping stone, not an end in itself. And that's death."

Even so, the New York engagement lasted through November 1964.

As New York's Second City was losing its players to the four winds, the folks in the Windy City were breaking in one replacement cast after another, thereby setting up a system that's ensured the troupe's continuity through the present day. The recruiting process, refined and embellished over the years, has never been less than a matter of utmost importance. At times it's been rigorous. In exceptional cases, not so rigorous. But its rate of success has been uncanny.

Actors have been drawn to Second City for any number of reasons. In the sixties, Valerie Harper followed husband Dick Schaal. In the seventies, Robin Duke followed high-school chum Catherine O'Hara, and Bill Murray followed older brother Brian Doyle-Murray into Second City: "There are people who still think of me as Brian Murray's brother."

Bonnie Hunt, an emergency room nurse; Steven Kampmann, a therapist at a state mental hospital; and Harold Ramis, a former psychiatric orderly, substitute teacher, and joke editor at *Playboy* had the requisite patience for the work.

Tim Kazurinsky, an advertising copywriter, took the workshops as a means of sharpening his presentational skills. Unexpectedly, Second City offered him a job. He accepted. "It represented an 80 percent pay cut, so how could I say no?"

Sandy Holt "was about eighteen when I was working as a waitress at a place called The Bear. John Brent and Howard Alk would improvise there. They had a fabulous kind of insanity. Everyone from Second City came to see them. I got to thinking it was what I wanted to do. Then I started stealing my mother's Chevy, and going to Second City, and hanging out."

George Wendt chose Second City by a process of elimination. "All I wanted to do was be in Second City. I didn't have any long-term goals. That's youth for you. It became time for me to think of what to do for a living. I didn't like anything. So I started thinking in terms of a process of elimination. I didn't want to be a fireman. I didn't want to be a doctor. Scientist? No. Teacher? No. I'd seen Second City a bunch of times when I was in college. Second City? I thought, 'Wow, that looks like I wouldn't hate it.' I was positive I wouldn't hate that, and I was pretty sure they got paid."

Eric Boardman and Will Porter, best friends since their days of teaching together, had given up teaching to pursue other goals. But the summer was open, and Porter suggested taking a Second City workshop. Boardman declined, "because my idea of actors was that they wore earrings and capes and sang 'Oklahoma.' Will said, 'Forget that. You might meet some girls.' They took the workshops, enjoyed them, and eventually joined the company. Miriam Flynn, a participant in the same workshops and later a member of their cast, is today Mrs. Will Porter. Eric Boardman is her writing partner and the godfather of their son.

David Rasche was a former divinity student from the University of Chicago. "It wasn't working and they told me they thought I'd be happier elsewhere, and I agreed. It was 1970, which was a continuation of the sixties and the asking of great questions. What was our country about? What was progress all about? The answers I heard were that ambition is a dead end. It was work, study, get ahead, kill. That was the progression that was around. So I had a lot of questions about what I was doing on the earth, and nothing seemed right.

"The summer after my senior year in college, I'd worked on a Great Lakes cruise ship. I was a porter. At night, I did shows with a waitress. I would rip off Mike Nichols and Elaine May—down to the inflections. I'd get ugly when the waitress didn't get the pauses right. Then I knocked around, and wound up in Chicago, and was in this film for a tenants' rights organization. I played the hero. Judith Flaherty—Joe's wife—was the heroine. She told me I might like Second City workshops, which cost sixty bucks. I couldn't believe it. 'I just give them my money and they'll let me do it?' I wanted it so much that I was scared to death about going. I finally got a friend to go with me and I paid his tuition. That's how much I knew it was what I wanted to do."

John Hemphill was improvising professionally long before an acting career ever crossed his mind. When he had a part-time job at an LCBO self-service store in Toronto, one that consisted essentially of stocking shelves, "I had to stand around a lot. Sometimes I would be asked about wine. If I didn't know the answer, I'd lie." What he really wanted to be was a schoolteacher. "I loved it. But for me, this was the right profession at the wrong time. No jobs. It was as simple and as sad as that." Then, in the late seventies, he heard Second City was holding workshops for new talent. "I'd heard there was a TV show of that name, but was unaware there was also a stage version. It cost six dollars then for one lesson of two-and-a-half hours. I took them because I thought they would be fun, rather than help me to a new career." They led to a long association with Toronto's Second City in several capacities, though at first ". . . to be entirely honest, I was terrible. It was three months before I got a laugh."

In 1960, Jack Burns was half the comedy team of Burns and Carlin, George Carlin having been the other half. Lenny Bruce had discovered them. They'd frequently pulled in fifteen hundred dollars a night. But Burns was awed by the level of intelligence displayed at Second City. "I think George is very intelligent. We both thought we were intelligent. Evidently Lenny Bruce thought we were intelligent. There were things George and I would try occasionally that were sharp, but we were playing some pretty rough clubs so you couldn't get away with a lot we wanted to do. I hadn't gone to college, my college had been the United States Marine Corps, and before that I'd been an army brat. But I was always trying to educate myself. In this respect, I was always sort of an outsider because who the hell did I hang around with on my corner of the street who read Kierkegaard or Proust. Mickey Spillane, maybe.

"So Second City, even more than the people who were in it, the idea of Second City, represented a whole new world to me. When you're in Second City, you read every paper, every magazine, every book. You have to—in order to be able to respond to the improv suggestions. And the ensemble playing and the improvisational aspects of it just knocked me for a loop.

"At one point, George and I went our separate ways, and I was in Chicago. So I asked, 'How do I get in?' They said, 'Well, there are many ways. You can work in the bar, or the kitchen, or sweep the floors.' I said, 'Hey, I just came from big bucks with Burns and Carlin. There's got to be an easier way.' But there wasn't. You've got to pay your dues if you want to be part of that company, so I went and auditioned in New York for two of David Shepherd's Compass groups. Alan Alda was at the audition too. We both got in. He went with the Cape Cod group, and I went to St. Louis, to the Crystal Palace.

"Larry Hankin was in the St. Louis company with me. This was the summer of 1962. Paul Sills came down to look for some minor league players to bring up to the big time. The night he showed up, we went crazy. It was every man for himself. Ensemble spirit fell apart. 'Paul Sills is here!' It was like God walking into this club. Then Paul asked Larry and me if we'd like to come up and hang around Second City and fill in once in a while, and we both went up."

When actors audition for Second City, they're judged on their improvisational ability, stage presence, and sense of timing. Auditions consist of tests like five-through-the-door, in which the quaking hopeful, without warning, has to concoct five different characters in a row. Do one. Leave. Do the next. Leave. Do another. And so on.

The qualities sought in the inquisition are, as expressed by Bernie Sahlins, first of all, intelligence. "A know-nothing person who doesn't know who he is, what's going on in the world or hasn't read anything, I don't use him. Then they have to use their environment, use their fellow actors, use what's on stage. Of course they have to have acting ability, and the ability to bring an ironic point of view to what's going on in the world, and stage presence, which is something unteachable and undefinable."

An actor auditioning in the early seventies was told to improvise Melvin

Laird (then U.S. Secretary of Defense) in a talk show format. The actor confessed that he wasn't sure who Melvin Laird was, and asked if he could be somebody else. "That's not the type we want, obviously," explains Sahlins. "I'd rather have someone with an academic background than a theatrical one, because our actors are also our writers. The man with the academic background uses his head and knows what to say. And with some actors, a strong theatrical background can be a hindrance. Some aren't used to performing without a script. Some can't create people on stage all by themselves."

Joan Rivers auditioned for Second City after waiting half a day in an outer office. She remembers being escorted to a conference room where Bernie Sahlins and Paul Sills sat in judgment. "The phone rang and Sahlins took the call while I stood there like an idiot. Paul Sills said, 'Improvise something.' " Rivers asked for a script. Sills said, "We don't work with scripts. Just describe something—anything—whatever you think is happening in this room." She exploded. "In this room there is a cheap ugly little man sitting behind the telephone without the manners to get off and watch somebody who has been waiting five hours. And the other man, so superior, is saying 'We don't have scripts.' " She waxed eloquent and chucked an ashtray across the room. Then they talked, and the following day she was offered the job.

As Second City grew, the recruiting process became an inverted funnel. Entry could be achieved at any of several broad-based levels, from the workshops to the kitchen. From these, the crème de la crème would rise to the top, through Children's Theatre, touring company, and E.T.C. (a later development, consisting of a sort of "resident" touring company in Chicago, with its own revues, presented on a stage adjacent to Second City's main building). Joe Flaherty, Tim Kazurinsky, Bill Murray, Harold Ramis, Betty Thomas, and George Wendt spent time on the Children's Theatre stage. Jim Belushi, Don DePollo, Tim Kazurinsky, Bill Murray, Brian Doyle-Murray, Harold Ramis, Betty Thomas, and George Wendt all worked in touring companies before playing Second City's main stage. Valerie Harper, Joe Flaherty, Ira Miller, David Rasche, and George Wendt specifically took workshops in hopes of being picked for the company. Joe Flaherty's first job at Second City was as stage manager. Ira Miller doubled as cook while taking workshops. "I figured if they saw me around all the time, they'd be more likely to use me. Also, I made terrific hamburgers."

Betty Thomas was a waitress. "I wasn't really interested in the theater. I was teaching school at the time. I had studied art and art history and I was teaching public school, substitute teaching, and I needed an extra source of

Left to right: Joe Flaherty, Debra McGrath, Betty Thomas (standing), Harold Ramis, Jim Belushi, Eugene Levy, recreating Funeral *for the twenty-fifth anniversary reunion. (Photo courtesy of Jennifer Girard)*

income—for extra money, a trip to Europe, those things—so I worked there a couple of nights a week. Then I think the bartender dared me, so I took a workshop with Jo Forsberg. The workshops seemed like the most fun I ever had.

"Then I went to Europe, came back, taught school, was a waitress again. I took Del Close's workshops because they were so interesting and fun. But it wasn't part of my life and I wasn't thinking of being in Second City. Then at school, somebody punched me in the mouth or something and I wanted to get out of there badly. Auditions were coming up, and Joyce Sloane called me and said, 'Betty, come down here and audition.' I said, 'Why?' But she got me down there, and I did the audition, and Bernie, after hemming and hawing, said well, okay.

"Then after about nine months, Eugenie Ross-Leming decided to leave the main company. They told me that until they found a real actress, until they found someone who could really do the roles, since I knew all the roles, I could do it."

Peter Boyle's ultimate arrival on The Second City stage was less an entry than the consummation of a pilgrimage. As a starving actor in New York in the early sixties ("the only way I could afford to see *Beyond The Fringe* was that they gave a benefit for the Actors Fund and you could get a ticket if you donated a pint of blood"), he took improvisation workshops and met David Shepherd. When Paul Sills opened the Game Theatre in Chicago, Boyle and Shepherd made the long, hard drive by car to experience it. "Of course I had to go," says Boyle. "It was like pursuing the Grail. The search to discover the real thing. Who is doing it and where can I find it? And all during the ride to Chicago, David unfolded the whole Compass and Second City story, the legend."

In New York, Boyle became a member of Elaine May's Third Ear at The Premise. Later, as understudy for the leads in the national touring company of *The Odd Couple*, he found himself back in Chicago again. By then, he'd spent time in California, where he'd participated in a few sets with The Committee ("I'd get a few laughs and think, 'Wow, maybe my sex life will improve' ") and where Avery Schreiber took him to dinner, paying with a credit card ("I was speechless. An actor with a credit card! I was unbelievably impressed"). In Chicago, Boyle took Game Theatre workshops with Viola Spolin. When *The Odd Couple* closed after two years, he was invited to join the Second City main stage company—completing the circle that all legends inevitably comprise.

Conversely, sometimes, it's a quick trip up from the minors. Don DePollo joined the workshops in early winter, by May was put in the touring company, and by September the entire touring company was promoted to resident company, which very rarely happens. Sometimes, the road to main stage is bumpier. George Wendt recalls being "kind of all over the place. I was in the resident company, then fired back down to the touring company, then we opened a gig at the Château Louise which could still be running as far as I know. Then back to the resident company, which by then was real smooth for me. I think the first couple of years I'd been kind of in over my head."

Melinda Dillon was a hatcheck girl at Second City while studying to be a serious actress at the Goodman Theater. As hatcheck girl, she was also an understudy. One night while she was hatchecking, Howard Alk gave her a note: "You're on tonight." She went on for Barbara Harris, leaving Paul Sills to understudy for her, checking hats.

Sandy Holt's entrance was, similarly, from the hatcheck booth. "After hanging out at Second City, I got a job in the checkroom for about a year.

Every single night I was like a sponge. I absorbed everything they were doing on stage. I was so terrible in the checkroom. I used to play in the coats because I'd get bored. People would come for their coats, which would be all mixed up. Besides, I'm allergic to fabric, so I didn't want to stay there. They had to put me in the show. I went from being a cocktail bunny at The Bear to appearing on the stage of Second City. Once I was in, there was no analyzing it. It was like being in love. 'This is where I belong. This is what I was meant to do.' "

Ann Elder made one of the fastest entrances on record. "I wasn't a theater major in school, I was an English major. And when I got out of college, I went to work in an ad agency, and I was a copywriter in Chicago. Two guys that I knew had been stand-up comics, and they wanted to get together a trio with a girl in it. They asked me. We got together a couple of weekends and we started writing sketches. We found a club, which happened to be around the corner from Second City, and this club was very anxious to have entertainment on weekends. So we three did our act, our little revue, and the only thing I asked of my two partners was that I had to sit down at all times. I suffered from total stage fright. If I stood, my knees buckled, so I couldn't stand.

"We played there about nine months, weekends only. Second City came to see us. I think it was Del Close and Sheldon Patinkin. Afterwards, they said 'Would you mind coming to sit with us and have a drink at the bar?' I was delighted because I heard the word 'sit.' My partners had much more talent—I was there just barely pulling my own—but Second City was a girl short. They were stuck. So they offered me the job that night. I think they were opening in three weeks. . . ."

When the pilgrims first stormed Los Angeles, then New York in 1961, a new gang took to the Chicago stage. Among them was Richard Libertini: "Macintyre Dixon and I had our own show, *Stewed Prunes*. We went to Chicago with it, then he had to go into the hospital. I hung around Second City, and that's when I joined. The company I went into was Melinda Dillon, Hamilton Camp, Zohra Lampert, Bill Alton, John Brent, and Tony Holland. Then, after a while, I left to work again with Macintyre Dixon. Then Paul Sills invited us both to join the company, which we did. But before that, when I first got in, we started out using some of the sketches our predecessors had developed and passed down. That was the core of the show, which would be followed by our own improvisations.

"When we inherited material, it was like the old vaudeville days. Someone says, 'You're going to do Floogle Street. Here's how it goes.' They'd kind of show you. So you're watching it, then you jump in, and you get the beats so you don't miss any of the important places, then you're on your own. Things continue to transform, because you're not working from a tape or a script, and it depends on who inherits what from whom."

A case in point is "Clothes Make the Man," inspired by the way men were suddenly becoming fashion-conscious and in tune with sartorial trends. Originally, Tony Holland played the salesman in a very chic men's store. Alan Arkin, a he-man type, was the customer. Holland pantomimed and described to him all the latest styles, waxing eloquent with exotically-rendered pants that had buttons or zippers down the sides. As Arkin absorbed the sales pitch and tried on the different outfits, he transformed inwardly as well as outwardly. By the close of the scene, he was a foppish dandy.

When Arkin left for New York, Hamilton Camp took over the part. (Prior to Second City, Camp played Bernard in *The Explainers*. In the cast with him, and later in Second City with him, were John Brent and Del Close.) Just as clothes make the man, the man makes the sketch, and you never get a carbon copy. Arkin and Camp are physically very different. Arkin looks like a truck driver. Camp could pass for an elf. On the other hand, the scene "was set and the laughs were there, so I had no reason to want to change it. I watched it a few nights, then went on and did it. Once an improvisation is finally frozen, all the permutations have been, practically, exhausted. In the main show, the idea was, as you do in any role, to step in and play it. The premise was an ordinary guy going into a fancy boutique and, as the clothes go on him, he's becoming more and more effete. I'm sure, within that, there were different values that came out. But the main thrust of it, how I handled each beat, I sprang off what Alan had given me.

"Then, after each main show, we'd take suggestions from the audience, improvise, and begin to build our own material." When enough that was new had been polished, the next revue was born.

As it was then, it is now, pretty much. A replacement cast has plenty to learn without having to start from scratch. With all the workshops known to mankind, a cast's first show, or shows, can be rough. Rough edges. Rough performances. Rough days and nights. This is part of the process that makes a cast a team. Surviving a shared disaster invariably forms a bond.

This means, by extension, that joining a cast already together is like being the new kid on the block. Joan Rivers was new on the block in the fall of 1961, smart (Phi Beta Kappa from Barnard College) and eager. The daughter of successful Russian immigrant parents—her father was a doctor and her mother a bastion of elegance—she threw her parents into a panic when she first mentioned wanting to act professionally. But the theater had held a special fascination for her since her first prekindergarten play, when she so much enjoyed her role as a kitten with pink ears that she refused to take the kitten hat off when she went home, or even when she went to bed.

When Rivers arrived at Second City, she didn't know anyone in town. She entered a cast consisting of Bill Alton, Hamilton Camp, Del Close, Tony Holland, and Avery Schreiber. She found herself being plugged into pieces created by others, for instance saying, "Baa, baa, baa" in "A Nation of Sheep." Because she was unassertive, she usually missed the action in the improv sets.

One night there was an improv suggestion for "a farmer and a hooker." Rivers approached Bill Alton: "Let's you be the farmer and I'll be the hooker." (1961 was perhaps too early to try it the other way around.) The scene worked. Alton was a married man with kids. He has children. So does she. He has pictures in his wallet. She doesn't have a wallet but she has a tattoo on her thigh. "If I flex my muscle, I can make my kid dance." The scene ends when she reveals that indeed she's a hooker—she hooks rugs.

With the success of the scene, Rivers felt more at home. Gradually, she developed new pieces with members of the cast. Tony Holland became her close friend and frequent partner. ("I was in shock that he wanted to be my friend. It was like Lenny and George in *Of Mice and Men*.") Together they created "Model and Tailor," inspired by the suggestion "A stitch in time saves nine." Rivers was Rita, the impatient model, standing on a chair. He was the tailor, pinning up her dress. Rita's aspirations are fading fast. When she was young, she figured to marry a doctor. Then, okay, a lawyer, a dentist. Then, what the heck, a CPA. Now thirty-three and still single, "If he walks and talks, he's for me."

Of the model, Rivers recently said, "Rita is the secret of my success. . . . Though I did not imagine it then, she was to become my stand-up comedy persona."

About Second City, she says, "I was really born as a comedian at Second City. I owe it my career. No Second City, no Joan Rivers."

But she also bade it goodbye in the face of competition that never seemed to end. Paul Sills left and Alan Myerson came in as director in November. The transition wasn't comfortable. "Model and Tailor" was dropped from the running order of the new show. Irene Riordan, new to the cast, was getting progressively more to do. Rivers was getting less. Irene Riordan became Mrs. Alan Myerson. Joan Rivers started moonlighting.

In December, to add to her income as well as professional credits, Rivers was performing two nights a week at the Gate of Horn. "The inner group of Second City was very upset because they thought I was commercializing my art, cheapening everybody's image. A single! At a nightclub!"

Depending on whom you talk to in the cast, the problem was not that she had a nightclub act but that some of them had given up nightclub acts to devote full time to Second City; that she'd get her Second City laughs at the expense of other people's scenes ("Dear, about our children . . ." "Jerk, we don't have any children"); that she'd step out of a scene to joke, out of context, directly with the audience.

Richard Libertini worked in the Chicago company when Rivers performed there: "I don't know if it was a misunderstanding, or a desire not to look uncomfortable. It can come from fear. But people won't want to work with you if they're afraid you're going to deny the reality of their scene, if

Left to right: Avery Schreiber, Joan Rivers, Bill Alton, Del Close. (Photo courtesy of The Second City)

you say, 'We don't have kids.' Even though I know it's not an easy thing to believe these six people are going to trust each other completely, particularly when there's this little thing called self-preservation that creeps in as soon as the audience sits down."

Severn Darden worked with her in New York. "Joan Rivers essentially wanted to do at Second City what she's doing now. She wanted a scene where people would simply let her alone to talk. But she was very good at that. Still is. I wouldn't say she wasn't a team player, but she wanted to do a different kind of comedy. She wanted more like the Catskills type of humor. And we didn't want that."

Bill Alton loved working with her. "She's driven, but she only drives herself. The point with Joan is that she is incredibly ambitious, driven twenty-four hours a day, seven days a week, fifty-two weeks a year. Inevitably, people who are like that in the business are mean. They'll kill their mothers if they have to. But *she* manages to be a sweetheart. I think it would be an oversim-

Joan Rivers on an early talk show, That Show. (*Photo courtesy of Howard Frank Archives/Personality Photos, Inc.*)

plification to say she just wanted to do stand-up comedy. She was literate, she read the papers. She was interested in becoming a star, and when she found her natural talent was for the wisecrack and the one-liner, it obviously made more sense for her to go that way than to do 'Football Comes To The University of Chicago.' "

Bernie Sahlins' feeling is that "Joan Rivers always wanted to be an individualist, a stand-up comic, someone who was there in a solo role."

Joan Rivers denies denying other players' realities. "You can tell from my scenes there that it's not the way I operate. I knew the medium and I knew the rules of improvisation, and the people who say I didn't never did scenes with me."

This charge in turn engenders variations: the response that the people who didn't do scenes with Rivers didn't because they feared she might deny their reality, step out of the piece, tell jokes . . .

Ultimately, Joan Rivers concluded that "I'm terribly sensitive. I want to please everybody. I cannot work on a set unless everybody loves me and I love everybody." She left in February and, except for a few months with the New York troupe, went on to other things. She left not the building she'd come to but rather, the one next door. Already—November 1961—the success of the company had warranted switching theaters with Playwrights. Joyce Sloane describes the original, smaller building as "bursting at the seams. We had to make the swap, after which, we had a sign outside pointing Second City this way, Playwrights of The Second City, that way. Sheldon Patinkin had to stand outside directing people from one place to the other. We had a traffic problem with the design of the new theater, because people would be waiting to come in, and other people would be trying to come out. Many's the night that Sheldon was announcing, 'Will those people leaving please leave?' and things like that. So we moved into 1846 North Wells, which had two hundred seats."

Playwrights continued in its new location, though not much longer, with offerings along the lines of Roger Bowen and Bob Brady's 'The Conscience of a Liberal,' a political revue presented on weekends.

The Second City remained topical, trenchant, abreast. The Berlin Wall with Del Close in a German helmet. U.S. involvement in Vietnam, with Roger Bowen as an "advisor." Fallout shelters, with Del Close marketing the franchise. John Brent, as the faith healer, heals the man with a deformed hand who pleads, "Make this hand like the other one"—only to depart with two deformed hands.

In one scene, Tony Holland is a goatherd in the Alps. Hamilton Camp is a karate salesman trying to sell him lessons. The goatherd isn't interested until the salesman asks, "What are you going to do if some guy comes out of the darkness and says, 'Your money or your goats?' "

The Second City remained true to classical allusions (with, for instance, Del Close as Euclid, Galileo, and Newton all in one evening) and its people scenes, whether Tony Holland and Bill Alton in "Lekythos" (about two men who were friends in college: One became a broker, the other became "the mole," a perennial student, who still had his ideals. Tennessee Williams loved the sensitive portrayals.) or Mina Kolb and Avery Schreiber in a *Zoo Story* parody, as a couple on a park bench:

Kolb: "You know, A & P and the Stop & Shop are merging. They're gonna call it Stop & A."

Or Tony Holland, his scarf thrown back over his neck, as the gay Rhoda Schaepiroe, who sometimes talked about her friend Svetlana, Stalin's daughter.

In October 1962, The Second City made its first appearance abroad, in the form of a two-month exchange with London, England's The Establishment satirical company. The Establishment had been founded by Peter Cook, Michael Frayne, and the *Beyond the Fringe* crowd. In London, they held forth in a ten thousand–member private club in Soho, and were an intellectual rage. On Chicago soil, and without the original players, it wasn't entirely the same. Awash with pro-Second City sentiment, Jean Martin protested in *The Nation* that The Establishment players improvised behind closed doors, only giving the audience the result; that they relied on words and visual jokes rather than on characters; and "the oddest and least expected difference between the two is that The Establishment is, for want of a better word, dirty— and Second City is not. This version of The Establishment is reportedly cleaned up some, but it still struck Chicago audiences as rather pointlessly off-color."

At the same time, at The Establishment, Second City was presenting *The London Show*, with Bill Alton, Del Close, Mina Kolb, Dick Schaal, and Avery Schreiber. The English were responsive, though with a preference for the off-color line. When asked why, critic Kenneth Tynan explained, "You have to face it. The English discovered their morality in the lavatory when they were little boys, and they never quite got out."

As Second City was opening in London, John Kennedy held forth in the United States, warning the Soviets to get their missiles out of Cuba. It was a swell time to be an American abroad. "We were just down the block," says Schreiber, "when the American consulate in London was bombed. Del had shots with his camera, from hiding under the car, as people raced by us shouting anti-American slogans."

All in all, it made sense to succumb to The Game. Says Schreiber. "We invented it just prior to going over to London. We were so excited, we had to have something to do. We started it, then it spread to the Royal Shakespeare Company, to the Old Vic, and to The Premise, then appearing in London. You each had three shots a day. They didn't accumulate. If you were caught firing more than three shots, you were out of the game. You could shoot anybody, and they had to die the most dramatic death they could in those physical circumstances. There were rules setting out the three times you couldn't shoot anybody: when they're working, when they're on the steps with a pot of boiling water, and when they're wearing an expensive camera, which was Del's rule. Anybody new who entered the game had to be known to everybody in it.

"It was going on all over London. All of the actors were shooting each other. I remember walking down the street, past Harrods, and I heard a voice. 'Av'ry.' I turned, and Leo McKern boomed, 'Bahng. Gotcha.' I fell in a puddle in front of Harrods. Another time, at The Establishment, Del actually fell down seven flights of stairs when I shot him. I followed him all the way down to the stage, because we had to go on.

Left to right: Dick Schaal, Severn Darden, Del Close. (Photo courtesy of The Second City)

"On our way back, we stopped in Philadelphia. Bill Mathieu shot Del Close underneath the Liberty Bell. Del staggered over to the guard, gasping. The guard just watched him fall."

When Severn Darden became involved in The Game, he added the qualification that once someone had shot you and you died, you couldn't get up again without the assailant's permission. It is reputed that, all over the world, The Game goes on today. Appropriately, if unintentionally, and even during their off-stage hours, Second City presaged the violent times to come. It stands to reason that they would have, since they presaged everything else.

In the same year, 1962, Second City won the "Man of the Year" Award of the American National Theatre and Academy in Chicago. Its members were Chicago celebs in their own right, attending Hugh Hefner's *Playboy* parties, appearing regularly on Jack Eigan's radio show, doing local WGN-TV spots filmed by William Friedkin (who later directed *The Exorcist* and *The French Connection*).

One night Friedkin took his camera to Second City to shoot something for TV. Every so often, he'd call, "Cut!" The actors would do the scene again. The audience would watch it one more time. A new dimension at Second City, to be sure.

Jack Burns, who joined in the fall of 1962, particularly remembers working with Friedkin for a "Love in America Day Parade" spot. "We did a film in the farm belt, using all Second City people. Billy Friedkin told this town we were going to do this little love story about love in America. He conned the whole town into bringing out the American Legion, the high school band, and it was one of the roughest days we ever had, because Billy, like most directors I know, once the camera gets rolling, what he wants to see is action. I was playing a newsman. Billy had hired some strong young Irish lads for protection. I said, 'Billy, why do we need protection?' He said, 'You never can tell what will happen. We'll improvise it.'

"We had this float carrying Julius Caesar. Dick Schaal was on it, Avery Schreiber, and some other people. I think, then, Billy told the town toughs to charge the float. 'Go get them. Go get those actors.' So the hired protection surrounded me, and I was okay, but Dick and Avery were fighting for their lives. Billy said, 'That was *great* material!' Then I think everyone wanted to drive us out of town, because they figured we were making fun of their high school band."

Avery Schreiber, too, remembers the film. "Oh, sure, Venus and Adonis,

Avery Schreiber strums guitar and Severn Darden makes a rare use of the trapdoor in Second City's stage. (Photo courtesy of The Second City)

George and Martha Washington. I think there was Elizabeth Taylor and five different guys. We had a wonderful time. We took a town. We *took* a *town*."

Schreiber had come to Second City by way of Playwrights at the Second City and *The Big Deal*. He soon developed a Samurai character that became Second City tradition:

"Dick Schaal and I did a scene called "Hibachi." It was a take-off on Japanese films. I was the Samurai landlord. Ann Elder was the woman in it. Dick was the husband. I came in to despoil his wife, and he picked a fight with me. We had a sword fight, and when Dick and I work with space, it's really magic, you see swords. He'd go for my feet. I'd jump in the air. I'd go for his head. He'd duck. We had this whole thing that was working, instant choreography between us. If I made a variation, I knew he'd be able to react.

"We had total trust. Sometimes it went on for a minute. Sometimes it went on for three minutes. Paul Sills would be sitting there, gritting his teeth. 'All right. Get it over with.' The ending we finally came up with—it happened one night in front of the audience, it wasn't planned—was that Dick couldn't get near me. I was all over the place. And he flung his Samurai sword into me. Then he and his wife stood together, and I backed into them with the sword sticking through me, impaling them, with the famous Japanese cry 'En brochette.' Then I wiggled the handle, the two of them went wuggle wuggle wuggle like they were getting whiplash on the other end of the sword. Then the three of us fell down. And down went the lights."

Here was a case of a character, more than a sketch, that would resurface with actors over time. David Steinberg would play a Samurai in "Rosh Hashanah-man," a parody of *Rashomon*. John Belushi would play a Samurai, at Second City and on *Saturday Night Live*. Shelley Berman had played a Samurai at The Compass: "Mark Gordon and I did a Samurai take-off. I did this terribly hokey thing with a sword. I kept pulling it out, out, out, it was maybe nine feet long. Mark would say, 'But that's in violation of the whole idea. We're doing a Japanese movie!' "

How much inheriting is involved, and how much develops spontaneously from improv suggestions, is anybody's guess, or secret. It's like what Jerry Stiller says about playing a camel driver in the St. Louis Compass (since then there have been camel drivers too numerous to mention), "But I never thought anybody took it from me." Adds Anne Meara, "We're generous enough to feel everyone has within them their own private camel driver. They've got that from themselves. Everyone has their own camel driver."

In 1963, David Shepherd launched a new Compass in New York, co-directed by him and featuring Jane Alexander, Macintyre Dixon, Paul Dooley, Richard Libertini, and Mary Louise Wilson.

In the Spring of 1963, The Second City appeared in Toronto, Canada, and won raves. (In fact, it was raves that had brought them there. Nathan Cohen, dean of theater critics in Toronto, had seen the group in Chicago. On the strength of Cohen's glowing praise, the Royal Alexandra Theatre booked a show.)

In September, 1963, a series of *Second City Reports* were produced on British TV. In the fall of 1963, The Second City appeared in London with *Looking for the Action (Peep Show for Conventioneers)*. "There were shows all over the place," recalls Richard Libertini. "There was one in New York, one in Chicago. I guess I left Chicago, came to New York, and they were putting together a London company. I had a choice either to do New York or London. I went to London, but I don't know how successful we were. The first company had played at The Establishment. This time, we were in a theater. We were censored by the Lord Chamberlain, in that we weren't permitted to improvise."

By the early sixties, The Second City had a roster of famous boosters. Studs Terkel hung out regularly at Second City, and Nelson Algren was a fan. There was one improvisation that Jack Burns did with Macintyre Dixon, based on a theater game called Camera. In the game, one person focuses on the other as though being a camera, then the focus switches to the other person. The game has a very interesting effect on the dynamics of a scene. In this one, a lunch counter scene, Burns gave Dixon a really hard time. The more aggressive Burns became, the more giving, as the counterman, Dixon would be. The scene concluded with Burns dumping an invisible garbage can on Dixon's head. Algren's comment was that it was like a scene from the New Testament, like watching Jesus behind a counter on stage.

Algren was more than a fan. He was even known to join in on an improvisation. Among other famous visitors to the cabaret were Sir Edmund Hillary, Margot Fonteyn, Supreme Court Justice Arthur Goldberg, Moss Hart, Tennessee Williams, Eunice Kennedy Shriver, Steve Allen, Joshua Logan, Mort Sahl, Jane Fonda, Chet Huntley, David Brinkley, Nelson Rockefeller, Saul Bellow, Mortimer Adler, theologian Karl Barth, a long list of foreign dignitaries, and "lots of people with pencils," of whom Schreiber was suddenly aware. "We'd see people in the audience, writing. A few weeks later, we'd see things that we'd done turning up on television shows. We thought, 'Well, this is interesting. It means that we're getting close to the commercial.' "

It was interesting, undeniable, and, some said, a mixed blessing. Being commercial means making money. Nothing wrong with making money. Making money means the actors don't starve and the show goes on. Making money means more people are coming—from a broader base of the population than the university campus. Then, as the general public was increasingly in evidence, improv suggestions reflected the trend. From "Rabelais at the Sorbonne" to "Jackie having her hair done" is a sizeable leap. To Second City founders in 1959, there would not have been much to commend the chain of events. Mainstream comedy was not their dish of tea.

But a few things had happened in the interim to alter the picture a tad. By the early sixties, The Second City was not unique in the entertainment realm in terms of having a social conscience. Pete Seeger and Bob Dylan had people putting their conscience to music, bringing things out in the open as they had not been before.

Likewise, mainstream comedy in 1959 had been represented by Doris Day and Debbie Reynolds movies and *Dennis the Menace* on TV. Mainstream comedy by 1962 was feeling the influence of, among others, Nichols, May, and Berman. A 1964 television show called *That Was The Week That Was* (political satire, sketches, blackouts, news reports, musical numbers) featured Second City alumni Bob Dishy, Alan Alda, and Sandy Baron. (Tony Holland and Andrew Duncan were in the British version; in the third year its name changed to *The Late Show, or for Those Who Are Too Drunk to Dance*.) Also in 1964, from Toronto television, came another series of *Second City Reports*.

A Chicago accountant first made waves in 1960 with his smash hit comedy album, *The Button-Down Mind of Bob Newhart*. (Just as well: "I was a lousy accountant, I always figured that if you came within eight bucks of what you needed you were doing okay.") Dick Gregory was using humor to change the social order. ("When I hit in 1961, there wasn't a healthy racial joke in America.") Mort Sahl was doing intelligent topical humor on TV, prime time. Lenny Bruce was challenging a mainstream he had no wish to enter, yet in the act of challenging, was redefining its bounds. (The night Lenny Bruce was arrested on obscenity charges, in 1964, Del Close went out on the Second City stage. He was talking, ostensibly introducing a piece. Another player came running out. "Del. Del. Lenny Bruce got busted for obscenity." Del replied, "No shit." Blackout.)

Mainstream comedy, in a few short years, was smarter and faster than before. If, in the course of these changes, The Second City was reaching television, it may be Second City wasn't being diminished as much as television was being improved. As Bernie Sahlins once observed, "It's not that we've changed. The world has taken a quarter-turn in our direction." A prime example of this effect is a sketch, direct from Second City, that Jack Burns and Avery Schreiber perfected. Burns played the fast-talking bigot. Schreiber was the long-suffering, ho-boy-do-I-get-all-the-nuts cabbie.

As Burns reconstructs the vignette, "One night during the improv set, we said, 'Give us some characters.' We got 'cab driver' and 'out-of-town conventioneer.' I don't even remember if we had an intermission that night. I almost think it happened on the spur of the moment. It may have been one of those moments where we just had a free-form thing and didn't have a break, because I don't recall ever discussing it other than sitting on those chairs, and we were in the cab."

Schreiber: "I thought the suggestions were 'cab driver' and 'bigot.' He chose this conventioneer, this character who came out of Boston, a sort of person he knew and didn't like very much. Jack had, and still has, a wonderful ability to pin people, and events, he doesn't really admire. And we had things

Jack Burns (left) and Avery Schreiber (right) in their famous cab driver scene. (Photo courtesy of Pictorial Parade, Inc.)

like albino jokes. Like Jack's line—'He's an albino.' And I grunt, 'Lookit, you can't be too white.' "

Burns: "And I started saying, 'Huh,' whatever he answered, as soon as I sat down, because I couldn't think of what to say next. Repeating myself. Very Boston Irish. 'You know what I mean?' 'Yeah.' 'Huh?' 'Yeah.' 'Huh?' 'Yeah.' 'Huh?' 'I know what you mean.' "

When they played Square East in New York, "Taxi Cab" was in the show. Reviews were enthusiastic. Agent Bernie Brillstein offered to represent them. In a week, they were on Jack Paar's show. Sensational. Doing an Archie Bunker-type character years before *All In The Family*.

Burns: "I mean, what we did, you can't do that on television. We were talking about prejudice and things of that nature. But we always felt the audience was ready because we'd been doing it for a year and we knew the results in clubs. So that was how Avery and I started. Paar said, 'Can you come back for eight more shots with eight more cab drivers?' "

Like Nichols and May and Berman before them—and merely by giving the world a taste of the socially satirical banquet routinely served on Second City's stage—Jack Burns and Avery Schreiber reshaped the broad-based public view of the nature and function of comedy.

Quite simply, they did what social satire is all about.

4
Developing Material, or If You Were Alive, Would You Laugh at This?

The Second City's most salient feature may be that it is a creative community. The fact that the members create comedy isn't insignificant—yet it's how they create it that really stands out. What they perform, they invented together—a process *The New York Times* has called ". . . turning themselves into something like stand-up playwrights for a theater of everyday life."

Each improvisation is the work of two teams—the team of players involved in it, and the team formed by the players and the audience combined. "It's collaboration," says Andrew Duncan, "collaboration theater. You know out there, the minute you start a scene, if you're going anywhere with it, you just feel it. If it isn't there, it forces you either to get out or change it. You can't do that with a stage play, where the script is already set."

Dave Thomas adds, "Even the games that were played on stage—they wouldn't wait until the game was over to tell the audience what it was. They'd tell them the game up front, so that the audience could be part of it, so that it wasn't something we actors could stumble across and take credit for. You actually had to try to make it happen."

As Bernie Sahlins explains it, "The actors make an offering in an improvisation. They receive a response and modify the next offering to include that response. Eventually the result is a kind of community theater."

"Second City has endured for over twenty-five years because it is the best training ground that I know of for young, would-be comedy actors, writers and directors," says Sheldon Patinkin. "They get to practice their craft and build their technique in front of an audience, six nights a week, fifty-two weeks a year." "As Second City actors," adds Murphy Dunne, "we had the chance to paint all the creative colors. Once you've been forced to do that—if you're wrong, you're going to know immediately, because no one will laugh." A psychologist would say this gives each performer, in the course of an evening, dozens of opportunities to be "notified" whether he's succeeded or not. Multiply this by the number of nights a performer ventures on stage, and the result is a staggering number of chances to see what works.

Mike Nichols has observed that it teaches you "to answer the unspoken question the audience asked—'Why are you telling us this?' "

There is no "season" in a regular sense. The company performs year-round. Second City never closes. Most shows consist of set pieces developed from previous improvs, followed by improvisations done on suggestions the audience calls out. This much of the form evolved before Second City was born. Roger Bowen explains that "The Compass Theatre was created to produce improvised plays. At first we did a new one every week, then every two weeks, then every month. Finally we ran out of ideas for plays so we stopped doing them. By that time we had a backlog of material that came from our late-night improvising sessions based on audience suggestions. We made a revue out of that and have used the revue form ever since."

Sheldon Patinkin's first taste of Second City was huge amounts of material being used up fast. "I started working at Second City right on its first anniversary, and the fifth show was already running then. We were doing the set show twice a night, at nine and eleven, on Tuesday, Wednesday, Thursday, Friday, Saturday, and Sunday, then there was also a one o'clock show on Saturday nights. And on Tuesday, Wednesday, Thursday, and Sunday, they improvised after the eleven o'clock show."

After improvs, the director gives notes, which is a matter of telling the company—generally, five or six men and two women—what can be saved, or improved, or jettisoned entirely.

Joyce Sloane, general earth mother at Chicago's Second City for over a dozen years, and now its producer, describes the process like this: "What happens is that they improvise, and the stage manager keeps a list. Bernie will come and say, 'What have you got?' Then the manager shows him the list, and he'll hate everything, usually, or pull everything apart. We'll be back to square one. Or he'll want to fix it. Or whatever. Then they start rehearsing, they start workshopping. At some point, that scene is ready to go into the show. It's really never ready, because they could rehearse it to death. The night before an opening we're still carrying on with 'What if you did this . . . ?' and 'This ending is better . . .' And you just have to give yourself a goal and you open, because we could never stop working otherwise. Then the show starts changing. They'll put in two or three new scenes that came out of improvisations, and they'll take out old ones. Then they'll put in more new scenes. When we're around 80 percent, we're in previews for a new show. Then we announce previews. And then when we get to 100 percent, that's when we open."

Since pieces are developed largely in the workshops, a Second City player can be chained to the stage day and night, which is why it really is a creative community, not just a job. "You never stopped working," recalls David Steinberg, "but no one ever said, 'I'm too tired to work.' That would be like saying, 'I'm too tired to get better.' "

Paul Sand remembers one such day of concentrated effort. "I was sitting in the audience with Paul Sills one afternoon, and we were watching Alan Arkin and Barbara Harris work out something. At this point, the group had been together a couple of years. What Alan and Barbara were doing was hilarious, but I wasn't laughing, because I suppose I was absorbed in the process. I guess we sort of got burnt out, not to the point where funny things weren't funny, but where if they were funny we wouldn't go 'ha ha.' So I was sitting, staring at the scene, and Sills turned to me and said, 'If you were alive, would you laugh at this?' I said something like, '. . . yeah.' "

When the cast has this kind of workshop, the focus is more on material than on games, although games might be used to warm up the players. The director presides at these workshops, not directing in the traditional sense, though certainly providing direction. As the opening of a new show approaches, the director decides which scenes are strong, and what their running order should be.

Ed Greenberg, a recent Second City director previously with the Committee, sees the role as being "like a mechanic, assuming you've got a good car but it needs a tune-up. You make little adjustments, and, as needed, you impose your vision and your attitudes and say, 'It's got to go in *this* direction to be more interesting.' As satirists or improvisers or whatever, I think we're functioning at a very fortunate time because things are changing so fast, even from night to night. I've noticed during the regular show that some lines have had to be adjusted just to keep up with what had appeared in the newspapers that day."

"Basically, as a director," says Don DePollo, who has appeared on the Second City stage, conducted workshops, and directed, "you *yes-and,* which is a term we use. You have to yes-and the actors and let them do their own material. Of course you'd like to present a lot of your own ideas, but usually the actors resist that, so you have to encourage ideas that they're working on and nurture their own stuff to bring it along. What I do is just give notes on how to make it funnier, or if it wasn't clever enough, to dispense with it. But it's always with their own material. I learned the hard way that you can't bring in your own ideas."

To Steve Kampmann, who first joined the main stage company as Don DePollo's understudy, DePollo taught volumes simply by infusion: "He was a big influence on me and had an enormous impact on the shows. His scenes were always strong, and from him I learned the finer points, like entering with a big laugh or bringing something important into the scene when you enter."

Harold Ramis found that "most people really resisted having anything imposed on them unless it was a great idea. I've never seen anyone resist a good suggestion. On the other hand, when Joe Flaherty and I got to codirect a show, more than 50 percent of the pieces had Joe and me in them. The rest of the company was not happy. I think Bernie actually stepped in then and finished that show."

It helps if the director cares about the actors. "Sheldon Patinkin," says Robert Klein, "was a wonderful director. As a child, he was a piano prodigy. He's a great intellectual and a fabulous force. He has a tremendous memory. He remembered our improvs and was a terrific editor. And he has sensitive feelings. He was the greatest comfort to the actors, which is important."

Robin Duke, who took workshops in Toronto with Patinkin, feels "they were the best basis for doing the stage that I could have gotten. He always taught wants and objectives. What are your inner wants and objectives? What you actually want and what you say you want. When you go out to do a scene on stage, you always have those two things to think about, to draw on. Then whenever you run dry or can't come up with anything, you have these tools. To want something and not ask for it directly was an inner want, and an objective was what you were asking for on stage."

The director has his eye on everything. According to Del Close, "My role as director was a normal one, encouraging the performers and helping the structure. See, the actors have the worst seat in the house—they're on stage. They need that extra eye out front." In a workshop, Del might suggest an alternate punchline, a story idea, a structure. A great believer in structure, he can diagram scenes on a blackboard: Here's the start—a housewife is washing dishes. From this, it can go to her husband comes home, or in walks a man from Mars. But it's got to go from a beginning to a middle, and from the middle it has to go to a logical end.

Close, who has performed, directed, and conducted workshops for Second City, instructs with a power akin to obeah. He is, personally, a mystical individual, who has eaten fire, studied witchcraft, and participated as a volunteer in the government's early experimental drug program.

A chief tenet of Close's workshops is group trust. He advocates the group spirit, the group mind, and the notion that the best way to make yourself look good is to make your partners look good. "You must learn to think like a group. You must learn to trust each other." Once, in San Francisco, he climbed a stepladder as part of a trust-building exercise. He asked everyone in the workshop to gather around and catch him as he fell. The fall broke his collarbone.

He says, "Other men have lived lives of quiet desperation. I have lived a life of wild desperation." Betty Thomas says of him, "His work goes beyond theater games. He has some of the greatest exercises in the world." John Belushi said of Close, "I like the man's style. He can create with you, unlike so many other directors. He can motivate people. He's been my biggest influence in comedy."

Paul Sills, extremely influential as a Second City director, is blessed with a vision of exactly what he wants, though he can't always convey it in words. Actors acknowledge his charisma, his genius, his amazing facility for putting players together in the perfect combination. On the other hand, they have occasionally shaken their heads wondering, "What's he talking about? I'll bet it could really help me if I knew what it was." Such is the nature of any transcendent truth. Mere words can fail. Mina Kolb thinks of him "as a kind of conduit. He's like the center of the wheel, and we're all the spokes. Somehow he coordinates everything. He gets a lot of people around him, and then he figures out what to do with them."

Hamilton Camp compares him to a dentist. "He's going for the nerve. Do all your tricks—he catches you. Some actors have almost fought Paul physically because he wouldn't allow them any space to lie. It infuriates him when he sees you putting a chain around your own leg when you're supposed to be going for the pure unknown."

Paul Sand remembers doing *Story Theatre* with Sills on Broadway. "It was time for notes, after the first preview or something. He said, 'Sand?' 'Yeah.' He said, 'Just, uh, be better.' Well, okay, nonverbal communication. Then another time, also *Story Theatre,* I was doing *The Robber Bridegroom,* which was the scariest thing I've ever done. Scared *me.* Because I had to figure out how to be a truly bad person. We were rehearsing a scene. I'm supposed to be a murderer who kills many wives, and I sort of observed myself, and what I observed was that I was just pretending to be a villain. I knew it was all wrong, and it wasn't working, and I was frustrated. Sills comes up to me and says, 'Look, Sand, I'm convinced you've been an actor for at least five thousand years. Now, you're going to squirm around and keep us all waiting for five weeks while you try to get this character. You're going to get it in five weeks, which means it's there. So go sit in a corner now and come back in five minutes, will you?' And I did. And came back with it. That's Paul Sills's kind of encouragement, his sort of brilliance."

"You had to listen to Paul," says Jack Burns. "He really made himself heard. I really liked the way he worked. Out of all the directors I've ever worked with, Paul probably taught me more about my craft than anyone else, as an actor. And he said something that always stuck with me. I don't know if he was the first person who said it, but he was the first person I ever heard say it. He said, 'The duty of an artist is to enlighten and ennoble, but he damn well better entertain.' "

Bernie Sahlins's name often comes up as the director who steers actors away from doing Perry Mason, Mr. Spock, and Sheriff Lobo, toward Portia, Plato, and Napoleon. Other directors have shared his feelings. But his is the name most thought of in this regard. "Let's do pirates and cowboys." "No, it's more fun doing Socrates on the Chicago City Council." It has occasioned friction as well as praise.

Ira Miller, who rarely got into trouble himself, was often at the scene of trouble, grinning furtively. One workshop in particular stands out in his mind.

"We were rehearsing one afternoon, and Bernie said something like, 'I want you each to come in tomorrow with five ideas for satirical blackouts.' Like it was a homework assignment. So Martin Harvey Friedburg was there, and Marty doesn't take garbage from anyone. Right away, he's real mad and he explodes, 'Okay, I'll give you five satirical blackouts.' And he reeled off these things, one or two words each, with a real beat and a rhythm. 'Here's your one. Here's your two. Here's your three.' The things were like President Johnson, a boat in the river, something else that made no sense. 'Here's your boom, here's your boom, here's your boom boom boom.'

"Then, for the fifth one, he turned around and pulled down his pants and mooned Bernie. 'And here's your fifth one!' Bill Noble was the stage manager. He was up in the light booth, and just as Marty said that and pulled his pants down, Bill killed the lights and it was a perfect blackout." Whereupon Murphy Dunne sprang to his feet with the cry, "He stole my jokes!"

Because Second City is a revue, there are musical numbers. Musical numbers also have to come from somewhere and are, like the rest of the show, team efforts. In this case, half the team is the man at the keyboard. Bill Mathieu, the company's onstage pianist and composer in its first years, played trumpet and arranged for Stan Kenton's band before joining Second City. He also wrote a column for *Downbeat* magazine, has arranged for Duke Ellington, and has written symphonies.

Fred Kaz, the pianist and composer for Second City for the past twenty years, began studying music at the age of four. He's written symphonic arrangements for Odetta and Peter, Paul & Mary, and the scores for movies like *Little Murders*. "Captain Kaz" lives on his boat, the *C Major*, has been described as one of the last living beatniks, and he lost the third and fourth fingers of his left hand when he was twenty-two. "Eventually I got talked into trying music again, so I reexamined my presence at the piano. I spent a couple of years reinventing my technique, and then I got into jazz really heavy on a new basis for a while. After a while, I clean forgot about the injury, and once again, playing the piano became an automatic extension of what I think." Kaz is, in the words of Harry Murphy, "the Chuck Yeager of The Second City. If anyone has the right stuff, he has."

Bob Derkach, pianist and composer for the Toronto company since 1983, estimates that by the end of his first Second City revue—a seven-month run— he had already improvised something on the order of nine hundred songs. In

Fred ("Captain") Kaz, left, with Alan Arkin, right, at the twenty-fifth anniversary reunion. (Photo courtesy of Jennifer Girard)

addition, he's played the occasional recognizable melody from a popular song, to suggest a mood or inspire a player. "I'm sure," says Derkach, "that I've committed two thousand or three thousand tunes to memory, but only know the first few bars of each. This works wonders on the Second City stage, but doesn't come in too handy at parties."

Mathieu and Kaz with Chicago's resident company, Derkach with the Toronto company, Ruby Streak on Second City's "resident touring" E.T.C. stage—and a very small, select handful of gifted musicologists through the years—have worked with actors who can't sing, and found notes for them. (Only a few actors have been so bad they were asked to mouth the words.) They've rescued improvs by coming up with the inspired musical cue, and they've worked outside of improvs on show-stopping musical numbers. They're so good that their contributions sometimes go unnoticed.

"It's like the guy who built the Taj Mahal," says David Rasche. "People don't walk in and say, 'What a great guy who built this!' You just assume it's there, and it's so exquisite that it doesn't call attention to itself.

"You didn't write songs in the workshops. We'd say, 'Fred, we need a song.' He'd say, 'Awahhh, man, I don't know if I can do it,' and then he'd stay up all night and come in with a wonderful song. You have an idea for a song. He writes it. You write half a song. He writes the other half. Like 'A Woman Is a Body Not a Brain.' We had this idea for a real revue number, top hats and canes, a parody of one of these torch songs where the woman sings, 'Some gals say they want a job but give me caviar and a mink stole.' He came up with the music, and lyrics like 'A wife is an attachment that you screw on the bed,' which isn't a bad little lyric.

"We wrote another one. Tino Insana came over to my house one time, and we both despised the sort of music the Carpenters were doing. I started playing some Carpenter-type chords on the piano, and Tino said, because they're such happy guys, we should sing about something disgusting. So we did this song about rape. Actually, we got about a quarter of the way through it, got a couple of lyrics, and couldn't make a song out of it. We gave it to Fred. Boom. It comes back. Beautiful, wonderful stuff. Fred gave us lyrics and wrote three-part harmony for it."

Bob Derkach had the rare opportunity, when there were three women in the Toronto company—Kathleen Lasky, Debra McGrath, and Sandra Balcovske—of writing something in an Andrews Sisters vein. "They were very excited with the concept and came back with suggestions for a 'Kung-Fugie Boogie.' We developed a very violent song—in three-part harmony—about women depending on Kung Fu to survive in this sexist society."

When these elements are pulled together—the reworked improvs, the director's input, the musical numbers—it's a show. Which is to say, it's the part of the show the audience pays to see. When this rehearsed segment of the show is over, the actors then take suggestions from the audience, leave for some twenty minutes to chew them over, then return. For this portion of the evening, admission is free.

Like the rest of the Second City format, suggestion-taking evolved over time. Early on, players employed devices like the Living Newspaper, which meant acting out newspaper stories on the spot—essentially an idea with roots in the Depression-era WPA (Works Progress Administration, renamed in 1939 the Works Projects Administration). "Of course," concedes Andrew Duncan, "we'd sort of worked this out. Everyone had crayons and we'd box items, and then we'd do things as diverse as saying the lines from the paper, or taking off on a scene." For instance, in a famous Compass rendition of the form, the same prize fight was reported in the jargon of *The Ring* and the then-newborn *Sports Illustrated.* The *Ring* version stressed blood and gore. A la *Sports Illustrated,* the story came off like a high-strategy chess match. Each time, the fight was acted out in accordance with its magazine description, by which point the fights had nothing in common.

In an early Second City "Living Newspaper," in one blackout presented when the headlines featured police corruption, an actress rushed on stage, breathlessly dialed a number on a pantomimed phone, and gasped, "Hello, FBI? There's a policeman hanging around in front of my house."

First-line–last-line suggestions became popular—and went on to amaze Broadway in the hands of Nichols and May. The audience provides a first line and a last line—anything from "Welcome to Oz" to "Change your oil?"— and the cast whips up the story in between. Variations on this are spot improvs

Left to right: Jim Fay, Richard Kind, and Mindy Bell performing a Second City improvisation at the twenty-fifth anniversary reunion.

from a first line of poetry in the style of whatever poet is requested, an obviously impossible task until you see someone like Garry Goodrow do it; and make-a-song, at which Avery Schreiber and Robert Klein excelled in their Second City years, as Bob Bainborough currently does. In this same vein, Del Close does an impressive Canterbury Calypso. The best of these can resemble master quality album cuts. The longest could fill an LP library. Legend goes that Toronto's Ron James holds the record for make-a-song verses in a single spontaneous ditty—twenty-nine.

In a recent make-a-song improvised by the Toronto company, Dana Andersen, from the stage, chatted with a seated audience member as an apparent warm-up preceding the improv set. "What's your name? How are you feeling? What did you do today?" Then the company emerged, offering a spontaneous operatic this-is-your-life version of the woman's answers.

"Sometimes," recalls David Steinberg, "you had to do opera in-the-style-of. I couldn't have known less about opera. The truth is, I still don't. But you had to learn about Wagner, Schoenberg, Berlioz. We had a musicologist at the piano in Bill Mathieu. He didn't care what you were saying, so long as you were singing the opera right."

Shelley Berman, at The Compass, remembers improvising operatic duets with Barbara Harris with no keyboard assistance at all. "I used to fight with her, disagree with her, because sometimes we couldn't stand each other. But when we improvised these duets, there was an incredible degree of give and take, knowing when to let the other party go, when to sit and listen, when to sing together, how to come up with rhymes. At the time, it was the most perfectly logical thing to do. After all, I thought, 'This is what we do. If we couldn't do this, they would have hired people who could do this.' But I think about it now, and I'm stunned. I remember doing it without piano accompaniment. Not a chord. I'm sure some people thought we were misleading them, and that we'd really rehearsed."

Suggestion-taking has been painful. There is, for instance, the very real danger of getting the same suggestion night after night. One way to avoid that is to say, "Let's have a relationship, like mother and daughter," hoping the audience will be more original than to yell back "mother and daughter." On the other extreme are the mystery suggestions, defined by Don DePollo as "the kind you can't figure out at all. We did a scene once where we were two experts, and we asked for suggestions of two things to be experts on. Every other night, we got animal husbandry.

"There was a show we did at the Château Louise, in Dundee, Illinois.

We asked the audience for several occupations. I can't tell you how many different nights we got Captain of Industry. It got to the point where the actors would be on the edge of the stage to see if the same person was coming back all the time."

For Del Close, the most bizarre mystery suggestion came during a tour. The tour hit several states, but he kept getting the same suggestion for an opening line. "Here we are in Spain." He began to wonder if he was being tailed.

Naturally, current events influence the suggestions called out. When the *Tropic of Cancer* censorship controversy was hot, it was offered every night for four months. When Goldwater was running against Johnson in the Presidential campaigns, "Goldwater" was a frequent response to "let's have an inanimate object." (Others were "husband" and "wife.")

One night, with The Compass Players in St. Louis, Irwin Corey was in the audience. Anne Meara asked for a suggestion. Corey shouted, "How about a group of improv players asking for suggestions from an audience?" The cast moved on to another suggestion.

Often enough comes the I'm-drunk-so-I-think-I'm-the-world's-funniest-human suggestion, offered with everything from good intentions to a desire to compete with the cast, to drinks hurled forcibly at the players' heads. One night while John Candy was performing, some invidious sot threw a glass at the stage, missing Candy by a few inches. This had the effect of silencing even the other drunks. The scene was followed by the improvs. Ben Gordon came out to take suggestions. "I wanted to get the house to warm up again. Meanwhile, they're leading this drunk away. So I did a couple of lines, 'Bring him back. He's got a couple more drinks to throw. The guy pays for three drinks, let him throw three drinks.' "

A suggestion isn't always taken literally, as when Joan Rivers turned "hooker" into someone who hooked rugs. Or the suggestion "brothel" might be answered with two witches over a cauldron, "Come to the brothel, where we make the broth."

"The best suggestions, though," says Shelley Berman, "are the simple ones. If the suggestion is already comedic—brothel, hooker, proctologist—you know the person who called it out either hopes that he or she is funny, or thinks that by giving you a funny idea, you will emerge funnier. The truth is, you don't need that, and if you do need that, you've got to examine what you're doing for your comedy.

"We did one—the audience was to throw a word at us, then qualify it.

The ball. The red ball. In this case, it was a bent key. It was Bobbi Gordon and I, and we improvised. She's sneaking me up into her dormitory room, which is obviously only for girls. We get into the building, and I'm raring to go with this girl. We walk up the stairs. It's miles. We walk up steps, we walk up steps. She keeps saying 'a little further.' I was coming up with lines like, 'If it's much further I may not be any good.' We finally get to her door, and she hands me her key. It won't work. I can't open the door. The key is bent. The desperation in trying to get that door open, the terrible desperation,

Andrew Alexander dons a wig to kid around backstage with the Toronto cast. Left to right: Peter Torokvei, Catherine O'Hara, Martin Short, Andrew Alexander, Bob Derkach, Robin Duke, John Hemphill. (Photo courtesy of Rick Alexander)

was agony. I chewed on it, to bite it straight. I stomped on it. I was brutalizing the key, and she's shssshing me because we're not supposed to make any noise. And I'm in pain because I *made* it, but I can't get in.

"I *had* to get in that room, but I couldn't, and eventually I gave up. I had to leave. I had to walk down all those stairs, too. Mind you, we'd improvised this, and now I was out of the picture and she had to end the scene. We hadn't discussed this part of it, so I had no idea what she was going to do. I frankly didn't know what would be next.

"Then Bobbi watched me leave, reached into her purse, and took out another key. She put it in the door, which now opened easily, and walked into her room."

Once suggestions have been taken, the cast adjourns backstage, a grim cubicle which, both in Chicago and Toronto, contributes to the sense of desperation. Says Ben Gordon, "It was a very cramped area. Cluttered and uncomfortable. You're under a lot of pressure not only from the audience, but you add pressure to each other with dares and challenges. Although you love and respect each other, it's still a snake pit." To Harry Murphy, "Sometimes, it can be like living in a submarine."

Backstage are a few props, like a few different hats and jackets. Several things happen here. Among them: Cast members kick around a piece they've been working on in preparation for the next show; cast members come up with sketches in response to the evening's suggestions; cast members go completely dry and valiantly hitch suggestions onto whatever remotely resembles a previous piece.

This phase of the process is the moment in time which George Wendt fondly labels ". . . the twenty-five minute bloodbath that occurs in the green room. It's a miracle anything good ever came out of that because it's kind of a high-pressure situation. In a funny way, it's higher pressure than in front of an audience, because in front of an audience, the pressure was so high that it was liberating. Back in the green room, staring at a couple of dozen suggestions, it was grim.

"When there was a suggestion that gave you an idea, you thought about it and who you wanted to do the scene with. Then you'd go off with whomever and sort of brainstorm it. Fred Kaz would help you shape it a little bit, and he was really good at putting some sort of button on it. Then you hunt for silly props and go do it."

Betty Thomas's recollection of the green-room blues is "pretty much cross talk at the beginning. 'How about this?' 'How about that?' Grab an idea, grab a person you think can handle it with you. Get in as many scenes as you can. Half the time, you were talking while another scene was on, trying to decide what you were really going to do. It's always high energy back there, and if you're not there, you're buried. What I learned was that you had to be right there, high energy, not going to get a drink, not doing anything else."

"My memory of backstage," says David Rasche, "was a bunch of guys walking around trying to think of funny things to say."

When the twenty minutes are over, give or take a hyperventilation or two, the actors return to the stage. This is when team spirit and spontaneity pay off, or else. Ready or not, they're on—

"Some people," says Andrew Duncan, "myself included, would go for weeks and nothing from the workshops, none of the games, nothing, had gelled yet. Then it would just click. One night I went out and it all fell in. This is one of the experiences people have when they come to Second City. Another is confusion about this scary job in front of an audience. The audience is going to judge you. And you do your scene, then the lights start to dim, and your scene has bombed. 'They're going to fire me.' Then you hear clap . . . clap . . . clap. Faintly. There were many nights like those. Then again, some nights, like Sundays, we could have seven people out there and it would be a great show, as great as a Saturday night with three hundred people."

For Pierre Epstein, it fell into place in a hurry. "This was in New York. The company was in New York, with Alan Arkin, Barbara Harris, I think Severn Darden. I was walking along Forty-seventh Street and Alan drove by in a Volkswagen. We were friends, and he said, 'Hop in.' Then he said, 'Do you want to do some Second City?' Second City was so new at the time that I said, 'Well, Alan, I don't even know how to do Second City.' He said, 'It doesn't matter.' I said, 'What do I have to do to audition?' He said, 'You'll go on stage with us.' I told him he was crazy. But he talked me into doing the improvs with them. He said, 'You'll do the dentist sketch with me. Don't worry about it. This is the outline of the situation. I'm the dentist. You're the patient. You come in. I try to open your mouth. You won't open your mouth. I do this. You do that. You never open your mouth, till I do this.' And he made this kind of sexy move. 'At which point you open your mouth, I get my hand in, you close your mouth. We struggle. Finally, I'm in the chair and you're the dentist.' I still thought he was crazy and I was terrified. But we did it and it got enormous laughs, and he told me it was a big success, and I'd added business no one had done before."

Arlene Golonka, who also joined when the company was in New York, remembers her chilling initiation. "I'd worked with Sills quite a lot in the workshops, but it was *nothing* like being thrown into the show. I was brilliant in my improvs in class. I was just terrific. But when I got out there with these guys I'd always admired, it took me quite a while before I really got good. Jo Anne Worley was in the same workshops with me, and joined the cast when I did. And we both talked about it, and we both felt that the first few times were blood-curdling."

The first time for Bill Alton was "terrifying. The first three months I couldn't look at anything but the ceiling. But what you come to realize is that you think funny and something will come. Also, the audience will accept your failure if you fail. That's part of it, like watching a bullfighter."

Derek McGrath, too, was "terrified" of improvisational comedy. "But I do like things that scare me. When I got into Second City, I couldn't eat dinner for two weeks."

For most Second City players, among them Bruce Jarchow, who is expert in performing the games: "Improvising in front of an audience is the biggest thrill anyone could ever have. The terror is like jumping out of an airplane. This is the theater's version of being a parachutist. You jump out and hope the cord works, and you do it for the thrill of it."

"There are nights," says Gilda Radner, "when in the middle of the show, you think, 'Oh, God. I don't want to improvise. I just can't take it. I'm tired.' Then suddenly, you get out there and an idea strikes you. You can get that resurge of energy, and then you can't wait to get out there and do it."

On nights when the thrill is there, you're more than welcome to enter someone else's scene-in-progress if it's flopping. On nights when you would rather be anywhere else but Second City, you can get pushed onstage anyhow. Fred Willard explains that "you could never tell if you were going to be good or not, because you'd get a suggestion, you'd think of a wonderful premise, and you could go out and do the first joke and be stuck out there and nothing would happen. Other times, I was literally pushed out in the middle of a scene. They'd say, 'Go out there and do something. The scene's dying.' I'd say, 'I don't know what to—' but then something would develop."

"Besides," adds Avery Schreiber, "it's fun to go nuts. I went through a crazy period. The thing I always loved about Second City improvisation is that you can go nuts in front of an audience and they don't know it. You totally trust your unconscious, and go for it. There were years of it, every night, I had an opportunity to go crazy in front of people."

One technique for getting into an improvisation is to develop a few characters. Alan Arkin admits to being "terrible for a long time after I got to Second City. I was amazed that I didn't get fired. I didn't know how to be funny. I had no idea. I can remember a couple of scenes early on that were unbelievably turgid and interminable. I finally, after many weeks, found a character that was just funny no matter what I did with him. I just played him for a while, then added to my library of characters. What I discovered is that after a while doing this, you realize you have about four different characters you can play well. You pretty much do one of those four characters in every sketch that comes up. Your job is to find who the characters are."

A character can provide anything from the handle on a scene to the key to a make-a-song. When you're doing a spot improv with no time to prepare, diving on an accent and expanding from there can work wonders. Elaine May, for example, has a broad character range, which served her in invariably good stead. Bruce Pirrie, in a pinch, can latch onto a James Bond character through a Scottish accent, do a few character lines—"Have I said anything witty about ma penis yet?"—and make a scene clever when the plot is not only not apparent, but in fact not there.

There are disciplined improvs, perhaps based on an exercise. There are two-person improvisations, consisting for instance of boy and girl, and also group improvs, about politics or corruption. For sheer insanity, there are "geeks amok" improvs. As described by George Wendt, they're "the kind we'll use for the middle of the second act, by which time of course the audience has fallen in love with the cast and we can get away with murder. We just go ahead and go bonkers and it will usually be the funniest scene in the show."

Fortunately, whatever the improv, you're never alone. You've got music. A scene can be led by a musical pun, or cued with appropriate musical references. You're on stage, absolutely stymied. The scene is dead in the water. Then you hear a few bars from *West Side Story*. Yeah, that's it. We're a gang. We're gonna rumble. Fred Kaz calls it "speaking English out of your piano."

Avery Schreiber worked with Bill Mathieu, who "was able to fit where our heads were, where we were in the space, and connect it with original as well as snatches of classics tunes that seemed to suit and fit everything." David Rasche worked with Fred Kaz, who "supports everything. You tell him it's sort of a Western deal, so it needs honky-tonk piano. Boom. You've got the best honky-tonk piano. Not only is it honky-tonk piano, but it's funny honky-tonk piano, and it's the essence of honky-tonk piano. It's not like a song you've heard. It's something else. 'Make it like if Bach wrote jazz.' He'll do it. If a scene is wilting and withering, he'll pick it up. He'll find something to do."

To David Steinberg: "They're simply not piano players in the usual sense. They are members of the company. I may have been more attuned to the music than anyone else around, because I didn't have those workshop things to go to like my where and my space."

As far as props are concerned, hats and jackets have been supplemented by the occasional surprise prop. One night, the suggestion was "shaggy dog." Tony Holland had a shaggy dog in his apartment four blocks away. During the break, they ran through the snow, got the dog, and set him on stage. Then the lights came on. In another show, Severn Darden was doing a scene with Barbara Harris. They needed a fur coat, which they borrowed from the cloak room. When the coat waltzed across the stage, a woman in the audience screamed, "My *coat!*" On stage, there was certain embarrassment, but the audience thought it dandy.

One of the most popular sources of improv is a visiting alumni or other celebrity, as when Groucho Marx visited Second City and witnessed a Khrushchev-Kennedy debate parody. Recalls Alan Arkin, who played the Khrushchev role, "When we asked for questions from the audience, we were getting all these responsible political probes. Then Groucho said, 'Where did Mr. Khrushchev get his hat?'

"We told him where Khrushchev got the hat.

"Then he wanted to know, 'What size is the hat?'

"We told the size. Next he asked, 'Can you tell me how long he's had it?' He went on and on. He wouldn't let us get past the hat I was wearing. We all finally got hysterics and ran off the stage."

Groucho became a fan, but didn't actually participate on stage. When celebrities and grads do get up on stage, results can go either way. They can be loose, wide open, undisciplined, or once in a while can lead to a piece for an upcoming show. Celebrity visitors Martin Mull, Dudley Moore, Peter Cook, Richard Pryor, Tom Hanks, Brooke Shields, Ed Asner, and Robin Williams have scored famously when they've winged it.

John Belushi's alumni visits to The Second City were always major moments. One night, Danny Breen was doing an improvisation on an audience suggestion about *Saturday Night Live* going downhill. "Nancy Kelly and I were onstage. We were playing a couple sitting there watching the show on television and putting it down. We were nailing everybody in it, all their characteristics. Suddenly there was a knock on the door onstage. I went to answer it, and John Belushi walked in. Well, we went so crazy we never finished the scene."

When Belushi was back in Chicago after starring in *Continental Divide*, he and the cast did an improvisation of Siskel and Ebert reviewing the movie. Backstage they discussed the details: "They always introduce each other." "Gimme some Ebert glasses." "Siskel always has his hair sticking up funny." Onstage, Belushi portrayed Roger Ebert slicing into Belushi: "He's overweight. He isn't an actor. He's no Robert Redford, let's face it. What's he trying to do? Belushi's a buffoon, not an actor." (In real life, Ebert praised the film.)

Betty Thomas was in the resident company once when John Belushi paid an alumni call. "I'd known him there since I was a waitress. It was great to have him want to do a scene with me. It must be hard for people who see a person as a waitress to accept the person as a fellow performer. But he was very generous, very open, and he did a scene with me which I loved.

"The suggestion could have been something like 'basement apartment.' Then he laid his idea on top of it. It was definitely his idea. It was about a rapist returning to the crime of the scene. I didn't mean that. I meant that he was returning to the scene of the crime. He came back to this basement apartment expecting I would be horrified and recognize him. But I couldn't place the face. I'm asking him, 'Have you changed your hair?' and he's come back to tell me that he thinks I gave him the clap. The scene was very controversial."

Andrew Alexander, executive producer of Second City International, has seen some alumni drawn to the stage like magnets, and others as happy not to go on. "It's not rare to find they're terrified, even the ones who have left here and come back. They can be kind of apprehensive. Danny Aykroyd came one night about six months ago, had a beard on and you wouldn't have known it was Danny, which was about the only way you could get him to do a set. It took people a while to figure out who he was. By that time, he was out of the scene."

Recalls Joyce Sloane, "Once John Belushi had done his movies and *Saturday Night Live*, he'd come back here and of course we would not announce him. He'd just come through the door. It would be fifteen minutes before the audience calmed down. Danny Aykroyd doesn't have that kind of instant recognition."

An alumni-visit improvisation with Dan Aykroyd occurred after his close friend John Belushi's death. Joyce Sloane describes the scene:

"A year or two ago, he and Jim Belushi did a wonderful scene about John. Jimmy came out on stage to great applause. Danny got nothing. Then all of a sudden, there was a rumble, and recognition was dawning. They did this great scene, with Danny saying, 'I was staying at the Château Marmont. Yes, I still stay there. And all of a sudden there was a flash of light, and noise, and it was John coming into my room. He said, 'Give me the keys to your

Gilda Radner and Dan Aykroyd (Photo courtesy of The Second City)

car and a hundred bucks.' Of course I gave it to him. I could never deny him anything.' Then Jimmy said, 'You know, I had the same kind of experience. I was taking a shower, and there was a flash of light, and there he was, showing me how to wash my hair, soaping my hair up.' It was a beautiful scene, and gave us all a thrill.''

Once, when Jim Belushi was with the resident company, Avery Schreiber stopped by. Schreiber played a master glassblower. Belushi was his apprentice. Schreiber demonstrated the technique, producing a pantomimed Pepsi bottle. Jim Belushi tried his lungs. Schreiber gaped. "A Bavarian crystal chandelier!" Belushi huffed and puffed again. Schreiber exclaimed, "Rheims Cathedral! I can sell this for twelve thousand dollars!"

Then the apprentice asked, "What do I get?" To which the bossman sneered, "Two sixty-five an hour." Belushi responded by blowing a bubble big enough to engulf Schreiber. Schreiber produced a pantomimed glass cutter, made a hole in the bubble, and yelled out of it, "You're fired!" Remember, this was all pantomimed. Remember, it was all improvisation. When team playing works at The Second City, it really works.

When an improvisation succeeds, everybody's happy. When it doesn't work, it can still be fun. For instance, playing on your teammate's neuroses can be exhilarating, as Andrew Duncan discovered. "Viola's whole thing was to use the stage and movement. She was constantly relating to environment. When Mike Nichols came in, he was scared. He really was. You can't blame him. By now, he'd been in New York and studied with Strasberg. Then we'd throw him out on stage—'Just do it.'

"So the joke was, you knew when Mike did a scene, because you'd come out and there'd be a stool or chair. And that time, he smoked Kent micronite filters. He'd root himself in the chair, smoking, and we would act around him. And then Shelley Berman did that too. I picked up on it. There was a scene Shelley and I did on Fuller Brush men, where I deliberately grabbed the chair and forced him to go around me. He was never funnier than when he was forced to use his feet."

Years later in Toronto, Derek McGrath undertook the "Elizabethan Option," based on a game called the option play. A player is engaged in an action. Another, sitting on the side, calls out "Freeze," then asks the audience, "What happens next?" The audience responds: "His manicurist visits." An actress comes out, improvising a manicurist. Play continues until the next "Freeze," followed by the next suggestion, until the next "Freeze." And so on. The distinguishing feature of the "Elizabethan Option" is its setting,

Shakespearean times. This particular scene wasn't doing too well. The players backstage had already strayed off to the kitchen.

"Freeze. Okay, who's going to help him?" "The queen." McGrath waited for the queen. Waited, waited. "The queen must be coming." Waited, waited, waited. "I hear the queen now." The queen never came. In desperation, he shot to the window. "If there's a woman within the sound of me voice, get your arse on stage."

Richard Libertini did battle with Improv Police. "That was a favorite trick. If an idea was dying, or if you personally were dying, they'd come out and arrest you in the name of something or other. Just drag you off the stage. That was quite common. The Improv Police would come out. Sometimes within the scene as characters. Sometimes they'd just drag you out. It wouldn't be as overt as an announcement that you were killing the scene. It would be a mysterious arrest. It happened to me one time. They were the plot police, and they nabbed me."

There are various ways, not all delicate, for leaving an improv that's sinking. Jack Burns learned of ditching the hard way. "I remember when I started, I was thinking, 'I'm really going to kill these guys. With all the night club experience I've had, I'll go for the laugh—' and I went on, the first time, with Dick Schaal. We were doing an improv, and I panicked. I was getting no laughs. Having come from night clubs, I couldn't—it was wrong. I looked at Dick. Dick is a real pro. He'd been with the company a while already and nothing was going to bother him, but I froze. Then I walked off the stage and left Dick Schaal standing alone out there, because I didn't know what the hell to say. It was my first real experience with that type of improv. What I'd done in St. Louis wasn't the same.

"Then Paul Sills lit into me. 'You *never* leave an actor on that stage to die.' I felt like a traitor. I said, 'You're right. It's just like the Marine Corps. You don't leave your buddy out there to die. What did I *do?*' Paul said, 'You're supposed to stay on the stage and listen to what people are saying, instead of just going for jokes.' "

Eugene Levy, with the first resident company in Toronto, was facing an improv that would be the last scene in the show. "It was a British war scene where you had to come on and do dialects and I could not do dialects. Valri Bromfield was brilliant at them. Danny Aykroyd, brilliant. Gilda didn't even have to be brilliant. The audience loved her anyway. I said, 'I don't know. I mean, dialects . . .' and they said, 'Oh, go ahead, you'll be fine. We'll start the scene. People will walk in one after another.' I said, 'All right. I'll make

Left to right: Debra McGrath, Martin Short, Steven Kampmann, Robin Duke, on Toronto's Second City stage. (Photo courtesy of Hugh Wesley Photojournal)

my entrance last.' They said, 'Yeah, fine,' and they started the scene, and I went home. I left the theater. I got in my car. I drove home. They didn't need me in the scene. I was sure they'd be on stage saying things like, 'Is that a knock at the door? Who's at the door?' trying to cue me on. But I knew that eventually they'd put two and two together and wrap it up.

"The next night they asked, 'What happened to you?' and I said, 'I can't do dialects.' "

Harold Ramis had a flair for exit subtleties like, "Op. Have to get the phone in the other room," then beating a hasty retreat in keeping with the character he was playing. "Op. Got to milk the cow." "Op. Got to moor my yacht." He found the experience liberating. "I actually liked some of our most humiliating moments. Some of the greatest crises were some of the best times I ever had. I never felt more alive. I loved the feeling of disaster, of impending disaster, and being in it with people you like and actually laughing about it, being backstage with Joe Flaherty and Brian Murray. There were shows we did our first year, they were so bad, we would try to leave the stage. Other actors would actually have to stand in the wings and throw us back out."

Mob scenes, on stage as in life, can be ugly business. In one, Joe Flaherty portrayed the town sheriff. A mob was to enter, menace him, and spring a prisoner. At a crucial juncture, he was to say, "Wait! You can't take the law into your own hands"—and the mob was to ignore him and continue with the jailbreak. Backstage, before the scene, Brian Doyle-Murray suggested a slight modification to fellow mob members, with the result that when Flaherty pronounced the words, "You can't take the law into your own hands," the mob agreed, "Yeah, he's probably right," and moseyed off. Flaherty reacted with total shock. The audience roared, and the scene became a standard blackout.

Paul Sand rather relished being abandoned. "I always sort of liked that moment. I thought that when the audience was in on the squirm, and you knew they were in on it, it became, ironically, a flawless way to end a scene that wasn't working. To see people jumping ship in a sweet kind of way, and leaving someone sitting there—you'd just look at the audience, and they'd look at you, and they would empathize with you—and Howard Alk would put the lights out."

Gilda Radner concurs. "There's this premise in Second City. If a scene is going real bad and the audience knows that you realize it and you're trying to find a reason to exit, they'll be on your side. They'll cheer you for getting out of a bad situation."

Abandoning takes many forms. It happened to Avery Schreiber the first night he set foot on the Second City stage. "Bill Alton and Del Close and I were in a scene about playing golf. Bernie had billed me, in the program, as the 'West Side Wit,' and I had this reputation for double entendres which, I swear, I did unconsciously. I guess it's because I want to make people belly laugh, which I really think is one of the most important things in the world. So perhaps I found ways to do it unconsciously.

"For this scene, we got a first line, a last line, and a place. The place was on a golf green. There were going to be two golfers and a priest. Bill and Del were doing their best to be duffers, and I came in as a priest. I was a wonderfully chubby, cherubic guy, with my hands together. They said, 'Hello, father, we're playing through. Can we help you?' I said, 'I'd like to bless your balls.' This was the early sixties. The place went up for grabs. Except that Del and Bill, totally horrified, walked off the stage, because Second City didn't do that sort of thing. I swear, I was talking about their golf balls."

When a scene is over, or is perceived to be over by the stage manager, the lights go down. This may occur because the scene has been terrible, and the first semblance of a joke will suffice. It may also occur because the man at the lights has been looking for a prop, or is inattentive, or drowsy. If he wakes up in the middle of a scene, he might kill the lights as a reflex, which may draw a "Hey! Pssst . . . bring them up" from the cast. But usually, once the lights are down, that's that.

"You could have murdered," says Paul Sand. "For us, it was Howard Alk. There were times, as soon as I got off stage, I'd reach for his throat. 'Howard, what are you *doing?*' 'Sorry, Paul. I thought I heard a laugh.' "

Adds Richard Libertini, "People tend to do that a little faster now than they did in the old days. As soon as you get somewhere near what is like a closing line, or a place where there's a laugh, bang, the lights go out. Doesn't necessarily mean a scene has happened. Usually the actors are saying, 'Damn, why did you take it out? We were just about to get there.' And everyone else backstage is clucking, 'Yeah, sure you were.' "

Conversely, the cast may conclude that the scene is as over as it's ever going to be. One of them announces, "Gee, it's getting dark." But the plea falls on deaf—or slumbering—ears, and the lights stay on, meaning the cast has to, as well. "Dark. Wow, really dark." It's not any darker. So someone thinks of a splendid new direction to take the scene, gets one word out, and— Boom. Darkness falls.

Without the risk, it wouldn't be improvisation. Surprisingly, the word *improvise*, contrary to surface appearances, is unrelated to the word *improve*. *Improve* means to increase the excellence of. *Improvise* means to do the unforeseen. The word to which it's closely related is *improvident,* which comes as no surprise to those who improvise professionally.

Richard Libertini, Macintyre Dixon, and Lynda Segal all served with Second City, before which they had an act—the name still conjures reverence—called *Stewed Prunes*. One sketch was about this improvident way of life.

Says Libertini, "We were doing *Stewed Prunes* at the Gate of Horn, and all the Second City people came to see us. Since they were out there, we thought we'd throw in a piece which we had done once in a while, based on an improvisational acting group. We took about seventy suggestions from the audience—time of day, characters, an impossible number of suggestions, one after another. And they were playing along with us, giving every suggestion they ever heard. When we had all the suggestions, Dixon said the first line, which was a suggestion they'd given us. This was followed by a long silence, with none of us knowing what to do or say. Tension mounted. We looked at

Both George Wendt (far left) and Shelley Long (far right) reached stardom on the TV show Cheers. *(Photo courtesy of Howard Frank Archives/Personality Photos, Inc.)*

each other. Sweat was forming. The other two backed off slowly, first one, then the other, abandoning me there. Ultimately, I broke the silence by saying the last line, which was the end of the scene. It was a satire on that type of thing, and the people from Second City loved it."

No doubt about it. An improvised scene can fail. Plunk. There it is. Nowhere. "Sometimes," says Mina Kolb, "you walk on and off and somebody should have pulled out the hook, because it's hopeless. When it doesn't work you just feel awful and walk around kicking stuff on the street."

Yet there are, in addition to first-time improvisations, chances to improve earlier efforts. Even a promising scene, on the first night, can ramble, or not really have a suitable end. But if the scene has sparkle, it comes back in another improv set. These are the scenes being readied for the next show. Not quite the same, but similar, are the hitch-ons when all else fails: "He said streetcar. You got anything for a streetcar? You? You? Me neither. How about the one we did with the bus?"

As to the scenes begun in previous shows, George Wendt explains, "You tape the improvs routinely every night. It's kind of a surveillance camera, like general blocking. No beauty shots, no close-ups. It's general blocking and sound in a fuzzy sort of way. Some people, like Donny DePollo, would always go back and watch those, trying to grab onto stuff. But it seems to me that you never forget the jokes. Never, ever, ever. I defy anyone who works there to forget anything that really went over well. You just don't.

"So you continue that process. The scene either works or it doesn't work. Then that evening, if there are notes, the director gives notes, sort of irrespective of what the audience felt. If the director thought there was a nice idea there, or a scene, he encourages you to try such and such a direction, this tack or that tack, to try the scene again or develop it. Invariably, the second time out, it would fail miserably. Del Close called it 'second time blues.' I guess that was because you were trying to remember the jokes and what worked the last time instead of playing the moment, the situation, the character. Then the third time, you at least hoped it would start to take a little more shape and usually by the third or fourth time, you'd have an idea of whether you wanted to keep the scene around. You can sort of smell a keeper the first couple of times out."

As to the hitch-ons, Wendt remembers being backstage "looking at the suggestions, and of course nothing would come to you from the suggestions,

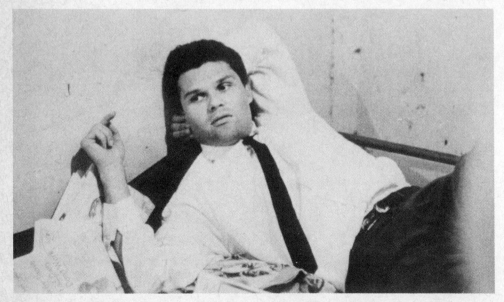

Fred Willard relaxing in the green room. (Photo courtesy of Fred Willard)

so then you'd start trying to think of some material that you had half-baked, and you wanted to pop it in the oven one more time, and tack on a suggestion that was remotely connectible to it."

Fred Willard had his own approach. "I always felt comfortable in knowing where everything went, which is the wrong way to do an improvisation. A lot of times we'd come in to work with ideas, and I had an awful lot of them. I'd come in and say, 'Tonight let's try to do a scene about a delicatessen. Someone comes in to rob it. You be the delicatessen owner, you be the robber.' I'd kind of talk it through. Then what happened was when they came up with suggestions that night, you'd see if anything fit. Then you'd say, 'Okay, let's try the one I ran through just now.' It got to the point that every time Bob Klein saw me, he'd say, 'Are you casting tonight, Willard?' And I'd answer, 'Gee, Bob, there aren't many parts . . .' "

Once a scene is sufficiently shaped, on stage and in workshops, it becomes part of the show. It is then, theoretically, fixed, but surprises are not without precedent.

Ben Gordon would get as far as the first few weeks of having a scene in a show, then want to mix it up. Once the scene was working, "I'd be bored with it. I'd want to walk out and throw new lines. I wanted to find new jokes, or new solutions. Or I'd come on at the wrong time, or I'd come through a different entrance. It caused a lot of pressure, and I'd get warnings. But for the most part, I found pressure healthy because it made you creative."

Jack Burns never ceased breaking up David Steinberg. Burns would be on stage "with my back to the audience. I'd just look at David's ear while he was talking to me. He'd be talking, then he'd start laughing. The audience wouldn't know why. Under my breath, I'd whisper, 'This is very unprofessional of you, David.' He'd be muttering, 'Stop looking at my ear.'

"Then I recall a scene we did in New York, when Second City was playing at Square East. I was an evangelist and Steinberg was a rabbi. I knocked on the door and said, 'Does Jesus Christ live here?' Then, in the course of the scene, he jumped on a chair. I jumped on a chair. We kept getting higher and higher on chairs. We did this whole scene just totally upstaging each other."

As Steinberg describes the scene, "It revolved around a Hasidic Jew who moved into Highland Park, and the reform rabbi came to talk him out of the move because he was embarrassing the 'normal-looking Jews.' I remember doing this scene with a lot of different people playing the reform rabbi. Robert Klein was one. Fred Willard probably was too. But I was the Hasidic Jew, and I was having a particularly good Saturday, and I'm walking around waiting for a visit from the reform rabbi, and there's a knock on the door. I didn't even know Jack was in town, and he peeks in and says, 'Does Jesus live here?' Then he turned me into a vaudeville performer. He'd try to keep my face turned toward him upstage all the time so the audience couldn't see me. The game became that. Great fun. He was always up to something like this.

"I would sum up our relationship by saying that anything you can do to another individual, Jack would do to me."

Surprises come in all shapes and sizes at Second City. When a visiting alumni is in the audience, a pun on his or her name might be worked into a sketch or improvisation. Nor does it have to be an alumni. In a recent sketch about Catholic school, reference was made to Saint Richard the Kind. Richard Kind being a member of the company.

As a surprise parting tribute to Joan Rivers on her last night with Second City in Chicago, during a scene called "Dentist," Bill Alton as dentist toasted her with pantomimed mouthwash and presented her with a book he particularly liked, Salinger's *Franny and Zooey*.

Another surprise, as jointly recreated by Burt Heyman and Ira Miller, went this way:

Heyman: There was a piano bar scene. I actually sang, and I can't sing. Remember me singing bad?

Miller: Yeah, sure. Bad. But it worked for that scene.

Heyman: Well, that's it. I was playing a real person, therefore as bad as I could sing, I can do that because I'm a person—who sings bad. I could be at a piano bar and I could sing like that, bad.

Miller: I remember. You were in it, and you sang bad. I was in it, as an obnoxious character at a piano bar. And Fred Kaz was in it, as the piano player. I was talking to Fred.

Heyman: Fred was at the piano, just off the stage, and we gathered around the wings and the side of the stage, and talked to him. Every night, my character ordered a pink squirrel. That was the guy I was playing. And this night was the last night of this show. It was chaos. I think there was toilet paper on the stage. And on *this* night, when I ordered the pink squirrel, in came my girlfriend—Judy Morgan, who was going to be in the next show—and she sat on my lap. She came in as a pink squirrel. They put a little tail on her or something.

A favorite Martin Short scene was "Hairdresser," in which he played the gossipy title role. Robin Duke, performing it with him, "had a speech at the end that I never wrote, and nobody ever got to hear. There's never been a speech at the end of the scene, because that's when Marty would dribble. I could never think of anything to say because he'd be dribbling, and I'd be

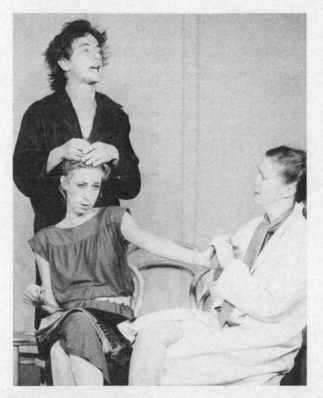

Martin Short (standing), Robin Duke (left), Catherine O'Hara (right) in the "Hairdresser" scene. (Photo courtesy of Rick Alexander)

laughing, and the audience would wonder why. Any time we do the scene at a reunion, I'll be backstage beforehand, trying to figure out what I'll say to him, or some fantastic response, but it just doesn't matter. I'll go out and try something and he'll make a face and the dribbling will start."

"John Candy," says Don DePollo, "can enter a scene anywhere and bring the house down. He'd just walk on stage and people loved him. So one night, he and I were in the wings but we weren't in the scene. We were talking, and the musical closing number was in progress. John said, 'Let's enter.' I said, 'No, we can't. It's the musical number.' He was kidding but I didn't catch on. I take everyone literally. Tell me there's a monster in the basement, and I find something to clobber monsters with and go look. So John said again, 'Let's enter.' I was concerned. 'No, no, no. John, it's their big number. They won't like us charging in on it.' He got hold of me and started marching us toward the stage. 'Come on, Don.' I was resisting, but it was like hanging on to Moby Dick. 'John, don't doooooo it!' He wouldn't let go of me. I was squealing like a baby. 'John, no, please, John, no,' and he stopped within an inch of our noses being out there. 'Oh. Maybe you're right.' "

Joe Flaherty was a master of surprises. Says Harold Ramis, "Joe would totally shatter the reality of whatever was going on at any time on stage. It often got out of hand and people would finally start warning him not to do it. He would come out on stage in a scene you'd done night after night and would change the major premise of the scene, or hit you with a line you could not do anything with.

"We used to do a father and son scene with this idea I got from a letter to Ann Landers. The letter said, 'My son disappeared for six months. Yesterday he walked in, went right to his room, and demanded dinner as if he had never been gone. What should I do?' I thought that was a wonderful premise. So I played a kid coming home after having been missing for six months. Joe played a very ambivalent father who both hated and loved his son. But it got really ridiculous, because I would walk in and Joe would go, 'Billlly!' He'd look at my feet. 'Where did you get those shoes?' It had nothing to do with the scene, and the audience didn't know that wasn't part of it. So it would leave me standing there like a fool, trying to either get back to the real scene or try to come up with something to justify this shoe business. But he was always doing that. He loved to crack me up on stage."

In another sketch, Joe Flaherty is the professor, giving a student a tough oral exam. Martin Short recalls being "kept on my toes, because Joe was always improvising. Very free form. At the end of the scene, the professor passes the student, because the student says he's afraid to go to Vietnam—or, after Vietnam, we changed the reason to his mother having eight kids—anyhow, the professor gives in and passes the kid. But sometimes Joe wouldn't pass you."

Nichols and May had a scene at The Compass called "Pirandello." It was in the style of Luigi Pirandello, whose plays explore the nuances of illusion and reality. When the scene begins, the two are children imitating their parents. Then they slip into being parents, having a fight. Then the fight becomes the actual performers fighting, until Elaine May looks disgusted and starts to leave the stage. Mike Nichols grabs her blouse. It rips. She says, "What do you think you're doing?" He answers, "Pirandello," and the scene ends to stunned recognition, followed by wild applause.

One night, the fight got away from them. Mike Nichols was hitting Elaine May in earnest, and she was clawing his chest. He thinks he must have blacked out before doing it, "And then they brought down the curtain, and we cried a lot. It never happened again."

There were times when surprises came from sources offstage. For a scene called "P.T.A.," cast members were planted in the audience. George Wendt, in character, smoked a cigar. "We were at the University of Missouri giving a show, and the security guard came up and told me to put the cigar out. I probably did, but it's a little rattling right before your cue to be dealing with a security guard."

On another occasion, Severn Darden was outside in the alley, shouting "Emma, where are you?" This was to create a long-distance effect. "It really sounded like it was way away. But a cop came with a gun. He said, 'What's going on?' I said, 'Let me show you.' I pulled a curtain and the audience was there, and he was staring at them, holding his pistol and flashlight. He was furious. I really hadn't done it to be funny. I did it because it would have been too long to explain, and he had a gun."

Another time, Paul Sand portrayed an underwater sponge collector. "We had blue lights, and I was doing slow motion, because I'd studied with Marcel Marceau, and the story had some joke ending. It had to do with running into Severn Darden or I forget what. But I remember being real quiet, and real proud of my slow motion technique. I was kind of stuck on myself about it, and thinking, 'Boy, are they quiet, they must really be impressed.'

"Then I heard, 'Tsk tsk.' I was destroyed. It was such a put-down. When the number was over and I got off, I said, 'I'll never go on another stage again. I can't stand it. I must have been the worst, and I thought I was doing so well.' Barbara Harris said, 'What are you talking about?' She went out there and did something and came back holding her head. 'I heard a "tsk." I won't go on stage as long as I live.' Severn did the same thing, and came back, asking, 'What are we doing? Somebody hates us.' So I said, 'I'm going to find this person,' and I peeked through the curtain, and saw a man eating a rye bread sandwich, trying to suck seeds from between his teeth."

Not all Second City shows were warmly received. When a touring company went to Louisville, they played a club named The Mousetrap. "Strange place," recalls Harold Ramis. "Like a Playboy club, only the waitresses wore mouse ears, little rat tails. The restrooms were marked Mice and Mouse. I could never figure that out. But we did some of our sacrilegious and antiwar material, which really got them steamed. We changed our show. Overnight, we threw out half the show, stuck in old blackouts. They cut our booking a week. I remember cocktail glasses hitting the stage, smashing off the back wall a couple of times."

George Wendt was "booed off stage" once. "That's an experience I think should happen at least once in everyone's career to every performer. It's a real lesson in humility. It was Ann Ryerson and Steve Kampmann and Don DePollo and myself, doing a particularly tasteless scene about nuns and priests getting into sexual situations. I don't know if it was religious fanatics or just shrewd theater-goers who started the ruckus, but they started booing us. There were maybe five or six of them, but it's pretty hard to go on with a scene when five or six people are trying to shout you down. We did all the standard improvisational quips to deal with hecklers, like 'Let's shut the window on those noisy neighbors,' things like that.

"They were going, 'Get off the stage, you boring people, boo, boo.' And the rest of the audience wasn't exactly sticking up for us. Eventually we had to take the lights down. We were all really humiliated and I wanted to quit. Bernie Sahlins rushed backstage and grabbed us. 'Get back up there, get back up there. You should feel good about that. You've got to understand, you hit home.' He tried to buck us up. It was a really bad experience."

Another scene that's caused trouble is "The Faith Healer," targeted at the people who commercialize religion. When it was included in Second City's Theatre Guild tour, 150 subscribers cancelled their subscriptions after seeing it.

David Steinberg played the faith healer one night. "There was this guy in the audience, every time I would say a line, he would hiss. I was getting angrier and angrier. And we weren't allowed to break the reality and say, 'Hey, jerk, who do you think you are?' He was ruining what we wanted to do. I was losing the entire show because this man was hissing every line I said. I stayed with the scene, but when it was over, I stormed off, went outside, slammed the door behind me, and walked out to the street. As I was pacing and fuming outside the theater, a woman stopped me and said, 'We've had the best time. We've come to Second City for four years, and my husband here is recovering from a tracheotomy, and it's so good to see him this happy.'

The husband said, 'I sss thought you were sss the funniest person sss.' Then he laughed, hsss hsss hsss.

"Then, later, I was doing the faith healer when we had faith healers out there. They were so offended at it, Sheldon Patinkin told me to go home through the back way."

Ira Miller was about to go on one night. "We were doing a transformation scene. We have a door on an axle, it turns all the way around. The idea was that J. J. Barry's character didn't like his body. Peter Boyle played the doctor. When J. J. said, 'I don't like my body,' Peter told him to stand against the door. Then he'd flip the door around, and the next actor would come out, pretending to be J. J. Then he'd say, 'No, now I'm too tall,' or whatever, and the door would flip again.

"And this time, I was on the back of the door, and it flipped around, and I walked onstage. I see Peter Boyle and a guy I'd never met before in my life. He was crippled, and he'd gotten onstage and said, 'Can you help me?'

"It was—I didn't know what was going on. For a few seconds, I thought it was J. J. or somebody with makeup. I was dumbfounded. Peter took the guy's arm and said, 'You'll be all right. Just come with me.' We all just stood there, and he led the man off stage as inconspicuously as possible, which was through the back of the set, through the kitchen, to his seat. We were in shock until intermission came, then we were asking each other, 'Describe to me what just happened.' "

There are compensations. If an audience was particularly unresponsive—deservedly or otherwise—Joe Flaherty would take the bull by the horns and insult the audience from the wings. "Farmers! They're a bunch of farmers!" This was aimed less at the audience than at unsettling whichever pathetic prisoners of comedy were onstage trying to please the folks out front.

George Wendt, in the infamous "P.T.A.," at least once exacted the satisfaction of revenge. For this scene, cast members blend in with members of the audience, portraying an assortment of unglued parents attending a P.T.A. meeting. "I guess the approach invited a lot of audience participation. We were out there, and some of the dimmer audience members may not have realized that we were the actors.

"We were right out there amongst them, and we could destroy them pretty easily. You don't want to heckle a bunch of professional wiseacres. We did that for a living. We would crush people. Danny Breen used to humiliate people if they were heckling. I got one guy real good once. On the Château Louise tour. It was a convention, so all the guys had name tags, 'Hi, I'm Joe Fabeetz from Kalamazoo,' or whatever.

"This guy was really drunk all during the show. He was disruptive, and I'm sure he was cutting his own throat with his organization, because he was really out of hand. So, in the course of the scene, I went up to him and started screaming in his face, and I read out his name. There was an audience of about five hundred people, and of course I've forgotten his name, but I hollered, 'Oh yeah? Okay, Mr. Joe Fabeetz of Albuquerque, New Mexico. I bet you'll feel real good in the morning. *Joe Fabeeetz*, Albuquerque, New Mexico branch' of this insurance company. I exposed him, and he probably still hasn't lived it down.

"That was a scene where we could get away with murder. If we saw people nodding off, we'd get right up next to them. Then when our cues came, we'd blast out our lines and watch them jump."

"Unlike Hollywood or New York," says Eric Boardman, "when we were with Second City in Chicago or Toronto, we weren't trying to impress producers or directors or talent scouts in the audience to get a job. Instead, the goal was to entertain each other and the audience and, if possible, make the piano player laugh. That was really the icing on the cake."

Ultimately, after the thrills and the failures, the humiliations and the compensations, what remains are the long-term results. To Bernie Sahlins, "My theory is that everything an actor does, from the way he looks at his watch to the way he moves across the stage, is in the service of advancing a story, and in that sense, it's all writing. In that sense we, while acting, write. I think improvisation is a technique and a tool. I think that even the best of them fail most of the time, and in the end the audience is not interested in how you got there but in what you're saying. The more clearly and concisely and artistically you say it, the more effective it is. The fact that they're making it up does not effect the actual content of what they're doing. Either it's something worth seeing or it's something not worth seeing. And if you get over the question of how, it doesn't matter if they're making it up or it was written, or they found it under a mattress."

A Second City scene is solid material, however derived. It's got a point. It's got a structure. Its humor comes out of reality, out of relationships. It's a vehicle for actors performing comedically, not a routine for stand-up comics.

What it's not is a bunch of ad-libs strung together. Ad-libs don't help the other players. They don't advance the plot. A Second City team player doesn't give the other player a line that shuts him or her out, but instead, offers one that presents a new way to get in.

"When you're alone," says Gilda Radner, "I know, you can always get attention in comedy. You just stick your finger in your nose. It doesn't matter what the other guy's doing. All eyes will be on you and you'll get the laughs. But in all of the work I've done, I've been a team player."

John Belushi, another team player, regarded the process with infinite praise. "In L.A. or New York, people look into the camera and forget to relate to the other performers. Here, it's a family. Ensemble acting, that's what Second City teaches you."

5
Duck Horns
and
Democrats
(1964–1969)

As Second City entered the latter half of the sixties, a subtle change took place. Sheldon Patinkin, who at various times has been a business manager, assistant director, director, and part-owner of the company, witnessed the evolution: "It is attributable to economics on the part of Second City, and a perception of what Second City *was* on the part of the people who were coming to see the shows. When you go to Second City and you see people being funny, you conclude that the point of Second City is to be funny. It evolved. It really did. There's no one point where you can say it stopped being pure. It stopped being pure long before Paul and Viola were gone. And there was a point, particularly when we moved to the second place, the bigger place, that it became more and more necessary to try and grab a bigger audience. The place had to become more commercial or die. And by commercial all I mean, and all that was meant, was that it had to start appealing to a wider audience.

"As a result, the workshops for the most part are and always have been about how to be funny, which is part of what drove Paul and Viola out. They became how to do Viola and Paul's work and make sure you were trying to be funny at the same time."

Into the widening crisis of identity strode David Steinberg, whom critics have described variously as "puckish," "beaming with fanged innocence," and "Woody Allen with sex appeal." Like Shelley Berman and Joan Rivers before him, he was accused in some quarters of sacrificing teamwork to comedy. By his own admission, he wasn't a whiz in workshop games, and "probably I was more concerned with the wit of the piece than the performing of it." He walked through people's wheres, stood in the middle of imaginary tables, marched through invisible walls. Yet he established himself as a verifiable drawing card—the sort of person who could leave Second City and get invited back.

Five-feet seven-inches and wiry, Canadian-born Steinberg was the son of a Rumanian rabbi. He himself enrolled in rabbinical school, then dropped out, continuing his general education later at the University of Chicago. Two events of this period turned him on to comedy. One was a Lenny Bruce

David Steinberg interviewing a very young Melissa Gilbert when he served as host of The Noonday Show. *(Photo courtesy of Howard Frank Archives/Personality Photos, Inc.)*

concert. "I felt he was a combination of James Joyce, Eddie Cantor, myself, yourself. I just couldn't believe it. I knew what I wanted to do." The other event was a Second City appearance on the university campus, with Bill Alton, Severn Darden, Tony Holland, and Joan Rivers in the cast. Impressed, Steinberg promptly auditioned and got into Second City.

His first night with Second City "was like learning to swim by diving off the *Andrea Doria*. Jack Burns told me, 'Don't worry. We'll look after you.' We were doing a fairy tale. You act it out in operatic style. That night the opera was 'Rumpelstiltskin' in the style of Wagner. Omar Shapli was the narrator. Jack said, 'I'll play Rumpelstiltskin.' Avery said, 'I'll play the prince.' Someone else picked another part. Everyone took a character and there was nothing left for me. I felt like a real jerk.

"Jack leapt on stage and started his aria about giving everyone three guesses to figure out his name. The whole point of 'Rumpelstiltskin,' of course, is that no one knows his name. Well, some divine guidance put my hand on a fedora on a rack. I put it on and crossed the stage and said, 'Hi, Rumpelstiltskin, I haven't seen you since college.' That meant thirty seconds into the opera it was already over. Everyone had to take their bows. For me, the lesson of that night persisted. Break any rule you can get away with."

Steinberg's improvisational style has been perceived, by some, as risk-taking, which he relishes enthusiastically. "If you try something that doesn't work, it can be a good indication that something is growing. In fact, the only way really to fail is by being safe all the time and never challenging yourself. It can be like skywriting. On a cloudy day, you can be writing like crazy and nothing comes through. But if you get just the right amount of sun and blue sky, it works. And there's no greater thrill."

Others wonder if the risk-taking is on the part of everyone sharing the stage with Steinberg. His arrival, recalls Ann Elder, "was a firecracker. An enormous energizer to a company of players who had maintained a kind of balance—we had gotten to the point where we had a very strong relationship, we knew each other. It was like one big happy family. Then came this kid, this very aggressive kid.

"The first week he was in the company, we did an improv together. As a rule, it was rare that I got off a line that made the audience really laugh out loud. But I did in this, and it was a major thrill to me. The rest of them were always spewing brilliance effortlessly, then I got off this one joke, and I was so excited. Something fell out of my mouth that was remotely funny and the audience seemed to think it was hysterical.

"The next night, we brought out the scene again, and before I got on stage, David said the line I had gotten the laugh with the night before. I said, 'I quit. You took my only joke.' I didn't quit. But I was mad.

"Of course, when I think about it now, David was just impish and mischievous and he didn't know I was so sensitive about it. I was practically in tears. If you told David now, I'm sure he'd cringe and say 'How could I do that?' because he's not the type."

Because he stepped into an extant cast, David Steinberg initially inherited material created by others. Arkin-type macho parts, Sand-type little-lost-schlep parts. "But you don't really get known for somebody else's scenes," says Steinberg. "You might by the audience, but not within the group. I stayed there long enough that eventually I was doing all my own things." This is accomplished in two ways—by starting from scratch and making your own things, or by vastly transmogrifying something and making it your own. For instance, a Severn Darden piece derived from Ionesco's *The Bald Soprano* evolved into a psychiatrist scene that not even faintly resembled it.

"I'd seen *The Bald Soprano*," Darden recalls. "Every idea took too long to build up. I said to Barbara Harris, I can do the same thing in seven or eight minutes, get the point across and many more laughs. Originally, the jokes were about this man, this teacher, who was a total tyrant, then he gets his come-uppance at the last minute."

Steinberg gradually altered the scene. "I used the duck horn. Severn never used a duck horn. Severn played a professor going 'honk' all the time. It was brilliant, I thought, but a little too intellectual for the audience to laugh at, though I can't imagine anyone not laughing at Severn. When they offered the scene to me, I added a duck horn. Then it worked all the time. The words seemed pretty much to be Severn's, as I remember it."

In this version, the student enters for his oral examination. "How are you?" asks the professor.

"Fine," the student replies.

"Wonkkk!" The professor blasts the duck horn in his face. "From a three-year-old, we're satisfied when we ask 'How are you?' to hear 'Fine.' From a Ph.D. candidate, we expect a little better."

No matter what the student does, or says, or thinks, the professor unsettles him with a resonant "wonkkk!" Over time, the Steinberg character became a psychiatrist, Marx Brothers-style, without the duck horn, but still completely wacko. The piece became one of Steinberg's signature roles.

A scene between David Steinberg and Omar Shapli explored the publish-

or-perish syndrome in academia. Steinberg, as the college president, lit into Shapli, the professor, for not getting his work into the journals. "Bernie always enjoyed the scene," recalls Shapli. "It was full of allusions to Blake and metaphysics. The audience never cared for it as much."

A piece Steinberg's name especially evokes sprang from an improvisation one night. "I was amazed when someone suggested I do an Old Testament sermon. Well, the thing about Second City is that you work from the top of your intelligence. So if you had pockets of knowledge about a subject, it would come out. I'd come from yeshiva—who would have thought you could use that on stage? But you could, and the audience knew what you were talking about. My impression was that the audience remained pretty smart all the way through.

"So I did a secular sermon one night, taking a suggestion from the audience. Moses. It was such a successful improvisation that I hardly changed a word of it for eight years. Then every night they would offer a different suggestion and, by the time I'd developed ten or eleven of them, they became the vehicle for me to do stand-up comedy."

In "Moses," the story is told of the prophet approaching the burning bush. He doffs his sandals out of respect, and gets a hotfoot. God instructs him to go to Pharaoh saying, "Let my people go."

Asks Moses, "Who shall I say sent me?"

Answers God, "I am that I am."

Sighs Moses, "Thanks for clearing that up."

Steinberg's sermons cinched his success at The Second City, and later, in the outside world. It's hard to resist a sermon that begins, "God, whom you remember from last week . . ."

In February 1965, while England's Oxford-Cambridge Revue filled in at 1846 North Wells, Second City undertook a ten-week Theater Guild tour that covered Boston, Cincinnati, Cleveland, Detroit, New Haven, Philadelphia, Pittsburgh, and St. Louis. The traveling cast was Bill Alton, Robert Benedetti, Severn Darden, Judy Graubart, Sally Hart, and David Steinberg. Reviews varied. A critic for the *Detroit Free Press* wrote that "David Steinberg has a bad habit of knocking his knees together in moments of stress but he's often a lot of fun." The program notes on Steinberg read, in part, "Despite everything you've heard about him, he is very well liked."

New recruits arrived in Chicago. In New York, Fred Willard and Robert Klein turned out for the same audition.

As Willard reconstructs it, "Sheldon Patinkin and Bernie Sahlins came and watched us. Lot of people auditioning. I think Alex Canaan was there. He got in the group. And Joan Bassie, who had a very proper British accent, though we later found out she was from Chicago. She'd studied at the Royal Academy in London. She got in the group. Billy Dee Williams was there, which I didn't realize till years later. He didn't get in.

"I'd never improvised in my life, and I thought I was going to be terrible. What they'd do—they'd take two people and stand them up in the middle of the audition and give them suggestions, just a situation. We'd start improvising. It seemed like every time it came around to me, I got something that I liked and could do, and by the end, when they said, 'Okay, who else wants to work on this?', I'd have my hand up. 'Lemme try.' So I was really hot, and in the back of my mind, I kept saying, 'Oh, they're gonna like me and I really don't know if I want to go to Second City.' Because I had an act with a partner, and it was doing pretty well. Then the act was slowing down, and Second City still wanted me, so I went."

Robert Klein, a middle-class kid from the Bronx, turned to the theater after a false start in premed. When he approached the audition, his experience included stand-up comedy as well as serious classics. "I was out of Yale Drama School, my fifth year of higher education complete, totally depressed, not in school for the first time in my life. I was substitute teaching, and I did some summer stock, like the play of *Herod,* a liturgical drama. I was on the cover of *Hi-Fi Stereo Review*, and the picture is hilarious. Me in chain mail and armor, one of Herod's soldiers, slaughtering innocents . . .

"I did that, and I went down to the Village for a few hootenanny nights. I went to the Bitter End and I was damn good, for about three weeks. Then I was bombing. I had no idea why. Obviously I didn't have the technique, didn't know how to recapture the thing. Then came this Second City audition, which appealed to me tremendously. My memory of the audition is a large room at the William Morris Agency, full of fifty or sixty people. Physically that doesn't seem right, but that's my image of it. That many people. We were given turns to improvise. I was paired with a person I'd never met in my life, named Fred Willard. He played a nightclub owner. I played a folk guitarist. We got a lot of laughs.

"What was wild is that the improv suggestions came from our competitors. Think about that. It's cutthroat. But it was a friendly atmosphere. The same day, Bernie Sahlins asked if I could be in Chicago by March. Whoooa! I said, 'Well, I have my affairs to tidy up.' Roughly, pack my suitcase. I had a garret with roaches. I had a girlfriend, but we weren't that close. Getting into Second City was the thrill of a lifetime, probably the most important thing in terms of training of all the jobs I've had."

Fred Willard joined Second City with second thoughts. "My first impression of Chicago was going to see Severn Darden, Howard Alk, Andrew Duncan, Alan Arkin. They'd do certain political humor, and references to Kierkegaard and Schopenhauer and Nietzsche. When I got the offer to go, I said, 'I'm not political. I don't know any of this. I'd be lost.' "

Robert Klein (left) and Fred Willard (right), who auditioned for The Second City on the same day. (Photo courtesy of The Second City)

Robert Klein was something akin to wide-eyed. "I loved show business, but already I was thinking—I wasn't that much of a radical but radicalized, I had friends who were at the time tremendous pinkos—and the whole idea of being unconventional appealed to me tremendously. Satire. The Second City looked like heaven to me. When I'd seen them on the Susskind show, they knocked me out completely. I was totally thrilled to be invited into the company.

"I remember, when I got to Chicago, Sheldon Patinkin warned me, 'Watch out for Steinberg. He's very talented, but he's trouble.' Then he came back to town from the Theater Guild tour, he was absolutely charming. Then we got down to business. I thought improvisation was my stock in trade, until I discovered how much I didn't know."

Robert Klein, physically somewhat taller than David Steinberg, was reduced by him to a height of about six inches in the duck horn scene. "I was cocky. I'd had some success at comedy already, but whatever I thought I knew, I knew nothing about this technique. And I found myself on stage, sitting in a chair, with David Steinberg parading behind me, back and forth, which was his favorite technique. Get the other actor in a chair, and go back and forth behind him, preferably with a Marx Brothers honker, not letting

Left to right: Fred Willard, Joan Bassie, Robert Klein, Judy Graubart, David Steinberg, Alex Canaan. (Photo courtesy of Fred Willard)

anyone else get a word in edgewise. He got tons of laughs. The audience wasn't aware of what he was doing to this other young man, me. He was brilliant on that stage. I give him credit for that. But the important feature of really improvising well is give and take. What he did was more like a monologue with someone to bounce off of.

"In many ways, the friction with him may have been good, in that it stirred me. It didn't make me complacent. But I can't help believing that a happy and content feeling is better. Even with that, from the instant I was on, I was made for it. The Second City was the most perfect experience I could have had—the show with the set lines, which was terrific acting experience, and the improvisations after each show.

"Then Steinberg left with the company that went to London, which was in August 1965. I had the chance to flower. I got more confidence because I didn't feel that competition, and I got more fluid, and I got used to the routine." Klein took make-a-song to a whole new level, got into characters, had fun. "When Steinberg got back, he had somebody quite formidable to deal with. From that point on, I more than held my own."

Fred Willard did scenes with Steinberg: "We'd try to come out to introduce a sketch. A lot of times, you'd tell a little joke to work it in. 'Now, we take you to a suburban home in Chicago Heights—' or whatever. So I told David, while we were standing backstage, 'I have a wonderful joke I may use.' I told him the joke. A few minutes later, he was out introducing a scene, and he told my joke. He came back, and looked at me, and said, 'I told your joke. We got a great laugh.'

"You couldn't be mad at him. He could borrow things from other people, but he was also the funniest, the best improviser I've ever worked with. When I would work with David on the stage, it would raise my level because I knew he would never suddenly fall apart or disappear. With some people, you have to be careful. You can't be too strong because they can't follow you. But David always had it under control."

Together, the group created a classic Second City scene, "The Amateur Hour." Fred Willard was the host, who introduced a succession of no-talent acts. Judy Graubart gave a show with a finger puppet. Alex Canaan did a bad Cagney with a Texas accent. Robert Klein was Herbie Shaloo, who nervously played a broom. Joan Bassie's talent was impersonating insane people, beginning with a woman in a catatonic fit. She went into the fit, and stayed there. Permanently. Host Willard observed, "Looks like she's become a regular." David Steinberg was a ventriloquist. His dummy was a hat on a stick. The scene became a favorite fixture in the Second City repertoire.

One piece, developed but not used, was given the heave by Paul Sills. Explains Fred Willard, "I created a *wonderful* scene. It was a computer dating thing where I'd been matched by computer with this girl, and the guy who was there and ran the computer was very smooth. The girl and I were starting to get along, but she fell for the computer guy, who had all the answers to everything. I thought this was great stuff, but Paul Sills threw it right out. He didn't like it. He said we were going to do a thing about Lyndon Johnson and Mao Tse-Tung in a swimming pool. To this day, I don't know why we did it, and I don't think it worked.

"We had been there a year and about a month before our last show opened, and right in the middle, they'd brought Sills in to direct the show. This was a show we'd been preparing for two months already, and it was ready to open, and he was going to throw out almost all the material. We had to do things like this huge swimming pool. And he had us play these really obscure theater games. For instance, you'd start with two people on a street having a hamburger, and then you'd establish that it was supposed to end with them sitting in a beauty parlor. But you couldn't say, 'Okay, let's finish eating and have our hair done.' If you did, he'd be screaming, 'You can't *write* the scene. It has to evolve.' There were arguments. It was like oil and water."

Says Robert Klein, "I did something like four different revues when I was there. Two with Sheldon Patinkin, then he took a leave of absence and Paul Sills came back to direct for a while. It was a great opportunity to work with Paul, although a very, very frustrating one. He was so tough on me, like a drill sergeant, and he seemed to be so nice to David Steinberg. Fred Willard he couldn't crack. Fred would listen, then continue to do it his own way."

While Judy Graubart, Robert Klein, David Steinberg, Fred Willard, and others held forth on stage, a future Pulitzer-prize winner worked the Second City beer garden as a busboy. Though David Mamet never participated in the workshops, he played piano a few Sundays for Jo Forsberg's children's theater, and asked Bernie Sahlins's advice about playwrighting. Recalls Mamet, "Bernie Sahlins tried to dissuade me from writing plays. I gave him my *first* play and he said, 'It's not about *it*.' " Sahlins failed to discourage him, while Second City concepts helped him on his way. "The blackout style inspired me in my early work *completely*, and the elegance of the actors I saw as a kid inspired me profoundly." As to friendships formed during these golden days, "David Steinberg continues to snub me after twenty-one years. . . ."

The Second City was still doing political satire—such as Robert Klein's portrayals of wrong-minded militants; and the "No Pictures" blackout, with an interchangeable public figure coming off a plane surrounded by photographers. He says, "No pictures, no pictures." They shrug, "Oh, fine," and walk away.

But there was a difference between the earliest days and these. What Compass and The Second City presaged in the fifties was, by 1961 and '62 and '63, actually happening. Comedy was smarter, true. But the world was shaping up to be no comedy.

President Kennedy was assassinated in 1963. Avery Schreiber was at Second City in Chicago then. "The night he was killed, I wanted to go on stage. I had ten ideas for anti-Johnson jokes, material, and sketches. Sheldon Patinkin said, 'No, we're closing down for three days.' I said, 'Damn it, why? We could pay homage to the man we loved, and get early licks in on Johnson.' "

Second City continued to address the issues, but deflected them, at least to some degree, with more silliness.

Sheldon Patinkin feels that "the transition really was the Steinberg, Klein,

Willard time, which was when comedy was getting sillier, because Vietnam was getting worse, and Kennedy was shot, and it was just getting harder and harder to do satire that could make an audience laugh, unless it was local or social."

Chicago was Mayor Daley's town and would be for a long time to come. Robert Klein did a Mayor Daley spoof. Also one of Lyndon Johnson, who scratched his ear way out—here. These were impressions in the sense of spoofing quirks and nailing ideologies. In the time-honored Second City tradition, mimicry wasn't the point. In the Kennedy-Khrushchev press conference, for instance, no one had set out to *do* either man. Because, as Jerry Stiller explains, "There are people who do impressions. They're very good impressionists. But once the audience is attuned to the thought that you can do Ronald Reagan and they throw Ronald Reagan at you, they're going to watch how good you do Ronald Reagan. Then mimicry becomes the objective of the scene."

Fred Willard portrayed another Chicago figure, critic/columnist/taste-maker Irv Kupcinet. "At the time he had a show called *Kup's Corner*. I had the big cigar, and I was sitting in the back. What they usually did on the show, they'd be talking on the panel, and he would get up, leave the panel, walk forward to the camera, and address the audience while the people sat in the background. I tried to do it but it didn't work. I don't think people got it. But I went back years later, and we did it again. Someone was Jack Nicholson. Someone else was Kupcinet. Kupcinet asked Jack Nicholson, 'Jack, are you any relation to that wonderful golf pro, Jack Nicklaus?' " The Chicago audience, brought up on a steady diet of Kupcinet's peerless style, howled with laughter.

In 1966, the cast packed their bags and took a show to New York—*20,000 Frozen Grenadiers*. Mike Nichols caught Robert Klein's act, and cast him in his Broadway production of *Apple Tree*. From New York, both Klein and Steinberg went on to major careers in stand-up comedy, riding the crest of the hip yet literate New Wave. Klein credits Second City with a lion's share of his success. "I learned everything. Discipline, improvisation, and the art of working up a comic routine. It matured me as a performer and gave me a feeling of control of the audience. Anybody with a little feeling for it can knock the audience dead two or three times. But the dynamics of doing it frequently, doing it in a systematized way night after night, are completely different. It's the difference between a professional and an amateur, and experience is the only bridge."

Also in 1966, an alumni cast visited Toronto with *Further Along: From the Second City*. The team consisted of Penny White, Jack Burns, Avery Schreiber, Bob Dishy, and Dick Schaal. Burns and Schreiber were already stars, and advance reviews promised "their popular taxicab scene." Schreiber, by then, was also appearing on TV's *My Mother the Car*. A Toronto highlight was a twenty-five-minute sketch, first performed in Chicago in 1963, from the growing Second City repertoire. In "Family Reunion," a young man (Schaal) entertains his small-town family after a relative's funeral. He tries to tell his vacuous mother (White), overbearing father (Schreiber), and dim brother (Burns) that he's gay. They choose not to hear.

In early 1967, a company played Toronto. This time it included Dick Schaal, Valerie Harper, Linda Lavin, Omar Shapli, and David Steinberg. They performed such classic pieces as "Museum Piece" (Lavin in the virginal Barbara Harris role, David Steinberg as the beatnik poet created by Alan Arkin), "The Amateur Hour." (Linda Lavin whistling " 'Twas the Night Before Christmas," Valerie Harper had the fit), two couples returning from seeing *Who's Afraid of Virginia Woolf?* (Harper as an Elizabeth Taylor double), and Zeus (Shapli) in a Broadway musical.

By now, The Second City connection had indirectly made major inroads into another area of the media—advertising. Bill Alton found himself spearheading the move: "I was back from England, in New York, and I ran into Elaine May on the street one day. She asked me to join something called The Third Ear, which was a little improv company she was forming on Bleecker and Thompson, where The Premise had been originally. The company was Louise Lasser, Peter Boyle, Mark Gordon, Renée Taylor, Reni Santoni, myself, and Elaine as director.

"Then Bernie Sahlins came to New York to start another Second City company, which I joined. Then we did the Theater Guild tour. Then it was back to Square East. One day, while I was there, I got a call from Mary Draper who was then head of casting at Doyle Dane Bernbach, a wonderful, creative advertising agency. She asked me to come down and audition for a commercial, which became a very famous one, for Thom McAn shoes. It was called "Man in a Shoe." I was walking around in a shoe as big as a large room. Gene Troobnick interviewing me from a booth.

"The commercial was a fantastic success, after which I kept getting calls, as did everyone, Alan Arkin, Zohra Lampert, Gene, all of us.

"Then, one day, I got a call—did I know any directors who could do a package of commercials for Gillette? I suggested me, and the guy said, 'I was

Robert Klein at the twenty-fifth anniversary celebration. (Photo courtesy of Jennifer Girard)

hoping you'd say that.' I did the package, and it won prizes. I started a company, which really took off, and I worked with Second City people like Andrew Duncan, Paul Dooley, Peter Boyle, Barbara Harris, Mina Kolb, Joan Rivers, and the others.

"We did a commercial for Arrid Extra Dry, in a sort of Santa Barbara think-tank setting. Different characters with different occupations, like Peter Boyle as a cop talking about perspiration and trying to get at his shoulder holster. It was called "Active People" and we improvised the whole thing.

"Then we did the Excedrin commercials. A woman came up with the idea of getting a group like us together in a radio studio. We just improvised, talking about headaches. We'd be milling around the studio, 'Oh, I got an idea. A man and his wife just got a washing machine and they're trying to hook it up . . .' We came up with these situations that produced tension and called for a good aspirin. I think it was Mark Gordon who came up with, 'I don't just have a headache. I have an Excedrin headache.'

"And they'd let you stay on as long as you wanted, then take the audio tape and cut it, and if they liked what they had, they'd call you back to shoot it on camera."

The Second City players had a whole new line, and a lucrative one, and on Madison Avenue, their reputations soared. "Only trouble, sometimes," says Fred Willard, "is you'd get a call from some agency, they'd tell you the product, and then you'd improvise. They'd laugh and they'd love it. Then they'd call you back in a few days to improvise a little more. This happened to me once, and the third time I was called, I assumed I'd gotten the commercial. But the woman was asking me to come in to do a different product. I asked what had happened to the other one. 'Oh, they cast it. They used some high school kids.' That's what they'd do, and not pay anything. But the practice stopped. The union put an end to it."

Second City players today get commercial parts in Chicago, New York, Toronto, everywhere. Burns and Schreiber, J. J. Barry, Lynne Lipton, Don Lake, Murphy Dunne, Hamilton Camp, Tony Holland, Burt Heyman, Ira Miller, Ben Gordon, Steve Kampmann are just part of the list. Robert Klein and Judy Graubart did "Ruffles have ridges." Zohra Lampert extolled the virtues of Goya beans and Ocean Spray cranberries. Paul Dooley performed in, and wrote, Martin Paint's "It ain't just paint." David Steinberg, who directs and produces TV commercials, works with Second City people whenever he can, and "I have never talked a client into a Second City person the client hasn't gone crazy over."

In addition to commercials came a new involvement in commercial film. Joyce Sloane had been working independently, in the United States and Canada, but always stayed in touch with Second City. By 1966, she didn't want to leave Chicago any more. "Second City was doing some film things and Bernie said, 'Take a look at them.' We had some young men doing wonderful experimental film programs here. Somehow, Bernie sold Bell & Howell on the idea that we should do a film program for them. Which we did. Bernie and I both went to work for Bell & Howell, doing these experimental film programs."

The notion, in part, was to bring the film industry to Chicago. The first feature film to come out of the project was Bernie Sahlins's science fiction satire, *The Monitors*. Second City acting talent was employed. The film had its world premiere in Chicago in August 1968, was deemed to be ahead of its time, and is now a cult film with a following.

Joyce Sloane was immersed in the project up to her elbows. "I learned a lot about film. That was the time for experimental films, and I went around to colleges, making presentations. 'The public will not stand still for Hollywood just turning the camera on. They want more. Film is art.' I made this big speech and showed our film of Alan Arkin and Barbara Harris doing "Museum Piece." The program was The California Underground, The New York Underground, The Teenage Underground, and so on. The brochure won an award. People would say, 'Thank you for your energy.' "

At this critical juncture—shows going to New York and Toronto, film and television projects—Second City had a choice. They could go on uprooting current casts and packing them off with suitcases, or they could start a touring company that had suitcases surgically implanted in their hands. They chose the latter course.

Ira Miller was among those in the first touring company: "I started in the workshops in 1966, and before that I did a stand-up comedy act, and I worked with another guy in coffee houses in town. Then I heard Second City was starting workshops to get new people. I took the beginning workshop, and a took job in the kitchen to support myself. Then I worked up to assistant stage manager. Then they started the touring company, which I was in for about eight months. Ron House was in it, who went on to do *El Grande de Coca Cola* in New York. Terrence Ford was in it, Harrison Ford's brother. Warren Leming was there, who married Eugenie Ross-Leming. And Jim Fisher was there, who later got into the company. And a few others."

The touring company was trained and dispatched to the field. By September 1967, there was also a Second City South, made up of actors from the New Orleans area, playing on Bourbon Street for a limited engagement.

When, soon after, Jim Fisher moved up to the main stage, so great was his eagerness that he tossed himself headlong into peril for his debut performance. "The show opened up with a song. The house went dark. The guys and the girls would sit on the piano where Fred Kaz was, then they'd hit the spotlights. My first night, I went out, and since I'd never done this before in the dark, I totally missed the piano and fell into the audience. Scrambled *up* on the piano and got there just as the lights came on so nobody knew what had happened. I almost broke my leg—as they say in the business."

Another memory associated with Jim Fisher is Betty Thomas, as a waitress, serving drinks in the front row. She was asked not to do it while he was performing. Thomas thought Fisher uppity until someone pointed out that between her six-foot height and her Afro hairdo, she completely blocked the shorter Fisher when she stood in front of him, even though he was on the platform stage.

In August 1967, The Second City was urban-renewed out of 1846 North Wells to 1616 North Wells down the street, in the heart of Chicago's Old Town district. The facade of the building at 1616 North Wells is three striking arches, designed by Louis Sullivan in 1892, and rescued by Bernie Sahlins from the old Garrick Theatre (previously the Schiller) which was torn down in 1961.

The new location was an area called Piper's Alley, with shops and boutiques and an ambiance which the developer felt Second City could enhance. He offered to build a new theater with a hundred more seats. The offer was accepted, and a theater took shape from the frame of the former Piper's Bakery and adjoining garage. Today, you can still see three letters of the word b-r-e-a-d on the wall. If you're the last one to leave at night, you may encounter the ghost of Second City. As Tino Insana recounts the legend, "Evidently, this woman fell into a vat of flour when the building was a bread factory. She was working for a penny a year or something. The run-in I think I had backstage with her was when I found, in a little corner, a couple of pennies. I took them. The next day, there was a bigger stack of pennies. I took that. The third day, there was a pile of pennies. This kept going on for a week. Finally, I told Fred Kaz about it and he said, 'That's the ghost. That's the kind of stuff she does.' "

Since the theater was 50 percent larger than its predecessor, and since even intellectuals aren't blind to the concept of financial risk, management saw some need to hedge its bets. It was imperative to fill seats. They would go right on doing smart humor, but with more appeal for the lunatic fringe. Tickets were now priced from two dollars and fifty cents to three dollars. The cast that opened the new building was J. J. Barry, Martin Harvey Friedburg, Sid Grossfeld, Burt Heyman, Sandy Holt, and David Steinberg.

Steinberg, who'd gone to New York from Second City, was back because his name was a draw for his alma mater. "I'd been on Broadway. I had starred in *Little Murders* and *Carry Me Back to Morningside Heights*, a play that I loved that did badly, but it was great fun. And I was in the syndrome of working less than when I wasn't successful, on that treadmill where once a year you start a Broadway play, and it felt awful. So I rushed back. That's when I created the psychiatrist scene, which worked out so well for me."

Now the psychiatrist scene centered on the nut case and the patient. The psychiatrist says, "Tell me anything." The patient confesses, "I'm a virgin."

Mike Hagerty (left) and David Steinberg (right) recreate Steinberg's famous psychiatrist scene for the twenty-fifth anniversary reunion. (Photo courtesy of Paul Natkin/Photo Reserve, Inc.)

The psychiatrist laughs hysterically, and calls out to the receptionist, "Hear that? He's a virgin!" The psychiatrist also jumps on chairs with demented abandon and makes "booga booga" noises.

J. J. Barry, Martin Harvey Friedburg, and Burt Heyman had been found by Second City at the Improvisation in New York. According to J. J. Barry, "We came from New York, where we'd been doing these improvisations with each other and Richie Pryor, without going by any rules. We just got up there and did what came into our heads. So when we got to Second City, we resisted the games. We were like the New York buffoons. Since that time, I've seen the light.

"But we made fun of the games, and then Paul Sills wanted to do a scene with a film of a pan of sauce. We were supposed to be ants and swarm over the sauce, react to it. We said the hell with that. We did a war movie. Now I see what he was trying to do, which was to show that the actor's function is in the moment rather than going for the laugh. I rejected it, because I thought the function of the actor was to get a laugh at any expense."

The revue began under the direction of Paul Sills. When Sills left to work with Viola Spolin on The Game Theatre, in 1967, Sheldon Patinkin took over. "His battle was in turning our heads around," Barry reflects. "We thought of ourselves as comics, and he had to make us into actors who did comedy. The reason they brought us in was because they were lacking, at that particular time with the particular company, the sort of humor we could do. So they brought in three loudmouths. They figured they could shape us up, and eventually they did, for which I'm very grateful. But when we came, I think that's when Second City changed from a satirical, intellectual group to a sort of broader-based Saturday night humor. As much as I like to be thought of as someone who is bright and clever, it is also true that we introduced what you could call a blue-collar approach to satire, down-home, nitty-gritty, on the street."

Despite differences from era to era, whether in 1959, 1963, 1967, or any other year, The Second City always responded to the world outside. Not always the same way, but in some way. Each cast can reasonably claim responsibility for some sort of transition. Bernie Sahlins sees the job of the directors and producers—and by extension, the job of the players—to be "the maintaining of a consistency in honesty of approach and quality, even if the ground rules are changing, or the attitudes are changing. It's quite interesting that they seem to change every four years. The attitudes toward drugs, toward sex, toward politics, are really school-generational, and if you're approaching something from a four-years-ago attitude, you're slightly askew, slightly out of synch."

Indeed, everything was changing. Anyone approaching 1967 from a 1959 perspective would have been out of touch. A longhair *then* was someone who went to the opera and played the oboe. A longhair, sixties-style, was a counterculture radical. Beatniks weren't even beatniks any more. They were hippies. Or yippies (from Abbie Hoffman's *Y*outh *I*nternational *P*arty) if they had a political bent. 1967 was dropouts and love-ins. "It was a real revolution for me," says Burt Heyman in reminiscent ecstasy. "When I came to Chicago and those hippies—it was like a dream come true. Hippies with tattoos on their bodies and love beads and long hair at the Lincoln Hotel."

In 1967, a musical opened in New York, off-Broadway, for ninety-four performances. It moved up to Broadway in April 1968, for 1742 performances. Called *Hair* and directed by ex-Playwrights harpist/composer Tom O'Horgan, it crystallized the spirit of the era. A song from the show, "Aquarius," became the theme of the love generation. It was the dawning of the astrological Age of Aquarius, an age of brotherhood and humanity that would have no room for national differences and racial strife. According to the song.

Out in the streets in 1967, riots raged, leaving 26 dead and 1500 injured in Newark, 40 dead and 2000 injured in Detroit. U.S. troop strength in Vietnam totalled 475,000.

Ira Miller moved up from the touring company, and got onto the main stage at the same time as Peter Boyle, who was brought in to replace a departing David Steinberg. With some other Second City players, Miller was involved in an unofficial show "at an anti-Vietnam rally on the South Side. On the stage were Martin Luther King and Jesse Jackson. No, they didn't participate in the show. They watched. I did Lyndon Johnson. Martin Luther King had a good laugh."

In 1968, following the assassination of the Reverend Martin Luther King and Chicago's ensuing West Side riots, Mayor Daley announced, "I have conferred with the superintendent of police this morning and I gave him the following instructions. I said to him very emphatically and very definitely that an order be issued by him immediately . . . to shoot to kill any arsonist or anyone with a Molotov cocktail . . . and to issue a police order to shoot to maim or cripple anyone looting any stores in our city." Tempers, not surprisingly, ran high.

Later in the year, Robert Kennedy was assassinated after winning the California primary for the Democratic presidential nomination. The Demo-

Peter Boyle (left) and Ira Miller (right). (Photo courtesy of M. H. Miller, Ph.D.)

cratic convention was held that year in Chicago, and the Windy City became a war zone. The peace demonstrators went up against Daley's cops, and lost.

Second City director Sheldon Patinkin had gone on to other things. Mike Miller, widely considered the hottest young director in town, came in to fill the position. Bringing with him an impressive reputation—earned in the field of drama rather than comedy—he introduced the company to innovations in lighting and theatricality. Coming into a revue already essentially planned and polished, he raised hackles when he tried to change it. Peter Boyle was fired after a disagreement with Mike Miller. Though Boyle was rehired almost immediately to star with alumni in a "Best Of" show at Ravinia, he wouldn't be participating in the main stage revue he helped create.

The revue at Second City in 1968 was *A Plague on Both Your Houses*. In one of its blackouts, a cop is beating up a young man. The young man begs, "Stop! Stop! I'm a reporter." "Oh," says the cop, releasing him. "Why didn't you say so?" Then the cop pulls out his gun and shoots the boy. Everyone who was there remembers opening night. By Ira Miller's account, "It was really an emotional time in this city, and in this neighborhood, and in this building. The police were out on Wells street, and the riots, and at the end of the show we sang the song, 'A Plague on Both Your Houses.' The cast closed by making peace signs, and the whole audience got up. Even Kupcinet and all these very straight Chicago people got up, really moved, and flashed back the peace sign. It was like an electric shock."

Jack Burns was visiting Chicago at the time of the riots. "I had been in *The Andy Griffith Show*, where I played Warren, the deputy sheriff. And I remember coming across the street from the Hilton Hotel, to the park where the kids were, and a cop said, 'Hey, you're Warren.' I said, 'Yeah.' He said, 'Well, stick around, we're going to kick some commie ass.' I said, 'I'm going over there, so you'll be kicking mine too.' And he sort of moaned, 'Warren, don't say that, please.' "

The old Second City theater and beer garden at 1846 Wells was being used for a field hospital to care for rioters hurt in Lincoln Park. Abbie Hoffman and Jerry Rubin were there. To some veterans of the encounter, Rubin gave rings made for the convention—a peace sign on a gold band. Peter Boyle got one, which he wore years later in the movie *Where the Buffalo Roam*.

In the same building at 1846 Wells, Paul Sills rehearsed a *Story Theatre* version of *The American Revolution*. Story Theatre—improvisational theater combined with a narrative line—has a remarkable capacity for reaching an audience for the first time with stories everyone already thought they knew. In the case of *The American Revolution*, the experiences of people on the streets of Chicago were pulled into focus with a powerful vision of redcoats and rebels.

The Second City main stage company remained no

Sandra Holt and Ira Miller. (Photo courtesy of M. H. Miller, Ph.D.)

less politically involved. Both Rubin and Abbie Hoffman guested in occasional improv sets. Sandy Holt spoofed Lady Bird Johnson to Ira Miller's LBJ. Ira Miller did a song as Hubert Humphrey: "Fred Kaz made me sing. I got so nervous, it made me crazy. In grammar school, I was the one the teacher told, 'Don't sing. Just move your lips.'"

J. J. Barry, who "accidentally happened to look like Richard Daley," became famous for his version of the Mayor. (Press conference: "Shut up. I'm not answering that question. You—you're next. What?")

"Since I looked like Daley, Abbie Hoffman and Jerry Rubin always wanted me to do improvs with them." Murphy Dunne joined the cast as understudy, then replaced Peter Boyle. Dunne's father was politically powerful in Chicago, but this didn't stop Dunne from taking his own political stance to the Second City stage.

The Second City, true to its roots, was reflecting the social texture of the times. Carol Robinson won hearty ovations for a monologue on the ages of woman, which took her from youngster to old age. It was a sensitive and perceptive tour de force. Paul Sills directed "The Trip," a kaleidoscopic representation of a nice Jewish boy on LSD. There was a spoof on another psychedelic drug, LTV—this one a string of TV commercial take-offs tied up in a musical extravaganza.

Just as true to its roots, the show continued with a whole range of character pieces that are timelessly human, from J. J. Barry as the obnoxious faith healer Holey Moley to Holt and Barry's "Mildred and Morris," a people scene in the tradition of "Museum Piece."

"Mildred and Morris" evolved from two workshop concepts, mirror (players mirror one anothers' movements to enhance mutual awareness) and space (the raw material of all improvisations). Holt describes the scene with affection. "These two very schleppy people never really had a relationship with anybody, and they were very awkward. They found themselves standing very, very close together in a narrow hallway, and I, as Mildred, was afraid to let him into my apartment, because my apartment was sloppy. He was smoking a cigarette and I had asthma. The space made us bump into each other. The juxtaposition of his face and mine forced these two people, who were afraid to be intimate, into their first intimate situation."

Barry too remembers "Mildred and Morris" fondly. "It was the first time I ever did a role like that, and it felt really great. We never did it as well as we did the first time, but Sheldon Patinkin immediately put it in the show. And that's when Sheldon told me he thought I was becoming an actor."

Sandy Holt wrote "The Gibberish Song" with Bill Mathieu, inspired by one of the oldest, most venerated Spolin games. In the truest spirit of gibberish, every "sjkduwing hiayehgiue ldku dkues" had a meaning, and every so often would lead to a recognized word. Bill Mathieu used every part of the piano. Holt used every syllable known to man. Mathieu later departed Chicago to work in San Francisco with The Committee and Fred Kaz took over on Piper's Alley. With him, Holt wrote "The Voice of the Flower," which found its way into the movie *The Monitors*.

In 1968, The Second City was hither and yon and again, with an August appearance at the Ravinia Festival in Highland Park, Illinois, and a three-week December stint at the Lindy Opera House in Los Angeles. With 1969 came a six-week tour ranging from San Francisco to the District of Columbia; a September engagement at the Eastside Playhouse in New York; man's first walk on the moon and the world's biggest love-in, at Woodstock music festival.

According to a calendar, the sixties were nearly over. In actual fact—and, by extension, on the Second City stage—the impact of the decade had yet to unleash its full force. The touring company, consisting of David Blum, Jim Fisher, Joe Flaherty, Gerrit Graham, Roberta Maguire, Judy Morgan, Brian Doyle-Murray, and Harold Ramis, was giving "best of" shows on the road while working up their own material from improvisations, and playing the main stage when the regular company was off Monday nights. When the resident company moved on, its replacements were culled from the touring group.

As the new resident company, this bunch would break with tradition in myriad ways—from what the men wore (including jumpsuits in place of the formal business-suit-and-tie of their predecessors*) to the length of their hair (Flaherty's was longish; Ramis's hair was a curly hippie mass) to the introduction, by Jim Fisher, of a VCR to record improvisations (which previously were audiotaped only).

These visionary iconoclasts would be billed as the Next Generation.

---

*Sahlins reasoned that a jumpsuit was essentially a suit and a vest without a jacket. Jim Fisher thought the outfit fine until a football scene in which Joe Flaherty and Brian Doyle-Murray lifted him over their heads. His jumpsuit, of one-piece construction, nightly threatened to rip him in half lengthwise at the crotch.

6
Cast
Chemistry

*D*avid Steinberg compares a Second City cast to a band. "You're connected to the company. It reminded me of what The Rolling Stones was, or Paul Butterfield, or one of those great blues bands. No one thought the singer was more important than the bass player. The audience might have come with those perceptions—'The guy who's out there making the most jokes is going to be the star'—but among ourselves, no one thought the singer was more important than the bass player. Fred Willard was so brilliantly funny, so wry, and he looked so straight. He was like that bass player. He was absolutely essential to the equation, the balance, of what we were doing."

Graduates may depart Second City. But the band plays on. Any player who has advanced through the ranks from workshop to touring company to main stage is, by definition, top notch. As Bernie Sahlins told Joyce Sloane, "This isn't the post office." Seniority does not buy advancement. Only ability makes the grade.

This being the case, consider what a team in fact is—six or seven extremely talented, extremely bright, hand-picked individuals who have their own opinions and intend to assert them. Next, consider what studies show about the relationship between assertiveness and humor. In one, conducted at Texas Tech University in 1981 by Paul E. McGhee, it seemed "clear that the need to dominate is one of the basic precursors for heightened humor development. The person in a small group or at a party who is the initiator of humor is really in control of the social situation: he gives people things that they respond to, so he's pulling the strings."

In a group of seven at Second City might be seven people like this. There are times when there's no playing follow-the-leader, since everyone wants to lead. Paul Sills has been quoted as saying the job of the director is to "keep the actors from assassinating each other." The dressing room is tiny, increasing each player's sense of the need to fight for a share of the pie.

Cast chemistry is axiomatic, but not automatic, at Second City. David Steinberg, at Second City with several different companies, felt the bonding more strongly at some times than others. "I don't think I ever really became a team player. Although, I didn't always have the strongest teams when I was there. It depended. Mina Kolb seemed to be as strong as anyone I ever worked with. Barbara Harris and I did operas together, and things in which she was so sexy on stage, and they were fantastic. Fred Willard and I worked very well together. Dick Libertini and I have wonderful chemistry on stage together. He has chemistry with so many people. Jack Burns and I worked great together. Bob Klein and I never worked well together. Maybe personality resistance more than even talent.

"I guess what happens as I describe it—I got along with the people I respected, and the ones I didn't respect, it wasn't so much that I didn't get along with them, but that they didn't get along with me. I wasn't sort of phony liberal about liking everybody. I wasn't altruistic. If I didn't feel someone was right for me, I didn't want to work with them. That was the part of the community that didn't work for me."

This is not to say that team spirit at Second City reigns less than supreme. Strong friendships have been born there. Great lessons in cast chemistry have been learned there. Collaborations have evolved there that transcend what any one person could do. But nothing forged in the fires of absolute creation is ever casually won.

At the very least, it's a discipline. Second City teaches sharing, so players share. They go on stage and share till their pores ache and the scene is a million times more delightful than it ever has been, which means that the other player has never looked so good. A talent agent in the audience sees the scene, does handsprings of joy, and hires—the other player. Drat. It can hurt. Likewise, a player can be backstage creating a scene, shape the suggestion into a clever whole, and go onstage with two other actors who quickly take over the piece. The audience concludes that this martyred third wheel is a tag-along object of pity.

What makes things so much more intense at Second City than elsewhere in the theater is the absence of scripted material. Elsewhere, an actor can grandstand a scene only within the bounds of the lines. When people are improvising, they can say anything, and do.

Jack Burns was "in my James Dean period. We did a scene in which I came off looking very well, but it had very little to do with the concept of Second City. It had nothing to do with anything except making me look good as an actor. It was a self-serving scene. Del Close had been out, Paul Sills was away. Those saner minds that might have prevailed weren't there to stop us. It was a week when we were saying we could do what we wanted to. In this scene, I was a sadistic fellow of the road at an all-night eatery, heading to Hollywood. I drifted in and out of people's lives. Sally Hart played a waitress, and I was bullying her. For instance, I recall bull-fight music, and I grabbed her apron and made her charge after it. I became a sadist on stage. It was well reviewed by *The New York Times*, but I alienated a couple of people for a week, probably including the actress. Del Close told me 'never to do that type of thing on this stage again.' And Billy Friedkin, who was in the audience, advised me that 'you could have done that scene with a tree.' I learned a lesson.

"So while there were healthy nights, there were some unhealthy nights. I don't think I was the only performer guilty in that respect. You could take out your hostilities on another performer in those improvs, and use very personal things to hurt and get reactions and be very real, and sometimes very funny. But playing on someone else's weakness is not supposed to be the name of the game."

It's no place for the faint of heart. Not in general, and certainly not in the men-versus-women arena. Historically, Second City's men in a given company have outnumbered the women more or less five to two. This was the ratio first time out. Departing players are usually replaced by others of the same gender. The odds have favored the guys. There were years when the men and the women were strong. There were years of strong men and weak women. There has yet to be a year at Second City where the women dominated five wimps.

Psychologists claim to have an answer here too. The inclination to be funny has been found to diverge by sex early in a child's socialization process.

Little boys clown more. Little girls, responding to pressure, want to know it's okay before they smile. A study of seven- and eight-year-olds at the University of Wales revealed that, even though the girls understood cartoons as well as the boys did, they were more likely to watch other's reactions before reacting themselves. Samuel S. Janus, in *The American Journal of Psychology*, concluded, "The fact that women in comedy account for at most 12 percent of the field, whereas in other areas of show business they represent at least 50 percent, attests to their lack of credibility as power figures."

Without taking sides, one may yet observe that the odds are not, in themselves, catastrophic. Among the finest Second City scenes have been "people scenes" with one boy and one girl, a combination not ruled out by a five-to-two cast. On a larger scale, if Second City is reflecting the real world— politics, jail, big business—it's not inaccurate for men to play most of the roles. On the other hand, the make-up of the company in part dictates the scenes. A cast of five men and two women can't scare up three Boswell Sisters unless one of the men goes drag. It stands to reason that if the cast were two men and five women, material would change substantially.

Which leads to the deeper tension. The majority tends toward guy humor. Hey, lezz do cowboys. Lezz be pirates. Lezz play gangsters. Who'll be the damsel we rescue? Who's gonna be the gun moll?

Then the reviews come out. One, for instance, in the *Toronto Telegram*, noted "a rather anonymous, flexible young actress who is used mainly as a compere." The woman in question was the only female in her company. The flexibility may have been her only weapon. The anonymity may not have been her choice.

A woman generally inspires respect backstage by knowing her craft, taking chances, and keeping up with the guys. Joe Flaherty calls Andrea Martin a "money player, whom I love on stage because she's got it every time. On opening nights, when everybody else is choking up, and you rush your lines a bit, and you don't relax, she'd be right up there. Bam!"

A knack for physical humor is a definite plus for a woman. "Gilda Radner," Flaherty continues, "was great because she would make anything work. You could give her a piece and she'd find a way of making it work in front of an audience. We did one where she played the daughter, who was retarded. She just had a way of playing her really cute, funny, not insulting. She did the same thing when we were in the National Lampoon show, which was a combination *SCTV–Saturday Night Live* crowd. Just give Gilda somewhat of a premise. For example, *The Mary Tyler Moore Show* was very popular then, so we said to Gilda 'You're a blind girl but you're out on your own.' Every night she'd go out, create it, make it funny. 'I'm blind and I'm going out on my own. Wheee.' "

Her blind Rhoda Tyler Moore won highest accolades from Bill Murray. "Gilda was great. John Belushi was her boyfriend, and he'd change his voice and pretend to be these thugs hitting her, beating her, cuffing her around on the stage. Then he'd change back to the boyfriend's voice and pretend to be saving her from the thugs. . . . She'd run, with a cane, full speed into this wall. To get a laugh. She was covered with bruises. You had to admire her."

Remarks this latter-day Lucy Ricardo, "I'd throw myself right into it. I don't want to die. I have a real strong will not to bomb. I want to do the job well, not waste anybody's time on the job, not waste anybody's time who's watching."

Women like Gilda Radner become great favorites for being great sports. Harold Ramis found that "women at Second City always felt slighted. The men would write scenes and say, 'All right. Oh, we forgot the girls. Okay, so the girls come in.' That's how it was treated. But the women who earned everyone's respect, like Andrea Martin and Catherine O'Hara and Gilda Radner, were the women who would do anything that the guys would do. Would take the big falls. Would do the mock fighting. Who would really debase and demean themselves for a laugh. Gilda had that. She did whole improvs with John Belushi that were solely based on him humiliating her in different ways, and she was a tremendous sport about it. She is a great physical comedienne, and a lot of fun."

Backstage in the green room, the unassertive female—or the new girl who hasn't asserted herself yet—can become lawn furniture in a hurry. She's plugged into scenes her predecessors played. Her ideas for responses to improv suggestions—if she makes any—don't carry much weight. Or if they do, the response from one of the men might be, "Okay, that's great. Yeah, I'll say that. And you can be, uh, my wife."

One of Joan Rivers's first roles was in "No, George, Don't," a piece created by Mina Kolb, then passed on by way of Barbara Harris. In it, a husband is leaving his wife. The wife is wheedling him to stay—No, George, don't. I'm sorry I caused a scene. No, George, don't. Please forgive me just one more time. No, George, don't, we'll make it like it used to be. At last, the husband softens, moving in for a kiss. The wife pulls away. "No, George, don't."

With this, Rivers "realized instinctively that these men would be perfectly content to let me fill in the secondary slots that needed a prop female, let me go on saying, 'No, George, don't,' while I slowly withered and eventually died. I could see that they regarded Second City as a male art form, that they did not want a girl pushing in and saying, 'I can do that scene.' " With realization came action, and she began to assert herself.

Betty Thomas, at first, "found myself doing TM between the two shows on Saturdays. I was unbelievable. I was a mess. I couldn't figure out why, because I was so successful in workshops and so unsuccessful in the company. One big reason was because there was so much competition, and so little cooperation. There was competition for a good reason, which was because you had to put a show together. There was never that pressure in the workshops. Everybody back there was into getting that done.

"There were five guys, and they'd go out after the show. If you had a boyfriend, you'd have to junk your boyfriend if you wanted to get anything in the next show because you had to spend time with the guys or you wouldn't get anything in the next show. Even then it would be minimal. Maybe you'd play a whore or a wife, but at least you'd be in it. At the beginning, I wasn't even doing that.

"Then I was told I had two weeks to get it together or I was going to be fired. What it did was put the pressure on me so much that I had to figure out how to turn things around.

"Cassandra Danz came into the company, and she was a feminist, which was new to me at the time. She said, 'Betty, nobody is going to offer us anything.' She saw it right away. She saw it in one second, and I really learned a lot from her. We put together some material, got it out there, let people tear it apart. At least we were doing something. To the best of my knowledge, it was the first time The Second City had funny scenes between two women. Once in a while in the past, they'd do something serious or weird, but nothing funny that I'm aware of.

"Then Deborah Harmon came into the company, right after Cassandra left, and I told her, 'Harmon, don't even talk to me. Don't ask me to do a scene or anything else because I am busy forming a power base.' Poor Harmon. She was so good. She said, 'Okay.' I went and did every scene I could do. I'd do scenes with Joe Flaherty. I'd do scenes with Brian Doyle-Murray. I didn't care what I was doing. I just wanted to be in them because I knew they would get on the running order and at least have a chance.

"*Then* I was able to go to Harmon and we came up with some really

"Guy humor" with, left to right, Bill Murray, Betty Thomas, David Rasche, Cassandra Danz, Jim Staahl, and Tino Insana. (Photo courtesy of The Second City)

successful, really solid two-women scenes. The guys would enter them. That's when I realized that guys would enter scenes they thought were funny. I knew as soon as they were entering my scenes that we were doing something right."

Barbara Harris, unassertive at The Compass, became more outspoken at The Second City. Elaine May always spoke up. Zohra Lampert could fight for herself. Mina Kolb found "a man almost always instigated a scene, so you had to make your ideas seem like somebody else's"—though the men who worked with Mina Kolb have all described her as brilliant, incredibly funny, and not afraid of speaking up backstage.

Sandy Holt joined Second City in the late sixties. "The women, at that time, were all vulnerable and very soft. Very strong, but you couldn't act too strong. Comedy was still very chauvinistic, and there weren't as many inroads even as there are now. The women had to fight for everything. I remember there were times when I fought for a particular concept, and Sheldon Patinkin would say no, then he'd compare me to the men in the company. 'Oh, you're getting to be just like David Steinberg,' which was a compliment, because

David was very successful, but that isn't what he meant. I was breaking the mold of the clichéd woman who doesn't know anything. I gave up being demure. It was giving me migraines."

Before joining The Second City, Miriam Flynn had gone to an all-girls high school and an all-girls college. "Never having experienced a prejudice against women, because I was simply never in such a situation in school, I never stopped to notice if there was one in the green room. I just said what I had to say and expected people to be interested. My naivete worked in my favor—the same way it does during improvisations. If you're naive enough not to conceive of the possibility of failure, it helps."

Accordingly, Miriam Flynn was a take-charge gal. Jim Belushi, at Second City in the seventies, was doing a newscast, with a late-breaking bulletin that the sun would go supernova in about eight minutes. For the rest of the scene, the cast was supposed to react with contrition and hysteria to the imminent end of the world. Unfortunately, he muffed the line. Instead of announcing there were eight-and-a-half minutes to zero, he said eight-and-a-half millenia. Since eighty-five hundred years is not much cause for panic, the scene had nowhere to go. Miriam Flynn stepped into the breach. "Jim is just a young boy. He just started, and he's going to be severely punished after this. He's going to Equity Prison for spacing out on stage."

"Ultimately," adds Robin Duke, "they can talk you down backstage but they don't have the control *on* stage. You can go out and if you've got a strong character, you're right there while it's being done. If they've asked you to be in a scene, and they're expecting you to do a cute little walk-on, you don't have to do that. You can do a little more. You keep in focus. You give them more to work with. You're helping the scene.

"They would usually start off, planning their scenes, and you'd get, 'Okay, it's us guys. You play the mother.' Then you come up with these great characters and walk all over them. It was fun. You get laughs. They get laughs. It's much easier than sitting in a room trying to get somebody to write your jokes down on paper."

The preponderance of men has held perhaps one—maybe only one— advantage for the outnumbered woman. To Ann Elder, it was "typical in those days for men to be 'male chauvinists,' because we'd never even heard the phrase, and never considered it to be out of the ordinary. But the men weren't a rival gang. They were fraternal, and they always looked out for the girls in a brotherly way. They were protective. They were caring people.

"When I first went out on that Second City stage, with so little preparation and so much anxiety, I would dry up. I couldn't talk. It was excruciating. But Avery Schreiber would work with me in the afternoons. Jack Burns would help me. Del Close would be supportive and say, 'Don't worry, you're going to be fine.' So would Sheldon Patinkin. They never played control games. I found them awfully concerned and considerate and sweet.

"Of course, the woman's 'typical' behavior in those same days was to have the mother instinct come out. You'd want to make sure the guys were eating right, and you'd worry if they were getting colds.

"And if you're really looking for a distinction between the lot of the men and the lot of the women in the company, it might just be that we women didn't have anybody doing our laundry or our grocery shopping. A lot of them had girlfriends looking after them."

Jack Burns enjoyed nagging Valerie Harper about women's lib. "I wasn't expressing my opinion, but I'd play that sort of character with her. If I said something antifeminist, I knew it would upset Valerie. I used to do it just to bug her."

This was one side of the coin. The other was Valerie Harper's experience in a Paul Sills workshop. "I was with Mary Frann, and I forget who else, but we were doing some exercise and Paul really lit into us for being so docile. 'Don't you know about women's liberation? Don't you know what's going on? Show some power!' and he was right. Then I began to be aware, then got really involved with the women's movement. Today I'm so radical about it that I don't even consider men the enemy."

On the level at which men aren't the enemy, Second City has been better than a computer dating service. The brightest, most talented men and the brightest, most talented women are rigorously selected, thrown into a crucible, and exhorted to create. They work long hours together, at the top of their intelligence, at fever pitch. Office romances can occur, even in the absence of whiteout and paper clips. Joan Rivers dated Richard Schaal before he married Valerie Harper. Paul Sills married Barbara Harris. Richard Libertini married Melinda Dillon. Bill Alton married Zohra Lampert. Bruce Jarchow married Nancy McCable-Kelly. Alan Myerson married Irene Riordan. Patrick Whitley married Sally Cochrane. Will Porter married Miriam Flynn. Joe Flaherty met wife Judith when he was in the resident company and she was in the touring company. Judy Graubart, now married to Bob Dishy, used to date David Steinberg.

The climate, recalled by Robert Klein, was "intensely close both figuratively and literally. David and Judy would be having a little quarrel, and

I'd defend her. And she'd tell me to mind my own business. She was a doll. She was a sweetheart."

Avery Schreiber met his wife, who was studying psychology, when she was a Second City waitress. During intermissions, he used to chide the audience—from a backstage microphone—to be generous in tipping. The two were married on a Sunday afternoon. They both went to work that night.

Valerie Harper discovered Second City and future husband Dick Schaal through her roommate, Arlene Golonka, when the two were appearing with the company in New York. Arlene Golonka was already married so when "I met this adorable man, Dick Schaal, I thought, aaaoooh, what a terrific guy for Valerie. I invited her and her boyfriend—they weren't doing so well at the time. I pointed out Valerie to Dick through the curtain. He said, 'Wow.' I told Valerie, 'Have I got a guy for you.' They met outside the theater in the street, and touched hands, and I knew this was going to be it."

"That night," recalls Valerie Harper, "I had one eye on the performance, and the other on Dick."

Even when Second City marriages don't last, as sometimes happens, the friendships tend to endure. The Second City bonds are that strong.

"Romances blossomed at Second City," says Ann Elder. "It was a passionate working atmosphere, no question about it. We had people falling in love one week and falling out of love at the end of two weeks, then falling in love with another person, and it was a very, very sexually charged atmosphere. I'm not saying it was a promiscuous situation. I'm just saying the whole art of improv and the whole idea of working together creates a certain bonding, and out of that bonding and that atmosphere, you're going to have a sexual situation occur.

"Then, when you break up, it can also cause problems. I recall one situation of a romance which occurred between one of the girls and one of the guys, and it was quite unrequited for her. They did an improv shortly after this relationship fizzled, and it was a really ugly improv. It was an improv where he annihilated her on stage, in character of course, and I remember she came off stage sobbing, because what he had done was taken the relationship and told her off in front of the entire audience. But she couldn't fault him, because it was legitimate within the terms of an improv. It was a perfect crime."

Rounding out the pressures—artistic, professional, social, romantic—is the pressure of the bottom line. Some players will hold that "bottom line" describes their salaries down to the dime.

Valerie Harper, with Mary Tyler Moore and Cloris Leachman, as she appeared on The Mary Tyler Moore Show. *(Photo courtesy of Howard Frank Archives/Personality Photos, Inc.)*

The Second City paycheck has never been meant to be grand. It's supposed to be adequate to the expenses of a young performer starting out. With luck, it's supplemented by occasional windfalls from trade shows, industrial films, and whatever else management or the performer can find.

Most players take the pay scale philosophically. They're not in Second City for the money. It was a long time in the life of Second City before entering actors so much as considered that joining might be a big career move. Before Avery Schreiber officially joined the cast, "I started working there for a hamburger a night. I was hanging out. Then I started working, I think it was about forty dollars a week for a year. It was survival time, it really was. That's when you sell your insurance policy."

Fred Willard, who joined when salaries were higher, got $150 a week for the first six months. "I'd only signed for six months, and then they wanted me to stay six more. I vacillated, then said, 'Yeah, I'll stay for another six months.' They said, 'Great.' I said, 'Should I be asking for more money?' The producer said, 'No, no. Everyone gets the same.' 'Oh, okay.' That's how I negotiated."

Conflicts have arisen when the extra work failed to pay windfalls. Bernie Sahlins, as financial mastermind of Second City, has harbored the constant conviction that belt-tightening was in order. He'd been there in the lean days when everything might have folded. There were times he held things together virtually by dint of his perseverance. He's consequently seen things in terms of the common weal. When the company would be invited to do a TV show that could promote Second City, he expected the troops to muster behind the cause. In his eyes, the benefit to the Second City family should have brought the players reward enough, *sans* extra pocket change. The players didn't always agree.

Joan Rivers remembers a point when success seemed sufficient to warrant a raise, and Sahlins told her, "You're very sick. I won't pay the raise, but I'll treat you to a psychiatrist." She combed Chicago for a psychiatrist, "hoping to find one who wouldn't bother to treat me but would bill Bernie for the time and then split the fee with me."

Before long, players organized Second City into AFTRA—no more TV shows for Second City unless it was a union job. Equity representation followed. Robert Klein, a former political science major, became the Equity deputy. Klein would argue, "We're gonna strike." Sahlins would say, "But we're a family." Klein replied, "Okay—pop . . ."

Betty Thomas, a later Equity deputy, never warmed up to the job. "The deputy is supposed to be the liaison between management and the cast. You check up to be sure people aren't coming too late, or that we're not doing too much free work. Then there was a thing about the meals. You're supposed to be given ten bucks or a good meal worth ten dollars when you're required to be at work through dinner time. I think that changed while we were there, but what happened was that Bernie wanted to choose the meals. We wanted the ten bucks, not the slime-ola meals.''

The use of material outside The Second City has caused the occasional stir. Sahlins's feeling is that if you create it on the Second City stage, it's a Second City creation which, if used elsewhere, should pay dividends to The Second City. "Our material," he reasons, "is what we have to keep going." Robert Klein compares the concept to going to medical school. You invent the cure for cancer. The school gets the lion's share.

When Jack Burns and Avery Schreiber rose to fame from Second City beginnings, and went on to have a TV show, they naturally wanted to use their signature cab driver routine on the program. The scene had been developed by the two of them from a Second City audience suggestion. The two paid The Second City when they used it on the air.

When Dave Thomas was on *SCTV*, and Bernie Sahlins was coproducer, Thomas came up with an idea for the Pocket Pal. "I wrote this commercial for a little device that projected mid-air collisions, sometimes as much as ten seconds before impact. It was another one of those useless products I saw coming out at the time. Bernie hated it. Bernie was very much creatively

Left to right: Dave Thomas, Catherine O'Hara, Martin Short, Ben Gordon. (Photo courtesy of Hugh Wesley Photojournal)

involved in the show then, and he said, 'People are afraid of airplane crashes. Forget it.'

"Then I was on the phone with Danny Aykroyd, who was on *Saturday Night Live*. He said, 'It's a hell of an idea. Give it to me. You'll be the only nonstaff writer to get a piece on *Saturday Night Live*.' He did it on *Saturday Night Live* and then Bernie called me the Sunday after. 'How did our material get on *Saturday Night Live?*' "

When matters can't be worked out through discussion, argumentation, and confrontation, there can be a parting of the ways. Because The Second City has and accepts its responsibility to each cast member to provide a worthy team, people have been fired for unworthiness. People have also been fired when tempers flared, and rehired again when things cooled off. Bernie Sahlins, who has been called paternalistic, avuncular, and pop, has always expected loyalty from the brood.

When Jim Belushi got a Friday night call to be in California by Monday for a TV audition, Joyce Sloane gave him four hundred dollars to get there. When Belushi got the job, called Sahlins and said he wasn't coming back, Sahlins is reputed to have raged, "He'll never step on stage again. I hope he breaks both his legs." The following week, Belushi called Joyce Sloane to say he'd never had a last night on stage. Could he? Sloane asked Sahlins who without hesitation replied, "I don't see why not."

Jack Burns describes Sahlins as being "like the Godfather in some ways. When I first went there, I had some tax problems. Bernie helped me, advanced me some money, took care of me. Then, when we went to New York, we thought we were being underpaid. We said among ourselves, 'The place is packed every night. We're gonna get some more money.' They said, 'Jack, you're the ex-sergeant with the Marine Corps background. Let's present Bernie with an ultimatum.' I said, 'Okay. I don't think it will work, but you're electing me your spokesman?' 'Yeah. We either get a fifty-dollar-a-week raise or we don't do it any more.' I said, 'Okay, but if we do this, we've got to stick together. The thing about unions is if one guy weakens, we're dead.' I went to Bernie and told him what we intended to do.

"He said, 'After all I've done for you, now you're going to pull a strike on me, Jack?' I said, 'Well, we just can't make it on what we're getting.' It was ill-advised and probably ungrateful, and Bernie said, 'You'll never work at Second City again.' He closed down the show that night. It reopened again with some of the other kids who were going to stay on and staff this great union. I was out on my ear.

"A couple of months later, Bernie and I were together again and we decided we'd go do the show in Chicago. It was almost forgotten. He never mentioned it again over the years and I certainly never did."

Dave Thomas has gone head-to-head with Sahlins more than once. "He was that way in negotiations. I always said, 'I'm quitting today. Will you tell me why I should stay?' I drove him nuts. But no one holds any real heavy grudges against the guy. We're a family, and it's like having an uncle or a grandfather who has quirks, or is a tightwad, or whatever. You just look at them and take them for what they are, and what they have to offer. Bernie did a lot of good, too."

Through it all, the family remains. Not only remains, but grows stronger, strengthened by the process—work together day and night, go out on stage together to stand or fall together, then get so wired that you go out after work to discuss what went well and what didn't. Strengthened not only by the process, but by faithful and caring den mothers like Fritzie Sahlins and Joyce Sloane, and complete with family reunions and other chances for graduates to converge. Festivities can range from Thanksgiving dinner for cast and staff and their families to alumni reunion revues, such as one the Toronto company did to benefit the United Way.

Joyce Sloane—the Rock of Gibraltar when it comes to family crises, the rock around the clock when it comes to organizing family fun—remembers an alumni company brought together to do a show at Ravinia, in Highland Park outside Chicago. "Paul Sand, Robert Klein, Fred Willard, Barbara Dana, and Peter Boyle were the company. I would drive them all out there every night. And as soon as Robert Klein got in the car, that was it. Nobody got a chance to sleep. He just broke us up all the way out there. Paul Sand had this imaginary severed arm that was supposed to be on the road, and he'd say, 'It's still there.' That was the only break in the conversation.

"One night, we were tired and crazed. We came to an intersection and I went through a red light. We wound up at a police station. Me and all of them. We had twenty-five dollars between us for bail. They were cutting up. They didn't stop. The police didn't know they were supposed to be funny. All I can say is I'm lucky I'm still not there."

Everything is a memory. For David Rasche, there was just before closing time. "I could never get enough of Fred Kaz. I used to sit late at night and listen. One of the most romantic things you can imagine. It's like a club. The place has emptied out. It smells of smoke, ashes, stale beer. The lights are down. People are drifting out. 'Good night.' 'Good night.' 'The bar is closing.'

'Anybody want one more?' Get a drink. Sit down. Freddy Kaz smokes a cigarette, saunters over in his way of walking, opens up the piano, plays. Just weaves a web of enchantment over everyone. It was great. Right out of a movie."

"It was a very happy time for most people," remembers David Steinberg. "We fought and screamed, but it wasn't with managers backing you up, and agents surrounding you, and every thought being a career move. You were really just trying to be as good as you could possibly be."

Jack Burns concurs. "There's never been anything that's compared to the intellectual stimulation, the creative stimulation, the joy and the camaraderie of Second City. You're certainly not going to find it in our business. We certainly weren't doing it for money. And of course, it's easier when you're young, not to do anything for money. It's very strange. I'm very antiwar, and yet in only two places in my life have I felt that camaraderie. One was in the Marine Corps and the other was Second City, and they both had a sense of discipline. They both had a leader like Paul Sills. It was like a commune. It was the sixties. Second City was, in many ways, the highlight of my life."

"It was a great life," asserts J. J. Barry. "You've got to believe it gets crazy. It gets very neurotic. But I can't remember a time in my life when I had so much fun. The fighting, the yelling, the screaming, the passion, the intellect, the insecurity, the craziness, the paranoia. As romantic as that sounds, it is exactly that."

For Sandy Holt, it approached finding the cosmos in a nutshell. "The whole idea of Second City is not to be competitive. In the workshops, it's not. But in our contracts was a two-week clause. You could be canned at any time. I had to fight for everything. Once I knew that I could fight for it, then I became part of the company. I had to recognize that everybody had a lot of fear. People were calling to get in the company. If you weren't up to par, there was always someone waiting to take your place. There were times when I was very depressed, and I had to force myself to be funny. I learned to come through, no matter what. That was wonderful experience. No matter how you feel, no matter how depressed, no matter what's going on in your personal life, you also have an obligation to an audience.

"It was intense and incestuous and we fought and we loved and we cared and we hated and we competed and we hugged each other. It operated on every possible level."

7

Chicago and Toronto: Bordering on Madness* (1970–1976)

CHICAGO

The dynamics of Second City invariably favor the uninhibited, both onstage and backstage. In the early years, the resulting intensity frequently resembled that of an electrifying ivy-league debating meet. With The Next Generation—launched with the new decade—the debate bore the trappings of a political demonstration. Their successors' fervor would evoke take-no-prisoners handball—a function of the times as much as the personalities.

David Blum, Jim Fisher, Joe Flaherty, Roberta Maguire, Judy Morgan, Brian Doyle-Murray,[†] and Harold Ramis, directed by Mike Miller, formed the Next Generation.

"Just around that time," says Joyce Sloane, "Bernie Sahlins's life changed

---

*Title of the Toronto company's twenty-fourth revue.

[†]At home and to friends, he was Brian Murray. "Doyle-Murray" became necessary when he took to the stage, to distinguish him from director Brian Murray. Brian Doyle-Murray's younger brother Bill had not yet joined the cast.

a great deal, and he went to New York. Sheldon Patinkin had left to go to New York. Though there were offers, I had no ambition to go to New York. I had a little girl, and while I was putting in long hours at Second City, the schedule allowed me quality time with her. Cheryl literally grew up here, and now she's general manager in Chicago.

"And suddenly, there was me, running this ma-and-pa operation pretty much alone. I had worked with other Second City companies, but this was the first company I was totally responsible for. We called them The Next Generation."

They certainly were. They were emphatically a TV generation, something their founders had been anything but. The comedy they grew up with had been televised. Only a hermit recidivist, by the late sixties, could have escaped the omnipresence of the television machine.

They were educated, but with different attitudes toward education. "I think," says Harold Ramis, "there were a lot of people in the audience in the

Joe Flaherty (left) and Harold Ramis (right), members of the long-hair "Next Generation." (Photo courtesy of The Second City)

early days who probably didn't get it as much as they pretended to. You know the herd effect. If someone laughs at an intellectual joke, others laugh whether or not they get it. Not everyone read *Steppenwolf*. Also, I suspect there was a lot of funny behavior when they did those things in the early days, too. Make a *Steppenwolf* joke *and* a ridiculous face. Like Severn Darden. His simple presence is funny. Half the time, people didn't have a clue what he was talking about.

"And with us, the issues were quite different. The earlier material seemed to be about a psychoanalytical point of view, how neurotic we are. A gentler kind of Eisenhower-era satire. In the fifties it had been black turtlenecks and quiet jazz. That wasn't us. We were radical. Our company was born out of the Chicago convention. We had a lot of radical statements to make about Vietnam, the Chicago police—and it was easy then. We felt we were the first long-hair group."

The label "Next Generation" underscored the transition, which of course was just the ticket in a nation whose touchiest buzz words were "generation gap." (The theme song of the TV show *The Monkees* extolled the young generation for having something to say. Parents heard the song and went rabid: "You kids think you invented conscience. Next you'll be telling us you invented sex.")

The Next Generation accepted the burden with quixotic zeal. They updated the audience-participation interview format. What had long ago begun as a Kennedy-Khrushchev debate with questions from the audience was now an interviewer (Joe Flaherty) and an Indian Swami (Harold Ramis) responding to audience queries.

The Next Generation also introduced a new approach to suggestion-taking for the improvisation sets. Recalls Jim Fisher, "At one point, we were saying the trouble with the other company is that they were so good, the audience sometimes didn't believe they were improvising on their feet. We were good, and we wanted the audience to know how good. So we were putting four pads on the wall, headed *who, what, where*, and *profession*. The audience was invited to come up and write on them during intermission, while we ran out to get sodas and drinks for ourselves. Then we'd return, walk around on stage, come up with what to do, and do it. There were times Brian Doyle-Murray would grab your arm and you'd start doing something, and you wouldn't even have time to know what he was thinking.

"The audience loved this, but we later discovered, as brilliant as we were at improvising, we could not get enough scenes to build a show, because the secret was, in the old style, developing improvisations you had done before. Using suggestions as springboards to build on material you played around with earlier. When it came time to set a new show, we'd be asking each other, 'What was that thing you were doing three months ago?' So we returned to the old way.

"Then, another thing we did—our company was so comfortable working together that all our scenes tended toward group scenes. We really had to work at coming up with some scenes for fewer people." Fisher's answer to this dilemma was to devise "The Wheel," a chart designed to evenly distribute the matching of players with other players.

The Next Generation's first show, wearing a radical heart on its sleeve, was less than a hugely successful event. It ended with a heartfelt plea to stop the Vietnam war, which was evidently not the way to leave an audience. Ramis recalls "playing to ten people some nights. Our show was kind of naive and idealistic. The critics were writing reviews like, 'Let's have the old company back. Bring back the varsity. Dump the second string.' But each show got better. The reviews got better. By 1973, we had a show that sold out every night and got uniformly rave reviews. Second City still does pieces from that show."

In one instance, The Next Generation played West Point. They piled into a small two-engine plane on a Sunday, flew out to West Point, flew back to Second City, became miserably airsick, and still had to give a show that night. At West Point, they favored cadets and commanders with an antiwar song based on a popular Brylcreem commercial. In the ad, people came back to the Brylcreem look. In the sketch, soldiers came back from the war. One's in a uniform. One's on a crutch. One's in a box. West Point missed the joke. It wasn't intended to entertain. It was a statement.

A scene performed in Chicago posed the notion that if a World War II prison camp could inspire *Hogan's Heroes*, "Here's what we predict TV will be doing to Vietnam twenty years from now." The *Bilko*-style scene—another statement—failed to ingratiate itself with the audience. A later TV spoof by the same company, a game show called "You Bet Your Organ," was far more successful in that department.

In the wake of the convention riots, Abbie Hoffman—one of the "Chicago Seven"—was on trial in 1970 for conspiracy, in a courtroom over which Judge Julius Hoffman (no relation) presided. Some evenings, Abbie Hoffman was back at Second City joining improvisations, at times having had to sneak in and out using the company's props to disguise himself. Hoffman enjoyed portraying the judge who copped his name.

Statements are terrific, to be sure. Yet The Next Generation realized in the long run—the very thing predecessors lamented as the sixties unfolded—there are fewer belly-laughs than one might wish in the blood and gore of planetary tragedy. As it happened, there were other statements to be made. A new kid on the block—brought in when Harold Ramis took a sabbatical—would help make them.

John Belushi. (Photo courtesy of The Second City)

In 1971, Richard Daley was elected to an unprecedented fifth term as mayor of Chicago, Charles Manson was found guilty of ritual murder, Del Close returned from The Committee to Second City to direct such firsts as a parody of *Hamlet* with a cast made up of ghosts, and the new kid came along.

John Belushi was the dark-haired, stocky, eldest son of Albanian immigrant parents, a born actor who could express more with his eyebrows than many people can say in words. In elementary school, a teacher found his horseplay so disruptive that she threatened to demote him from sixth grade to the second. In high school, he was football team captain, a rock musician, a drama student, and king of a homecoming dance. In college, other actors thought him so intense, performing as Danford in Arthur Miller's *The Crucible*, that he seemed capable of hurting them. He held various odd jobs, from trucker to janitor to busboy in one of his father's restaurants. For a time, he seriously considered a career in professional football.

Whatever the all-American Everyman did, he did with unbridled energy—"like a grizzly bear in heat," some said. Not surprisingly, improvisational theater provided the natural outlet for his audacious drive.

With Tino Insana and Steve Beshekas, Belushi formed an improvisational trio at the College of DuPage, a junior college. The impulse behind the enterprise, as described by Insana, "was the sixties, rock 'n' roll, Cheech and Chong. It was something like let's have a band but let's be actors. I don't know what it was, but it wasn't to make money, I don't think. We started rehearsing at a friend's home, and did pep rallies and things, sketches and improvisational stuff. Then we transferred to the University of Illinois Circle Campus and we opened our own theater and called ourselves the West Compass Players. We worked there for about a year and toured a little bit.

"We were so young and naive, everything was spot improvisations. My father was the conductor with the Grant Park Opera Guild and the Grant Park Symphony, a classical musician, and he played piano for us on Fridays and Saturdays. Our make-an-opera was outstanding because my father would do these wonderful overtures. He had a great time.

"We did political satire, and we did a lot of old immigrant characters because we were mangy-looking hippies and we'd go to the Salvation Army and Goodwill and those kinds of places to find used clothing for a dime or a nickel that we could use for costumes. It made for a lot of shabby street characters.

"And we didn't have any money. We had this little coffee house where we played. It would be a dollar to get in, and maybe a hundred people would come. We'd serve things like brownies and coffee. Then we'd take the proceeds, we and our girlfriends and our friends and hangers-on, and go to a Greek restaurant, Diana's. We'd always spend the bankroll. They kept the restaurant open just for us because there would be fifty of us. The Greek waiters would be breaking plates and dancing."

Before each night's performance, Belushi would be out front at the coffee house entrance, soliciting customers and promising to return their admission if they didn't like the show. Onstage, he would let fly with take-offs on Joe Cocker, "Elton Taylor" (a combination of James Taylor and Elton John) and Mayor Daley, characterizations which—along with other West Compass material—would soon find their way to Second City.

Joyce Sloane was touring campuses in connection with the Second City film project. "I went to the College of DuPage to show our program to their director of student activities. While I was there, I thought about the touring company and said, 'How about booking the Second City touring company?' He said, 'We don't need your touring company. We have a student here who goes down and sees your show and comes back and does it for us.' I said, 'What? Where is this student? I'd like to meet him.' Then he said, 'As a matter of fact, he's over there' and led me over to John, who was fiddling around playing foosball. The man said, 'John, there's somebody who would like to meet you. This is Joyce Sloane from Second City.' John looked up and said, 'Well, I've seen a few of your shows. Why don't you come and see us? I've got my own group.'

"After he transferred to the University of Illinois Circle Campus, he'd be bringing me flyers, and saying things like, 'We're playing the church tonight. Come and see us?'

"Around that time, we went to the Plaza Hotel in New York, where we played the Plaza Nine. We were auditioning for a replacement company. We looked and we looked and I said to Bernie, 'I know who to call.' I called John. He auditioned and Bernie was completely blown away. So John worked in the replacement company, then when we came back from New York, he was in the resident company."

At the age of twenty-two, John Belushi had such natural talent that he bypassed the touring company entirely, beginning his tenure on the main stage. Tino Insana was hired into the touring company, "and we'd tour with Joyce Sloane in this van. Cheryl was a little girl then. She was twelve. We used to go to her school and tease her when she was in the playground. She was real proud, though, because she liked us."

John Belushi essentially stepped into the spot vacated by Harold Ramis. Belushi was admiring of the senior ranks, of Joe Flaherty and Brian Doyle-Murray and Harold Ramis. But he had few qualms about making the stage his own. Betty Thomas—in the touring company when Belushi came to the main stage—remembers that "he was pretty good from day one. He didn't have to wait to learn to be at their level. Of course, he'd steal a line as soon as it was up there if he could . . ."

Ramis remembers: "When I met him—it was hard to get him off the stage once he got on. The other actors could wander on and off, he didn't seem to notice. He really loved it. He was solid and it was fun."

"John had that kind of magnetism where there was nobody on stage with him," says Joyce Sloane. "He didn't have to play by the rules because the audience was always looking at him anyhow. He grabbed an audience. He had a mesmerizing personality. He always said, 'You attack the stage like a bull,' which is the way he used to come through the door on that stage."

"He took incredible risks onstage," says Fred Kaz. "To risk everything the way he did requires a heart of tiger meat, which is what Johnny had."

Chicago critic Roger Ebert found in him a "remarkable range . . . where he was that rarity, a physical comedian with a quick intelligence, capable of transforming a scene with his own imagination, able to move between slapstick and great subtlety and tenderness."

Belushi's characters and characterizations became favorites—the taxidermist who takes his girlfriend home to meet his stuffed parents; his Marlon Brando, his sort-of Del Close, his Mayor Daley ("If a man can't give his own son a job . . ."); his Hamlet ("To be, to be, sure beats the shit, out of not to be"); his Archangel Gabriel at the Annunciation, walking with just enough spring in his step to make his wings flap (and just enough mischief to have the occasional glass hurled at him by an outraged patron); his Truman Capote to Joe Flaherty's William F. Buckley (Buckley: "If the good Lord wanted us to be homosexuals, he would have made Adam and Steve." Capote: "Oh, don't be silly, Bill").

His improvisations could be crude-going-on-shocking. Some that were, were legendary, though never turned into scenes that got into a revue. Tino Insana became the first to utter the "f-word" as part of a regular show, in a reference to his high school letter sweater. ("Let's face it. By then, it was colloquial. That's how we spoke.") But Belushi used it as a verb, an adjective, an adverb, and a condiment, pushing the limits of taste much farther than Second City had ever gone.

Bernie Sahlins, as producer and sole owner of The Second City—and no big fan of cheap language—drew the line, but not where it rested before. "Bernie," says Harold Ramis, "was our strong link to the past. We often thought some of his ideas were really dated and stale, but he was also generous enough to let us be what we wanted to be, and he was practical enough to see that when something worked, even if he didn't agree with it, it belonged in the show. Certain obscenities got built into certain scenes because they weren't gratuitous, or the laugh was so irresistibly good it couldn't be denied."

"That was the times," explains Sahlins, "and Belushi was an exemplar of the times. His attitude was bad boy, and he freed up the work a bit in that direction, and it infected everyone else." Even so, there was much that Belushi would say onstage only when Sahlins wasn't around.

Harold Ramis returned to the resident company shortly after Belushi joined. "There had always been certain slots at Second City. When I started there I had long hair, and I was like a freaked-out zany, a freaked-out Henry Aldrich. Then, when I came back to Second City, Belushi was so weird he sort of filled the zany slot. He'd even taken my place on the stage, my favorite spot, upstage, eleven o'clock. So I got a little more subdued and writerly, sort of more everybody's tutor in a way, which was a good role actually when it came to later doing *SCTV*."

The Next Generation left its stamp on The Second City, in language and material. They created classic scenes that became Second City standards— the New Year blackout in which Baby New Year (Fisher) guns down Father Time (Flaherty); "V.D." (about a singularly unsympathetic clinic where a person can get rapped across the knuckles by a nun for having a social disease); and "Funeral," in which the family tries to keep a straight face to bewail the departed, who died when he jammed his head in a can of baked beans. (The scene developed when the cast returned from a funeral and Del Close remembered that he'd frequently speculated on the possibility of a person dying by getting his head caught in a gallon can of Van Camp beans.)

Harold: *(friend of son of the departed)* I'm a friend of John's, Mrs. Smedley. John told me what happened to your husband. Seriously, Mrs. Smedley, it's really a crime what happened, somebody oughta look into it, maybe the Pure Food and Drug Administration. To make

a bean can the size of a person's head . . . They
should put a warning on the label.

John: *(son)* That's it. I'm leavin'.

Judy: *(wife of departed)* Johnnie, you stay here with your
father and mother.

John: What kind of father is that?

Judy: Johnnie, your father loved you.

John: Then why'd he do this to me? What kind of legacy
is this, a bean can over my head for the rest of my
life? Do you know how I found out about it? Do
you know how I found out? I was in school, in bi-
ology. They announced it over the P.A. system.

In "P.T.A." sex education is discussed by prurient parents: "I would
just like to say that I for one would not like to sit around all day and look at
sex organs. . . ."

Gus: . . . I think that the adults of the community should
get together and talk about sex. I mean a little oral
sex is necessary in any community. But this guy over
here is talking about birth-control devices—the next
thing you know he's going to be passing out those
condominiums to our kids.

Wife: Marty, may I be recognized?

Marty: I recognize my wife.

LeVine: Good for you, Marty!

Wife: Thank you. Now as you know, Marty and I are both
devout Catholics.

Coach: Right on!

Wife: Now, the Holy Father says having intercourse should
be for procreation only. Now, Marty and I find we
enjoy having sex . . .

LeVine: Good for you, Marty.

Wife: The result is four boys and three girls that I wouldn't wish on anyone! Now if Mr. Luveen . . .

LeVine: The name is *LeV*ine.

Wife: Oh, *LeV*ine. If Mr. *LeV*ine can show me a way to have sex without having babies, then I'm for Mr. *Lev*ine.

LeVine: Call me Russ.

Jim Staahl, in the touring company, understudied the men. "They would go on vacation. Each person would take a week. About the third week, I forgot who I was playing. I went rushing on stage in my Roman centurion outfit, and Eugenie Ross-Leming looked at me, and said, 'No, Staahl.' I had committed the cardinal sin of being in the wrong sketch at the wrong time. The lights went black. I rushed off, then returned as the husband in the sketch, in which the wife is giving her husband a *Cosmo* quiz. About two scenes later, I came back in the centurion costume. Maybe the audience sensed something, but I don't know if they really caught on."

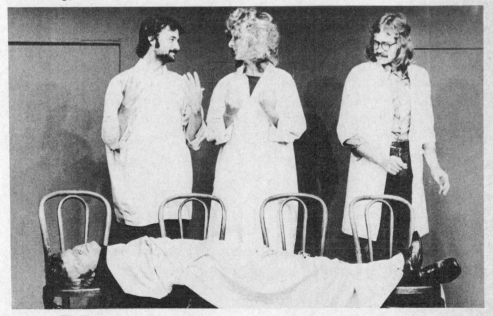

Left to right: Bill Murray, Betty Thomas, Tino Insana; David Rasche on the chairs.
(Photo courtesy of The Second City)

With Staahl in the touring company at various times were Tino Insana, David Rasche, Suzanne Rand, and Betty Thomas, later joined by Ann Ryerson, John Candy, and Bill Murray. Through a friend of Betty Thomas, some members of the group were invited to perform at a maximum security prison, Terre Haute Penitentiary. Recalls Staahl, "It's a weird feeling to be there and realize they're locking the gates behind you, shutting you in with the prisoners. A guard told us not to go to the bathroom alone, to take at least two guards with us. There were mats between the seats and the stage. We said, 'Oh, are we going to sit on the floor?' They answered, 'No, that's to remind them they're not to come any closer.'

"We got to the cafeteria, and there's this guy with purple hair, obviously dyed it with hydrogen peroxide and got a bad blonde job. Tino at this time had hippie hair to his shoulders. This guy saw Tino and said, 'Ah wan him. . . .'"

The prisoners served dinner, which they had cooked as well as, apparently, stolen. "They stole flour and made us a cake," adds David Rasche, "and they sent us a big board with all our names engraved on it, and stars made out of metal, that they made in metal shop. Very sharp edges. A very strange experience."

Eugenie Ross-Leming had replaced Roberta Maguire in the resident company. When Ross-Leming left Second City, Betty Thomas moved up from the touring company to take her place. There was a sketch Thomas did with Brian Doyle-Murray. "Brian was witty, fast, real smart, real laid back. Great stuff, so left-handed. I don't know where he got it.

"We did a funny improv. We were at a country club during the gas shortage. Brian played the guy having an affair with me. Flaherty was my husband. I'd left my husband to come out and talk with Brian in the parking lot, and his big thing was, 'If you really loved me, you'd siphon the gas out of your husband's car and put it in mine.' It was very soap opera, very high-style. Brian loved style. I said, 'I have no siphon.' He said, 'Here's a hose.' He had me down with the hose trying to siphon the gas. Full of innuendos."

The Next Generation had come some distance from Barbara Harris and Paul Sand in the woods, talking about nature, rescued by a bus driver sounding the horn.

As on Chicago's stage, some of Second City's early lights and founders were elsewhere reflecting the times. Mike Nichols, by now a successful director, had made *The Graduate* (1967) and *Carnal Knowledge* (1971; script by Jules Feiffer), both films incorporating some improvisational technique. Roger

Bowen had been Henry Blake in the movie version of *M*A*S*H* (1970). Tony Holland and Andrew Duncan were regulars on the satiric late-night *ABC Comedy News*. Paul Mazursky directed *Bob and Carol and Ted and Alice* (1969). And Premise/Second City people had served up politics, national security, and the phone company in *The President's Analyst* (1967; directed by Theodore J. Flicker, with Godfrey Cambridge and Severn Darden).

Members of the Next Generation began, one by one, to drift off in their own directions, to explore the different ways in which that might be done. John Belushi, for instance, had left after twenty months, to work in New York. He loved Second City, but not at the expense of his ambitions. He believed that his talent qualified him for the big leagues. "After a year or so at Second City," he said in 1973, "you start to get this fear that you'll die there. That you'll never get any better. And you start wondering when you'll leave and what you'll do." He went directly into *National Lampoon's Lemmings*, initiating a connection that would very soon prove a goldmine for his Second City pals.

In 1972, in Washington, D.C., a handful of men were arrested for the Watergate break-in and Richard M. Nixon was reelected to the U.S. Presidency. In 1973, the Vietnam peace pacts were signed in Paris and U.S. troops left Vietnam. The Watergate hearings began. People established in the business of political satire were saying, "What's left? How am I supposed to satirize a cartoon?" The incoming company of Second City had a ready response.

In time, a new team was formed from the touring company, with Ann Ryerson, David Rasche, Betty Thomas, Tino Insana, Jim Staahl, John Candy, and Bill Murray. All seven were over six feet tall, and gentile, earning them the nickname "The Seven Giant Goyim," and Bernie Sahlins's plaintive "What happened to the neighborhood?" Bill Murray remembers the company learning to tap dance because, "We thought if we could capitalize on our size we'd be really funny. So we took tap dance lessons from a guy on Dearborn Street. We took tap for three months and never got it in a scene." Recalls Jim Staahl, "We took tap in a class with all these serious students in leotards and leg warmers. We were there in our street clothes. The teacher was always yelling at us to stop making the class giggle. But it was so tempting, like the time Tino and Jim Fisher and I did a step with Fisher in the midde. Tino and I lifted him and he tapped in the air, Three Stooges–style."

Political commentary took the form of the "Alderman's Ballet" (Tino Insana, David Rasche, and John Candy in "fat suits"—huge stuffed coats—

singing and dancing while removing money from each other's pockets), and "The Watergate Symphony" (a Watergate spoof in the style of Spike Jones). For this, the cast took great pains to develop proficiency on their various instruments, ranging from clarinet to slide trombone to autoharp. When it came time to assign an instrument to Bill Murray, nothing was left. He was reduced to breaking balloons in time to music, expending precious little effort and getting most of the laughs.

The team inherited the usual ration of classic scenes, a favorite one being "The Amateur Hour." This time, it was Betty Thomas who specialized in having the catatonic fit ("I always tried to take my nylons and roll them down, but one night I didn't have a chance to find nylons, so I took my pantyhose and rolled them down. That was the end for me. I couldn't even stand up there straight.") When she played it, other cast members specialized in trying to break her up.

Left to right, standing: Ann Ryerson, Bill Murray, Tino Insana. Seated: Jim Staahl, John Candy, Betty Thomas. Foreground: David Rasche. (Photo courtesy of The Second City)

The team also contributed classic material to the ongoing repertoire. David Rasche's songs, "I Hate Liver," and "It Was Your Fault" are prominent on the Second City hit parade. "I Hate Liver," a country and western song developed with Fred Kaz, Tino Insana, and Jim Staahl, makes the point that no matter how you cook it, liver is appallingly inedible. The ditty closes on a sonorous yuck, pluuu, yuck. The song "It Was Your Fault," probably the most frequently performed ever at The Second City, is a rueful torch-type ballad in which the singer confesses that there's no repeating often enough— I'm terrific, you're dense if you haven't caught on, why did I put up with you for so long? It's over and it's your fault.

With Tino Insana and Jim Staahl, David Rasche appeared in "The Ventriloquist." Insana was the ventriloquist, Staahl was the talent agent, Rasche played a rude dummy. In "The Rat Catcher," Rasche was a bookworm nerd and Jim Staahl was an exterminator with a gun: "All right, you dirty rats. Come on out, you dirty rats."

With Betty Thomas—foreshadowing their future roles as TV's Officer Lucille Bates (*Hill Street Blues*) and Officer Sledge Hammer (*Sledge Hammer*)—Rasche played a male rape victim, while she portrayed the cop. The scene took a swipe at the miserably unsympathetic treatment of women in such circumstances: "You were walking down the street in *those* pants, mister? Pretty tight, aren't they?" (It was with a modification of this scene that Thomas auditioned for *Hill Street*.)

Betty Thomas, with Deborah Harmon, created several two-woman scenes that were funny, daring, and attentive to the times. In one, two young girls are in the ladies' room of a drive-in movie, discussing whether to take birth control pills for protection before going back to their dates. Comments Thomas, "A lot of that came from my experience teaching school. I saw that the girls knew nothing about birth control, and probably a quarter of them were pregnant at one time or another. They thought if you took a Thursday pill, then on Thursday you were covered. I actually had a student say that to me. So we did a scene about that."

In "The Curse," a mom (Thomas) tells her daughter (Harmon) about another of the fun things she can expect from being female. Bill Murray played the brother: "I know what's going onnn-nn. You have the cur-rse." The scene, a thematic innovation, also introduced a deft strategic move— while a guy might *enter* such a scene, only a woman could play the major roles.

Though "The Curse" wasn't tied to the headlines—instead, qualifies as one of those time-honored Second City "people scenes"—speaking about it was more a phenomenon of the seventies than the fifties. Says Thomas, "Women in the audience just never had any things of their own up on that stage to laugh about. Maybe I could have started in a more general way, but I think the way to be funny is to be specific. In terms of my own work, I didn't exactly know how to be funny about general things until I could be funny about specific things. I had to take my own life, which happened to be feminine. The things that embarrass you, when you look back on them, become very funny. And Del Close always told us, 'Use your own life.' " And the business of Second City is to act as ironic observer.

Toronto-born John Candy was tall and heavy-set, with long blonde hair that sometimes reached his shoulders. His face, when in its beleaguered mode, suggested Beaver Cleaver grown up. Candy came to The Second City by way of low-budget Canadian films and Toronto's satirical underground revue, *Creeps*. He auditioned for Second City at the suggestion of a Canadian friend, Dan Aykroyd. For Candy, the move stateside was unsettling: "I'd never really been away from Toronto, and before I went there, I had all these weird images of Chicago. I guess it went back to my TV infatuation with *The Untouchables*. But once I got there I realized Al Capone and Frank Nitti weren't around anymore."

Yet he suffered a mishap in the unlighted wings of Second City when he moved up to the main stage. As Tino Insana describes it, "We were both big guys, and the first night, after either the first scene or the second scene, I collided with Candy. You get on and off quickly. In an improvisation, or when there's not enough laughs for the blackouts, you get out fast. God forbid someone should get in your path. And I slammed into John, and knocked him out cold. We'd always bump into each other in the dark, until we got our routes down."

Adds Jim Staahl, "Tino was notorious for getting offstage in a hurry, maybe because he used to be a football player. If there was going to be a blackout, we'd ask which way he'd be exiting so we could leave in the opposite direction. Then John Candy arrived, not only new to the company but new to the country. He was sort of an outsider. He didn't know about Tino and he'd hardly been with us at all when Tino flattened him in the dark. I was onstage for a scene I was supposed to be doing with John, wondering what was keeping him.

"The funny thing is that we felt so bad about his accident that it instantly broke the ice. That—and his cavalier attitude of 'I guess I was in the wrong place.' Then we figured, 'He's okay. Tino knocked him out.' "

Once on stage, Candy developed a habit of getting himself and fellow players comfortable in a scene by opening an imaginary liquor cabinet, or a bottle, or whatever, and casually offering drinks. From such humble beginnings emerged his *SCTV*-famous Johnny LaRue.

After performances, the cast often stopped off at John Candy's apartment, winding down from their high-level exertion until the sun came up. Candy's quarters attracted them because, with his girlfriend still in Toronto, he lived like a bachelor with very little furniture and "there was plenty of room to stand around." Came the time his girlfriend decided to join him. The group heard a TV ad for incredibly inexpensive carpets and drapes. "Hey," they said, "you ought to do this. For fifty bucks, you'll have a great place." Candy called the salesman, who played "bait and switch" and stuck him with thousands of dollars of merchandise.

John Candy and Bill Murray. (Photo courtesy of The Second City)

A frequent stage partner of John Candy's was Bill Murray (kid brother of Brian) in pieces like "New Delhi," about a deli in India, which was, says Bill Murray, "the dumbest thing I've ever been part of. It was just endless, incredible death."

Bill Murray, the fifth of nine children (six boys, three girls) grew up knowing the value of a laugh. "No drunken audience could ever compare to working our dinner table. If you got a laugh, it was like winning a National Merit Scholarship." He received his primary education from Franciscan nuns, his secondary schooling from Jesuit priests. Often enough, his parents were summoned to school to discuss discipline problems. He engaged in school drama programs. "You got to get out of class for a few hours . . . and there were girls." At various times, he earned money for the family by landscape gardening, hauling concrete, and working in a pizzeria. His deadpan expression belied his volatility—a little-boy playfulness in a strong, rambunctious man, who wasn't averse to fist-fighting when the need arose, such needs including the letting off of steam.

He looked at medicine and baseball as lifelong professions. Improvisational comedy was considered only because Brian worked at Second City. Bill Murray enrolled in Jo Raciti Forsberg's workshops. "He dropped out of the class and went off to the mountains once," says Jo Forsberg. "Another time he dropped out for some other adventuring. He wasn't very stable at first. He wasn't serious enough to really focus on it until the third time. He had matured somewhat by then.

"He was a good student, a very good student, once he decided to stick it out. And I saw he had something very special. I thought there must be something we can do to develop his charisma, which led me to create exercises aimed at that, so people would be aware of what it was they were packaging. They seem to have worked, though really, he had it anyway."

Bill Murray took the route of workshop, children's theater (where children participate on stage and enjoy such role reversal treats as *Sleeping Handsome*), and the touring company (says Joyce Sloane, "When we played a girl's college, we left without Bill. He came back a day later"), then graduated to the main stage.

In Murray's work and the parts he played, Bernie Sahlins found "an enormous intensity. In the kind of work we do, you don't have the luxury of two hours to build a character, so you concentrate more on a few characteristics. They have to be just as true as the characteristics in a longer work, but there are fewer of them and they have less depth. You also therefore leave a little bit of yourself showing. You, the actor. You're not totally the character. Well, Murray was totally the character. There was such intensity it was sometimes frightening.''

Joyce Sloane found in Murray "a great sense of clothes. He could buy a six-hundred-dollar sports jacket and make it look like it came from the dime store as soon as he put it on. At first, he and Dick Blasucci lived in Bernie and Jane Sahlins's basement until there was a fire, which started in the basement, at which time we thought it best that they move. After Bill had left Second City, if he was back in town visiting, he'd leave a message on the tape in the box office, 'I'll be in town for a wedding Sunday. You might find me drunk and throwing up in front of the theater. Bill.' "

Sometimes, taking curtain calls with the other members of the cast, Murray would introduce Joyce Sloane to the audience as an Olympic skier.

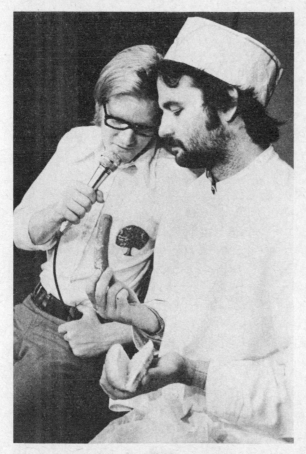

Jim Staahl interviews Bill Murray and his hot dog.
(Photo courtesy of The Second City)

In a popular Second City scene, Murray played a hot dog vendor to Jim Staahl's sportscaster. The premise was a game delayed by rain so long that air time had to be filled by instant replays of "the rain drop that started it all." In desperation, the sportscaster interviews the vendor about his technique for applying mustard, then reruns it in slow motion. The vendor concludes with the inside scoop that his shoulder has been giving him trouble, but this season he expects to make a comeback because he can throw peanuts four rows now.

From Murray's Second City days came a Todd Di LaMuca prototype with a red shirt pulled up over his head while he slurred, "I'm a lobster." This odd specimen of humanity began not from an improv but in a bar, where Murray disappeared into his shirt, spilled drinks on people and created general havoc among customers, because "I can't *help* it. I'm a *lob*ster." Someone suggested, "Hey, that's funny, why not do it onstage"—a process Del Close calls "positive exploitation."

Another Murray trademark, the obnoxiously oily, greasily cordial lounge singer, brought new dimension to the word "superficial." In "Read 'Em and Weep," Murray played a singing weatherman with chains on his neck and ruffles on his shirt. Tino Insana, as his sidekick, wore a tuxedo and a fake dog leash. "The first couple of times Murray did the lounge singer," recalls Betty Thomas "I thought, 'Oh please, I can't listen to this again.' It was bad. Then it got progressively better, until it was really good—in that painful way—on *Saturday Night Live*."

When, a few years later (1976), Pauline Kael saw Murray on *Saturday Night Live*, she wrote that he "seemed like something out of the swamp—cold-blooded yet sweaty," the kind of person who "would think up fraternity-initiation rites." Yes, indeed. These very characteristics, properly channeled, would one day make him a superstar.

TORONTO

As Chicago's Second City braved the challenge of the seventies, the plot had been slowly thickening in Toronto, Canada, a city which, in many ways, paralleled Chicago. It had a sort of second city attitude vis-à-vis Montreal. It had an artistic community. There wasn't much else besides The Second City available in terms of cabaret. And Toronto was "only" a second city, permitting a certain freedom among performers to take risks, bomb, and take risks again. By coincidence, like Chicago when The Second City began, the hot theatrical offering in Toronto in 1973 was *West Side Story*.

"One day," Joe Flaherty recalls, "Bernie said, 'How would you guys like to open a theater in Toronto?' We said, 'Toronto?' He said, 'Ah, it's great. I love it. I was up there last week and I watched a play, an entire play in Greek, on television.' This is Bernie. I don't know how well that bodes for doing improvisational cabaret.

"So he booked a group of us at the University of Toronto to play one night there, so we could go up and take a look at the city. The show went

Bernie Sahlins and Andrew Alexander in 1983, at a cast reunion celebrating the Toronto company's tenth year. (Photo courtesy of Rick Alexander)

over really well, we really liked the place. Brian Doyle-Murray and I volunteered to help get a cast going. So we came up in 1973."

Toronto differed from Chicago in its political stance. After all, it was located in Canada, not the United States. Canada wasn't involved in Vietnam, wasn't involved in Watergate. Her 1967 was marked by the "Happy Birthday Canada" centennial celebration and Expo Montreal. Her 1973 was marked by the hundredth anniversary of Canada's Royal Canadian Mounted Police. Toronto had local politics and national issues, but they weren't those of the United States.

According to some, among them Catherine O'Hara, such conditions facilitate satire. "There's so much going on in the United States, it's hard to parody. In Canada, because things are taken seriously, there is something to rebel against. Canada is a good straight man."

When The Second City first scouted Toronto in 1973, *Godspell* was the biggest show in town, made more impressive by the way its producers had cast it—opting for unspoiled young performers in lieu of flashy stage types. Slick entertainers didn't get in. Charismatic innocents did. *Godspell* would prove an excellent training ground for Second City hopefuls—improvisation and mimicry were encouraged during rehearsals.

Gilda Radner auditioned, and got in with a rendition of "Zippity Doo Dah," instantly projecting the upbeat, lovable, simple quality that underscores her personality. Lorne Michaels, a frequenter of Toronto's Second City and later producer of *Saturday Night Live,* calls it her "Muppet factor." This waiflike onstage aspect isn't far from the offstage Gilda Radner. She walks with an uncertain tiptoe walk. One time, she confided that when the cast of Second City came to the University of Toronto and went to dinner afterwards with a mutual friend, "I was watching you leave with my nose pressed against the glass. I was *dying* to go with everybody." On another occasion, she asked Joyce Sloane, with abject humility, "I know times are bad, but do you suppose we could afford a better grade of toilet paper?" During the same Second City days, her pets included a three-legged Yorkie and a cat without a tail. She used to explain that his tail fell off one night.

The Gilda Radner who went out for *Godspell* was a mere snub-nosed slip of a young woman. As a child growing up in Detroit, she had been overweight, at one point turning down a modeling job for Lane Bryant. She draws a connection between her weight and her comedy: "If you can decide to be funny, I decided it at age ten. When I was ten, I said to myself, 'You're not going to make it on looks. . . . That's why I'm not afraid to do anything comedically. I'll walk into a wall. I'm not afraid of anything. I don't worry about femininity. I think I am feminine. But I know I have scared many men off because of humor. I'll be funny instead of feminine. You're not likely to see me sitting back at a party being pretty."

Martin Short—who dated Radner during *Godspell*—was the youngest of five children in a family whose credo is "Maintain the Merry Theme of Life." He was born and raised in Hamilton, Ontario, where his granddad had been one of the first to wear Bermuda shorts, thereby—and because the man grew corn on his front lawn—earning the reputation of a town oddball. As a boy, Martin would loan money to brother Mike if Mike could make him laugh within ten minutes. The Short household, in every way, emphasized the value of being happy.

By the age of fourteen, Short was the star, producer, and writer of his own imagined television show, performed in his room and taped on his own audio equipment on alternating Mondays at 8:30 P.M. Applause was provided by a Frank Sinatra record, *Sinatra at the Sands*. "When I sang," explains Short, "I would put on the applause, and then introduce one of my guests, like Tony Bennett or Barbra Streisand. Then I would put on a record and they would sing, there would be applause, then I would sing another song. Then I would put on a Jonathan Winters record. After creating a couple of shows, I would type up the listings for *TV Guide*."

As Short grew older, he worked with disadvantaged children and, impressed by Richard Chamberlain on *Dr. Kildare*, enrolled in the premed program at McMaster's University in Hamilton. At McMasters, he drifted into dramatics, meeting Dave Thomas and Eugene Levy while in a production of *Macbeth*. Together, the three became the hub of theater arts at McMasters, collaborated on original musicals, took shows on the road, and cemented a lifelong friendship.

Eugene Levy strayed to Toronto, lured by the hope of film work with McMasters classmate Ivan Reitman. ("I heard that my old school chum was about to direct his first film in Toronto. So I called him up to see if he had a part for me. He told me there was only one job left on the film and that was as coffee boy. The operative word was 'on' the film, not 'in' the film. It paid sixty dollars a week, which I jumped at." In 1971, Levy won an award for his role in Reitman's *Cannibal Girls*, "which makes you wonder what the losers were like.")

When *Godspell* held auditions in Toronto, Levy called Martin Short—still attending McMasters—who came down to try out as well. They both got into the company. Remarked Short subsequently, "I couldn't believe it. I was in show business for about an hour and suddenly I had a job." Also signed were Andrea Martin, and Paul Shaffer at the piano. Dave Thomas got in as an understudy.

During *Godspell*, Short, Levy, Thomas, and Shaffer would gather for regular "Friday Night Services," sharing dreams for the future and speculations on who would be the first—and who would be the last—to succeed. "We'd get some beer and pizza," Short says, "and the object was just to try to make each other laugh. We'd stay up till our eyes drooped." Short taped the proceedings. The other three kidded that he'd tape the first fifty years of his life, and spend the remaining fifty listening to the tapes.

Cast members of *Godspell* became local celebrities, with their names in the columns and their voices and faces suddenly in demand for commercials on radio and television. When open auditions were held for Toronto's Second

City in 1973, *Godspell*'s Jayne Eastwood, Gilda Radner, and Gerry Salsberg tried out and made the team. Eugene Levy auditioned and didn't ("I think Gerry Salsberg was more extroverted than I was") but consoled himself nicely by stepping into the leading role in *Godspell*. Short, not ready to tie himself down to the routine of improvisational comedy cabaret, chose not to audition. Instead, he became the host of a CBC-TV program called *Right On!*, a rock show for teenagers on which guests, and Short, sang. "I had long hair," he recalls, "but I was totally unfunky."

A comedy team not from *Godspell*—a quick blonde fox named Valri Bromfield and the tall (six-foot one-inch) dark presence of Dan Aykroyd—also made the grade. They improvised with the precision of a well-oiled machine, rapid-fire, pure, and untouchable. Their routines included a mother and father telling their son his First Joke, a major event in the child's life and one not to be taken lightly.

Aykroyd possessed, says Fred Kaz, "the most brilliant mind I've ever

Left to right: Eugene Levy, Dan Aykroyd, Gilda Radner, Rosemary Radcliffe, John Candy. (Photo courtesy of The Second City)

known. He was absolutely lightning quick. Total control. He has the mind of a calculator, the metabolism of a hummingbird, and acts like it ain't all there."

Aykroyd, who looks like your brother-in-law if your brother-in-law happens to be an FBI agent, in fact would soon have to decide between The Second City and the Royal Canadian Mounted Police when the latter approved his application. (His father was an assistant deputy minister of transport and his grandfather was a Mountie.) He was born in Ottawa, then raised in Hull, Quebec ("where Montreal sends its old gangsters to cool out"). According to his younger brother Peter (who before long would also join Second City), "My parents have a photo of Dan when he was about three and I was just a small protein unit, and in the picture he's riding a small motorcycle, carrying a machine gun, and wearing a cowboy hat. In other words, even then he had at least three characters going at once."

Aykroyd's was a strict Catholic upbringing, complete with the occasional whipping. For his twelfth birthday, his father gave him an electric lawnmower with a bow on it so that he could do the lawn. The first record Dan Aykroyd ever bought was *Hymns of the Army, Navy, and Air Force.* Cohorts of his youth had names like Ray the Green Beret and George the Thief. For acts of mischief early in life, Dan Aykroyd was expelled from the St. Pius X Minor Preparatory Seminary. Undaunted, he moved on to the study of criminology and deviant psychology at Ottawa's Carleton University, which brought him in touch with a wide assortment of underworld types. Says Joyce Sloane, "I once watched a movie with him and he knew every weapon that was used. Then, another time, I got a letter from the Solicitor General of Canada. I thought, 'My God, what have I done?' It was from Danny Aykroyd, who was working in the prison over the summer." His twin fascinations for law enforcement and lawbreakers have inspired friends to kid that his perfect fantasy is to rob a bank, then arrest himself.

Aykroyd also found time to work as a railroad brakeman and a road surveyor in the Northwest Territories. Other interests have included the occult, seances, and UFOs. Because he is webfooted (a membrane connects the second and third toe of each foot) he isn't entirely convinced that Earth is his home planet. "You look at the floor and see the floor. I look at the floor and see molecules." From such a mind came the original script of *Ghostbusters.*

With this background, it was perhaps inevitable that Dan Aykroyd would form a comedy team with Valri Bromfield, that the two should set their sights on Second City, and that they'd one day get in.

Joyce Sloane knew Bromfield and Aykroyd from her earlier visits to Toronto: "I met Danny when he was about seventeen. He was partners with Valri and I'd be going to Toronto to look for locations. They'd know I was coming and he'd carry my luggage. Valri would rip off flowers and leave them in my hotel room. They were just wonderful kids. And they'd be setting up auditions for me to watch. Initially, we'd brought them down to Chicago to audition. They did the set and they were great. We knew before auditions in Toronto that they'd be in the show. They were really excellent."

The first Toronto Second City cast was pulled together—Dan Aykroyd, Valri Bromfield, Brian Doyle-Murray, Jayne Eastwood, Joe Flaherty, Gilda Radner, and Gerry Salsberg, with composer-lyricist Fred Kaz. Three women, four men—a rarity for which Bernie Sahlins obligingly modified some traditionally male roles to give them to Valri Bromfield.

The first Toronto edition of The Second City gave their first show in a bleak neighborhood on Adelaide Street. Eugene Levy, in the audience, was wildly enthusiastic: "I went to opening night and was completely knocked out. I'd never seen anything as funny, as bright."

A *Toronto Sunday Sun* review singled out Gilda Radner, noting that she combined "a subtle and highly unusual physical beauty with an impish humor of devastating restraint. Sooner or later her pent-up potential will explode with a blinding flash into a blaze of fame."

Over the next two productions, the company did some of its best work improvisationally. Attendance, sparse for the paid show, picked up dramatically for the improvisations, which were free. The audience for the improv sets was supportive. Unfortunately, the troupers hadn't a ghost of a chance of surviving. The theater had no liquor license, no air-conditioning, and could barely sustain its run. As Eugene Levy observes, "You can only drink so many Cokes in a night."

The show folded, abruptly, in bankruptcy, which the cast discovered by going to work one day and finding a sheriff's notice and a padlock on the door.

Andrew Alexander, a Canadian in his early thirties, was indirectly connected with some of the people involved, and interested in the Toronto entertainment scene. "I'd dropped out of university after doing some small concert promotion, started selling advertising, and went quickly back into the rock and roll business. I became involved in a festival called the John Lennon Peace Festival in 1970, which introduced me to a few people. It was a large event that never happened, but I had met these people and I ended up becoming the producer of a very small theater in Toronto, Global Village. That involved me in producing late-night improv. Young people would come for poetry reading, jazz, really a potpourri. Danny Aykroyd and Valri Brom-field started there in 1970 doing their work. Gilda Radner was working in the box office. This was when I really got the bug. Then I started doing some theater promotion, got a job offer from Chicago, went to Chicago in 1972."

Joyce Sloane would run into Andrew Alexander on airplanes. "I got to know him, and I would ask him for Canadian advice. Then came the day that I had a call from Gilda Radner. 'We're locked out. What should we do?' " Joyce Sloane made a few phone calls.

All was not lost. Bernie Sahlins, who had always wanted to see a Second City thrive in Toronto, made a licensing arrangement with Andrew Alexander for a reported two dollars and a contract written on a napkin. For a more substantial investment, Alexander also acquired space in the century-old Old Firehall on 110 Lombard Street in Toronto.

Recent program notes describe The Old Firehall as a "Toronto landmark, built in the last century, probably before you were born (there will be exceptions to that of course) (not you madam) as the fire house for this district." Various legends describe it as having a haunted belfry. "Well, not haunted," says Don DePollo, who has both performed and directed there. "But no one ever goes up there. 'What's up there?' 'No one has ever looked.' " The building additionally has a cabaret theater, a restaurant, and at one point an after-hours bar.

With a theater and Toronto rights to The Second City, Andrew Alexander had to reassemble the cast: "They had a pretty rough experience at the other place so obviously they were all a little horrified when I approached them to come back. Then, it was really terrible trying to get started here as well, because we had to rehearse the preview between rock bands, which was how it was set up then. In between the sets we would do our comedy. I think they were saying, once they started, 'Ohmigod, this is even worse than the last place.' "

Joe Flaherty had left before the padlock incident. ("I'd be reading the papers and every once in a while I'd see an interview with Bernie where he said that Joe Flaherty and Brian Murray, the Americans, would be phased out. This was weird to me, because when Canadians worked in Second City in Chicago, there was never any talk of phasing them out to make an all-American cast. I only planned on being there a few months anyway. I took off and went to Europe.") Andrew Alexander invited him back. Flaherty returned to find that indeed, it was worse than the last place: "Once again, we were starting from scratch. It was a restaurant and a sort of bar downstairs where they would dance, serve drinks. Before we were technically opened, when we were getting material together, we performed for this audience of people dancing and drinking. They didn't know who we were, what we were doing. We'd get up, do some scenes, then it would be over. They'd just sort of scratch their heads. 'Where's the beer? Let's dance.' Andrew was saying, 'You guys have got to get three good reviews here, because it's critical.' "

Andrew Alexander, with concert promotion in his background and an uphill trek in the foreground, wasn't about to chance it to word-of-mouth alone. He brought in telephone solicitors to push the first dinner-plus-cabaret show. Dinner served upstairs. Cabaret downstairs. Eugene Levy wrapped up his *Godspell* stint and John Candy, now a seasoned improvisational performer, his hair as long as ever, returned to native soil to join the Toronto cast. The new show opened with John Candy, Joe Flaherty, Eugene Levy, Rosemary Radcliffe, and Gilda Radner, with Bernie Sahlins and Joe Flaherty directing. Reviews were strong, and got better, and the uphill grade gave signs of leveling off.

When Second City played Adelaide Street, there had been complaints that the show lacked Canadian content. On Lombard Street, the cast took note and presented *You're Gonna Be All Right, You Creep, Leaving Home and All, Eh?,* which satirized several Canadian plays that were around. Flaherty played the tyrant daddy, Angus, Radner was the retarded daughter, Colleen, Candy was the hockey-freak son, Johnny, Levy was Leonard, the son who was gay, Radcliffe was Bea, the mom who was getting the worst of the deal:

> Bea: Oh, I wish today had been a little happier. I've been cooking and cleaning and getting ready for Johnny's homecoming and still it seems that we're always fighting. You know Angus is always a little hard on us when he gets to drinking. Still I know he loves me, eight times a day sometimes. You know he's nearly fifty and he's as frisky as a little piglet. Still I wish his standards for the children weren't quite so high, he's never been happy with Leonard and he's always been a little disappointed in Colleen. He says she's not right in the head. I say she's just a little socially withdrawn. (Hubbub.)

Angus: Shut up and sit down.

Bea: Angus, Colleen has learned something today.

Angus: Ohhh, so the wee lump has learned something today.

Bea: Tell Daddy what you've learned today, Colleen.

Colleen: To take out the kitty litter!

Angus: And where do you put it?

Colleen: On Daddy's pillow.

Angus: On my pillow! What the hell do you want to do that for, you retard? Oh, Colleen, you make me want to puke. Johnny, pass the vegetable there. Sit down, sit down. (Hubbub.) That's a right funny joke, John. You know I love it when you pick on your sister like that. You're right, too, lad, you know. Look at her sitting there like a damn brussel sprout. Colleen, Colleen. You're not my daughter. Leonard's my daughter . . .

The cast went on to do wonderful things. For an interview sketch, Gilda Radner created Miss Eleanor Teably, the prototype for her *Saturday Night Live* Emily Litella. Levy was the interviewer. Teably demonstrated how she taught inanimate objects to talk. "Originally," explains Radner, "it was a turtle. The turtle walked off the table, crashed onto the floor, and I had it scream and talk as it fell. Then we went to a snow shovel. The shovel talked. Then it was a tea kettle. We found out that with the tea kettle, which had a lid that moved up and down, that it was funnier when you made something move for talking. And then we went to a shoe."

A Radner/Teably character also did a scene, set in France, with Levy. She was a dotty woman, and he portrayed a gigolo trying to pick her up.

Some of Joe Flaherty's best scenes with Gilda Radner stemmed from his refusal to let her off the stage. He'd define situations that trapped her, forcing her to stay. In one improvisation, he had her upstairs in her bedroom, weighing

Gilda Radner, as Emily Litella, with Chevy Chase on Saturday Night Live. (Photo courtesy of Howard Frank Archives/Personality Photos, Inc.) Eugene Levy and Gilda Radner. (Photo courtesy of The Second City)

six hundred pounds and unable to come down the stairs because she was too wide. Since the rules of improvisation forbid denying a reality once someone has created it, she was stuck. In another scene, he was the narrator.

"And Trixie danced." Radner danced.

"And Trixie sang." La-la.

"And Trixie turned somersaults, because show business was her life." Radner did it, edging her way offstage, shuffling-off-to-Buffalo, just about in the clear.

"And," Joe Flaherty gamely announced, "There were such great applause, Trixie gave an encore." Because he was narrator, she had to do what he said. According to Joyce Sloane, "Gilda was always looking for ways to escape. Joe was always clever enough to keep her on."

They were doing a new show every few months. The sun shone brighter on Lombard Street, by gradual degrees. But it was far too early to rest on laurels. They ignored no detail. They called one revue *Alterations While U Wait* because it started with *A*, which would put them at the beginning of the theater directory listings in newspapers.

The Toronto cast made headway, not only on stage, but as members of the Toronto entertainment community. Like their Second City predecessors before them, they were getting calls for extra work on radio and television, spots with a comedy slant. In the ensuing years, Toronto's Second City faces and voices would appear in endless commercials (Derek McGrath for Super Loto, Canadian Tire, Speedy Muffler King, and more; John Hemphill, Don Lake, and Debra McGrath for a staggering range of products; Ben Gordon and Steve Kampmann for appearing in a series of Philishave spots that won numerous television commercial achievement awards in Canada and the U.S.; Catherine O'Hara and Robin Duke, separately and together, including as two old women, for Pepsi. They used gray wigs and glasses, but no makeup. Their friends said, "You looked great. The makeup made you look *so* old." Ben Gordon alone has recorded over 200 radio spots, appeared in over 30 commercials in Canada and the U.S., and has created award-winners—through improvisation—for products ranging from Wranglers to Toyota.)

In 1974, the Toronto and Chicago companies of Second City arranged a brief exchange. Down to Chicago went John Candy, Catherine O'Hara, Dan Aykroyd, Eugene Levy, Gilda Radner, Rosemary Radcliffe, and pianist Allen Guttman. Up to Toronto went Bill Murray, Mert Rich, Ann Ryerson, Betty Thomas, and Paul Zegler. William Leonard, in the *Chicago Tribune*, thought the Canadians were great: "There are three gentlemen and three ladies in the company, and they work with such ensemble that it would be silly to nominate anyone as outstanding or as a star. There are probably a few names in the youthful company you will be hearing about again, on a somewhat grander scale."

The Chicagoans, duly heralded in Toronto, managed to create one of their more outrageous scenes. Bill Murray and Betty Thomas developed it from a backstage suggestion. Says Thomas, "Del Close came in backstage just before and he said, 'You know, there are no more taboos about incest, because of the pill.'

Joe Flaherty as Sammy Maudlin. (Photo courtesy of Rick Alexander)

That's all he said. A typical Del thing to say. We all looked at each other and said, 'Okay.' Murray and I said, 'Let's do a scene. I'll be the mom. You've just come back from college, and you find out that I'm on the pill, and we'll see what happens.' Most of Murray's scenes were come-on scenes anyway, so he fell right into it.

"In the scene, she's saying, 'I take the pills to regulate me because of the hormones. It has nothing to do with anything else. They're very low dosage.' Inch by inch, we break down the idea of the fact that we could never make love. There were no big consequences. We weren't going to have an idiot for a child. It was a lovely scene. I always thought it was fun to do. The slow seduction of your mother."

On another stage in 1974, in New York, the cast of the *National Lampoon Show* was taking shape. John Belushi was director as well as one of the performers. He'd brought with him—by way of the *Lampoon Radio Hour*—Joe Flaherty, Bill Murray, Brian Doyle-Murray, Gilda Radner, and Harold Ramis. Says Ramis, "John, even though he was younger than everyone, was a little bit like Michael Corleone in *The Godfather*, where the younger son sort of takes over the family in a way. I felt that strongly when he hired us to work with him on the *Lampoon*. And it was funny, because he sort of knew our strengths. He knew what a strong combination that would be."*

An episode of Gilda Radner's characteristic supportiveness stems from this period. "In London, Ontario," recalls Bill Murray, "we were supposed to do the show twice in a night to two different audiences. But there was only one audience's worth of people in the whole town. And they hated us. But one night, all of a sudden as we turned around, we heard this cackling. This girl in front was laughing! And we looked out and it was Gilda. She had sneaked away from us and down into the audience. And we realized that if *we* were watching us, we'd be funny. She gave us the will to go on against this nasty, ugly crowd."

John Belushi had also wanted Dan Aykroyd for the *Lampoon Radio Hour*, but Aykroyd had just re-signed with The Second City in Toronto and was honoring the commitment. Besides his Second City engagement, Aykroyd was managing a grimy after-hours saloon, Club 505, decorated in forties-style sofas, armchairs, and a barber chair. There he "slept in lofts above whatever crept on the floor at night. It bordered on serious squalor at times." (A rat once emerged from the toilet there while Aykroyd was using the seat.)

Club 505 shared a store-front at 505 Queen Street with Marcus O'Hara, Catherine O'Hara's brother. It was Marcus O'Hara who introduced Dan Aykroyd to Bill Murray, and John Candy to Gilda Radner. Marcus O'Hara owned a truly monumental collection of squeeze toys, which he displayed in the window of 505. When O'Hara once had the bad luck to pass out, Dan Aykroyd and John Daveikas (creator of the *Ghostbusters* logo) propped him up in the window with a sign reading, "Buy this man." O'Hara came to in the window, smothered in toys, with people staring at him from the sidewalk.

When Belushi hit Toronto, recruiting for his show, Dan Aykroyd took him to Club 505. The meeting was fortuitous. Aykroyd has said, "The friendship was almost instantaneous. Clearly here was someone who understood me and someone whom I understood."

Though they wouldn't be together on the *Lampoon*, they decided to stay in touch. In the next few years, they would work together, jointly own a bar

---

*Belushi developed his samurai during the *Lampoon* period. As described by Harold Ramis, "There was a retrospective on television, I think on PBS, of Kurosawa films. John started doing the Toshiro Mifune mannerisms, and that became his samurai on *Saturday Night*. That's one I distinctly remember actually watching him develop."

John Belushi and Dan Aykroyd, in Chicago to film The Blues Brothers. *(Photo courtesy of Paul Natkin/Photo Reserve, Inc.)*

(the Blues Bar in New York, named for their phenomenally lucrative pairing as the Blues Brothers), and become the closest of friends. Aykroyd would bestow on Belushi a whole string of nicknames—among them Bear Man, Black Rhino, and the Black Hole in Space. ("If you ever lend him a watch or a lighter or something, it goes through him into another dimension. You ask for it back five minutes later and it's gone and there's really no way you can find it.")

Bill Murray briefly joined the Toronto company where, on one unfortunate evening, a heckler went too far. Generally, the stage manager is responsible for quieting or removing audience members who simply will not back off. Despite various efforts, this one kept hammering away. Finally, Murray had heard enough. He stopped the show, grabbed the man, and marched him out into the alley. When the two returned—bloodied and bruised, their clothes torn—the man resumed his seat and Murray continued onstage. No repercussions followed the incident, and the man's date allowed, "Well, good, he deserved it."

By April 1975, Toronto had entered its second year, the touring company was in its eighth, Chicago was in its fifteenth. Another foray by Sahlins's stalwarts was inevitable. A phalanx of Second City pilgrims set out to conquer yet another frontier. They planted their flag in Pasadena. Joe Flaherty remembers it well: "We opened this place in a shopping center. Bad idea. Didn't work. Used the name of the show we had in Toronto when we left, *Alterations While U Wait.* People would bring their clothes in, their cleaning, and yell because we didn't do laundry. It was a good cast—Betty Thomas, John Candy, Eugene Levy, Doug Steckler, me, and a good understudy whose name was Michael Douglas. Later he changed his name to Michael Keaton. He did pretty well from that point on. But the whole thing was ill-ventured, ill-gained . . . just ill, we all got ill from that experience."

What did come out of the Pasadena trip—in fact, from an improvisation—was the original *Sammy Maudlin Show,* which would later become an *SCTV* staple. In this spoof of a talk show, Joe Flaherty played host Sammy Maudlin: "At that point, Sammy Davis Jr. had a show on the air that was a frenzy of self-congratulations and mutual admiration and I just wanted to do something on it so badly, to get it out of my system. I didn't want to do Sammy Davis Jr. per se. I just wanted to do something suggesting that type of show business guy. Then we all picked parts and said let's just go out there and talk each other up. John Candy was the announcer, William B."

Eugene Levy came on as Vegas-style comic Bobby Bittman. Says Levy, "The improvisation was modeled after *Sammy and Company,* which was syndicated in the States and never seen in Canada, so we didn't really discover the show till we went down to Pasadena. I played this comic, Bobby Bittman, who comes tiptoeing onto the stage. 'Howaya? I was just doing a special in the next studio. HoWAya?' And he said these pompous things like, 'As a comic, in all seriousness.' I wore a loud sports jacket, an open-collar type thing, and whatever ring I could scrounge up backstage. Then the show was just the patting-on-the-back syndrome, this mindboggling, 'Let me tell you about this man. This man has done more charitable work . . .' "

Dan Aykroyd had planned to go to Pasadena. What changed his mind were calls from fellow-Canadian Lorne Michaels, who was going to be producing something called *Saturday Night Live,* and from John Belushi, encouraging him to audition. (Gilda Radner had already been hired for the program, and had chosen between Michaels's offer and one from another Canadian—and fellow Second City graduate—David Steinberg, who wanted her for his syndicated talk show.)

The scene "Parent-Teacher," which introduced Edith Prickley (in leopardskin). Left to right: Andrea Martin, Ben Gordon, Dave Thomas, Catherine O'Hara, John Monteith. (Photo courtesy of Hugh Wesley Photojournal)

For a while after Aykroyd joined *Saturday Night Live*, he commuted between it and Canada. When he stayed in New York, he slept in John Belushi's apartment, on a foam slab at the foot of John and girlfriend (later wife) Judy's bed.

Until Aykroyd left, there were Dan Aykroyd, Ben Gordon, Andrea Martin, Catherine O'Hara, John Monteith, and Dave Thomas on the Toronto stage.

Dan Aykroyd and Dave Thomas were something of a team. In a dual improvisation, they'd claim to be graduates in sound effects from MIT: "We challenge the audience to give us any sound effect at all that they think we'll have difficulty doing, and we'll do it, jointly or individually." And they did. Everything from chain saws cutting '57 Chevys in half to Saturn V launches.

Almost immediately, their onstage collaboration was spilling over into the outside world, and back onto the stage again. Dave Thomas was fresh from the advertising business, where he'd been a copywriter, "and Danny had some connections at CBC. We were both entrepreneurial actors even back then. We wrote for CBC kids' shows, we wrote commercials. I got a lot of freelance thrown my way from when I was in advertising, and Danny and I sat down and wrote them and performed them together.

"We found that we could write backstage and during the day, enough to really quadruple our income. We'd be writing backstage between scenes and one night I remember doing a scene called 'Cadets.' Danny and I played

John Candy (left) and Dave Thomas (right). (Photo courtesy of Hugh Wesley Photojournal)

two police officers. We're sitting there, but the focus was over on the other side of the stage where something was going on. Danny turned to me and said, 'You know what we could do—' and he was continuing the thought we'd left off before we came on stage. It was clear he'd been doing his lines and still thinking about that conversation."

Dave Thomas and Ben Gordon did a scene about Canada's national identity, anticipating the "Canadian content" considerations that would lead to *SCTV*'s McKenzie Brothers. Says Gordon, "We played two Canadians, two real Canucks, sitting on the Scarborough Bluffs, which are the bluffs that face across the lake to the United States. The premise was that Canada had gone to war with the States by sealing off all entries to Canada in hopes of maintaining our Canadian identity. Everything in Canada that was American had to be shipped back to the United States. We tore the U.S. Steel siding off our homes and sent it back. Hershey's chocolate bars went back. My wife was from Detroit. I sent her back. You know the movie *The Apprenticeship of Duddy Kravitz* with that American guy, Richard Dreyfuss? They cut him out of the picture. Now it's just a bunch of Canadians talking to a hole. Doesn't matter—they've been doing that in Ottawa for years."

Canadian 1: Well there's nothing to watch on T.V. since they blacked out the American programming.

Canadian 2: Ya well I heard the other day that that Canadian stuff is supposed to be pretty good.

Canadian 1: No! They've got Elwood Glumer and the detective series now called Elwood-O. And then that other boring thing The Streets of P.E.I.! What are they doing?

Canadian 2:   I know, I know. You know, they are ruining sports too, you know. They've got the Expos playing themselves now.

Canadian 1:   Ya, I heard about that. I saw the headline. Expos play with themselves.

Canadian 2:   Ya and they still manage to lose five games. . . . I don't know.

In a scene called "English Lesson," Andrea Martin portrayed that most dedicated of language students, Pirini Scleroso. Pirini spoke no English. Her teacher was of the new school of linguistic instruction—say the same thing clearly, over and over again, and the student will mimic you until she gets it right. One gives Pirini full credit. She came close to every inflection, with phrases at least as lucid as "Whey risky bops?" ("Where is the bus?") and "Yorky McGee Reggae" ("You're giving me a headache"). While teacher went slowly crazy, Pirini took pride in her progress.

According to Andrea Martin, "I would love to be able to give myself full credit for that but alas, the scene was created by Danny Aykroyd and Valri Bromfield, improvised one night. And Danny played the part Pirini did. I made it into my own after doing it. Danny's words were 'Canoe trachami tootholowtow'—which means, 'Can you direct me to the hotel?' That's the only expression I kept from the scene. I think Catherine O'Hara gave me the name

Catherine O'Hara (left) and Andrea Martin (right). (Photo courtesy of Rick Alexander)

Pirini Scleroso. Unless I'm forgetting something, I believe that everything else I did was either my creation or we improvised it on our own. But I couldn't resist that scene, because people really liked that character."

Del Close came up to Toronto direct, and introduced a special Halloween set. In it, Andrea Martin did a trick along the lines of the great Carnac. The audience provided a batch of questions on slips of paper. Just before Martin opened each slip, she'd spout a brilliant response to the question she was going to read, then read the question, which "miraculously" fit. Audience members were flabbergasted as they recognized their questions, because it meant the trick wasn't fixed. The "trick" was that she appeared to answer the first question, then opened the slip of paper to read out what it said. But what she was giving out loud was a bogus question. Silently, to herself, she read the real question. Then for the next slip, she answered the question she had just read to herself—always getting one ahead with the slips of paper, therefore always answering an authentic question, but after rather than before having read it.

That's what the trick was supposed to be. But she tricked herself by forgetting questions as soon as she tore them up, and had to wing the whole thing.

For another Halloween scene, Close wanted to create an atmosphere of horror. From the back of the theater, while the audience was distracted watching something else, he threw wet spaghetti into the rafters, so that it would later land in the laps of the audience, when the cast talked about hideous white worms. The scene turned out to be a hideous embarrassment.

Symbolically, it also marked a shift in emphasis between earlier and later Second City. According to Ben Gordon (who before joining Second City had written for *Laugh-In* producer George Schlatter in California), "This is something previous groups of performers in Second City may have been interested in—a chance to stretch the bounds of the actor-audience relationship. It isn't something we were interested in. We were interested in exploring the bounds of comedy. How many beats we could delay the punchline and still get the laugh? These were the things we were experimenting with. Comedy, not the intellect as such.

"We were the first wave in Canada after the initiation. Our cast, different probably from most casts or any cast in the past, at least to my general knowledge, was composed of people who were already working professionals. Sheldon Patinkin saw me doing a comedy routine with a girl downtown and

John Belushi as the samurai, with Bill Murray and Garrett Morris in the background, on Saturday Night Live. *(Photo courtesy of Howard Frank Archives/Personality Photos, Inc.)*

hired me for Second City on the spot. Andrea Martin did all kinds of shows. Then later, when Marty Short and Derek McGrath came in, they were already successful working professionals in town. We all had commercials and voice-overs, which are very big in Toronto. Some of us would take time off to do a film. Andrew Alexander brought us to Second City to be entertainers in the Second City mold. We went after that type of audience. All the focus was on bringing people into the show."

It's hardly the first time a cast sensed a break with tradition, hardly the first time a company went after laughs. It's no doubt true, but no cause for damnation. As Andrew Alexander is quick to add, "All the focus was on attracting people to the show by offering quality entertainment. I concentrated on bringing in extremely talented performers, and they justified my faith in them by working at the top of their—and Second City's—form." The orientation that set them apart from their predecessors was only a matter of degree. Pirini Scleroso is as perceptive a piece of academic satire as Professor Valter von der Voegelweide. They just go to different schools.

From Chicago's Next Generation to Toronto's renegade satirists, Second City was up to its same old tricks—preparing tomorrow's stars. By the end of 1976, Dan Aykroyd, John Belushi,* and Gilda Radner were spearheading a comedy revolution on NBC's *Saturday Night Live*. Bill and Brian Doyle-Murray had appeared, less auspiciously, on a short-lived embarrassment in TV variety called, ironically, *Saturday Night Live With Howard Cosell*, on ABC. Jim Staahl, Jim Fisher, and Tino Insana had distinguished themselves as the comedy threesome The Graduates (originally intended to be The Graduates of Second City, until Bernie Sahlins suggested that the name "might confuse people.") And John Candy, Joe Flaherty, Eugene Levy, Andrea Martin, Catherine O'Hara, Harold Ramis, and Dave Thomas were mounting television's quintessential satire of television—*SCTV*.

*Belushi barrelled into television insisting that he hated the medium as it was then being done, and that the only TV he ever owned was black and white, covered with spit, and had to be tuned with a fork.

8

Chicago, Toronto, and *SCTV* (1976–present)

Second City's history has been, among other things, a perilous series of life-or-death moments on which its survival depended. With each move to a larger theater, the need to fill seats was more pressing. Each time a theater opened and couldn't count on selling most tickets to a university crowd—which was every time but the first—material necessarily became broader-based.

Not once was the step undertaken without someone saying, "There goes tradition."

Yet not once was the step undertaken that tradition did not in fact keep Second City on course. People scenes remained observant people scenes. The humor continued intelligent. The references changed because headlines did—which is strictly in keeping with tradition, since Second City from day one has kept up with the headlines. Not much point embalming the news.

CHICAGO

Mid-seventies in Chicago, the likes of Miriam Flynn, Ann Ryerson, Eric Boardman, Danny Breen, Don DePollo, Michael Gellman, Bruce Jarchow, Steve Kampmann, Tim Kazurinsky, Will Porter, Mert Rich, Jim Sherman,

Jim Staahl, and George Wendt were impersonating the Reverend Billy Graham (Staahl), Edgar Allen Poe's raven (DePollo, who also had a fetish for a fish suit), and a test-tube baby (Wendt: "No, it wasn't diapers. It was a tasteful sunsuit. I did other impressions, but those guys all died, like Leonid Brezhnev and Cardinal Cody of Chicago").

Right along, they pursued ancestral footsteps in the usual favorite ways—improvising commercials, distrusting politicians, doing pseudo-macho humor, exploring the dynamics of a father and his son, and invading Canada. Recalls Wendt, "We freelanced a lot of industrials. Winged it, really. Go into business meetings, a room full of executives, literally not having written one thing for them, and you've already spent the money. And they'd say, 'What do you have for us?' and we'd say, 'Well, there's the . . .' then someone would say, 'The baseball scene . . .' 'Yeah, yeah, the baseball scene,' and then we'd just sort of wing it right in the meeting. We didn't get much repeat business."

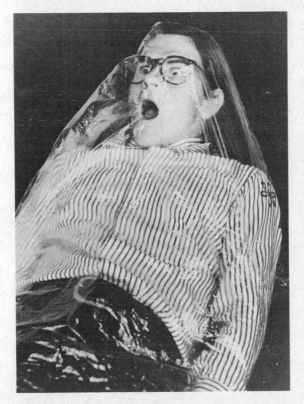

Tim Kazurinsky in "Sperm/Egg," from the revue entitled Another Fine Pickle. (*Photo courtesy of The Second City*)

There was one scene about a politician named Phil Crane. Says Don DePollo, "George Wendt portrayed a videotape in the window. A videotape of politician Phil Crane. You just saw the top half of him. Tim Kazurinsky was the videotape master. I was just the agent. I asked, 'I've got this tape here. My politician, Phil Crane. Can you make him look good?' George delivered this speech for about a minute, then Tim said, 'Let me run it backwards.' George did the whole thing backwards. Tim said, 'All right, we'll edit out certain parts.' By editing, when we played it back, George said things that were totally different. It was very funny.

"Six months into the run, everybody got bored. George got weirder and weirder. One night he jumped out the window, grabbed me, threw me back in, jumped back in with me, and said, 'All right, I'm holding him prisoner until you meet the following demands.' Tim was just staring, and I was laughing so hard, I couldn't get out of the window. He finally let me go. I crawled out of the window and screamed, 'This thing must never fall into the hands of other people. You've created something evil!' "

Pseudo-macho humor ranged (ranged?) from pirates to cowboys. Described by Wendt, "The pirate sketch never got very far. It would just be a bunch of guys going 'Aaargh, aargh,' putting on silly hats, hooks on our hands, rubber chickens on our epaulettes, and trying to affect peg legs. We'd capture the Jewish princess, who would eventually conquer us all, or something like that. The cowboy bit was kind of a fantasy that Kazurinsky and Jarchow and myself had. We threatened to try a cowboy scene in the improvisation for a good year before we did it. Whenever the boys decide to get silly, it tends to be like Visigoth scenes, and they never work. They always sound like such fun, and they never work.

"We were determined to get a cowboy scene that would work. So Tim Kazurinsky got into the silliest cowboy outfit, with a blowdryer for a gun, and Bruce played it relatively straight, and I looked pretty silly, and we decided to just go out and mime that we were riding on horseback along a trail, and that it was a really boring, long day, and we were looking for a place to camp. Fred Kaz played this kind of doung-de-doung-de-doung lonesome-on-the-range music, while the three of us ambled abreast, doing different silly little horse walks, and we didn't talk. We wanted to see how long we could get away with just not doing a thing. We were very successful. The audience just kept laughing. The longer we didn't talk, the harder they laughed.

"So finally, after about five minutes, we'd cut it off by starting this dialogue, and they stopped laughing altogether. It turned into a scene of seeing how long we could get away with not doing anything, and the audience loved it. Then Fred Kaz wrote us a barbershop-harmony cowboy song with three of us instead of four, and that was the piece."

A twist on the concept of a father-and-son scene involved Don DePollo as a vampire: "Miriam Flynn played a psychiatrist. I played Dracula. George Wendt played my son. He'd probably never admit that he was in it. The premise was that he wanted to open a Burger King. He was being very normal. So I took him to the shrink, because instead of wanting to be a vampire, he

Left to right, standing: George Wendt, Don DePollo, Larry Coven, Audrie Neenan, Tim Kazurinsky. Seated: Maria Ricossa, Will Porter. (Photo courtesy of The Second City)

wanted to open this Burger King. George wasn't the original actor in it. First it was Mert Rich. But whenever I said, 'Mert-ty, look me in de aye,' he'd laugh and squeal and run into the wings to stop laughing. So they had to put George in."

Among other vignettes were Eric Boardman as clergyman Lincoln Good-heart in a comment on "modernized" religion (he'd changed the sepulchre to a salad bar and hung up a poster of the Fonz); newscasters confessing all when they mistakenly read that the world would end in 8½ minutes instead of 8½ millennia; musical numbers about Jimmy Carter in Wonderland and Caesar's court deciding who would be mayor after Daley's death; a Russian ballet in which all the dancers are trying to defect; and Steve Kampmann's fund-raising announcement for public television.

The fund-raiser spot provided Kampmann's breakthrough on Second City's stage. "I was added to the cast as its seventh member. The scenes were already set, and I just came on for the improvisations. It was tough, because the audience wouldn't have seen me all evening, wouldn't know who I was, and probably didn't care. I knew I had to bring something to the party right away, so I came up with this plea for funds."

In it, the announcer begins his pitch calmly enough, offering an incongruous book bonus to patrons who come through. When patrons don't cooperate, he threatens to reveal the names of people who are having illicit affairs. Finally, he takes a gun to a boy scout, played by Eric Boardman, and instructs, "Call now."

When the Chicago and Toronto companies swapped stages for six weeks, the Chicago folk took props with them for the "American Gothic" tableau (Miriam Flynn as Mona Lisa, Steve Kampmann and Ann Ryerson as American Gothic, Don DePollo as Blue Boy, Jim Sherman as a Picasso, George Wendt as a piece of sculpture, Eric Boardman as the security guard). This required taking a pitchfork through Canadian customs. The customs agent inquired, "What's this?" "Uh, we're actors, sir." Whereupon the agent called out, "Hey, Charley, first pitchfork this morning."

TORONTO: *SCTV*

In the years from 1959 to 1976, the single biggest change in the world may have been not the Bomb, not the Pill, but the influence of TV. It was simply no longer possible, in 1976, for satirists to dismiss it as unimportant. In the fifties, a major city might have had as many as eight daily newspapers. By the seventies, a city was lucky to have three, and people were getting their headlines in part if not wholly from the home screen. A President's electoral victory had been attributed largely to TV (consensus was that the televised Nixon–Kennedy debates had showed Kennedy to advantage, and overstated Nixon's five o'clock shadow); a war in progress had been televised (with on-the-spot coverage of death and destruction shaping public attitudes toward Vietnam); through television—neither radio nor the papers could have done it—the world watched man's first walk on the moon.

In 1976, it was not only possible but inevitable to recognize TV for what it was, for better or worse—the common literature. Where it was categorically impossible for Second City players to successfully face a broad-based audience with an intricately constructed scene-in-depth about Schopenhauer, they could explore the nuances of *Leave It to Beaver* in compulsive detail, with the audience devouring each morsel. It's a fair guess that by 1976, there had probably been even more bad TV written than bad books.

Here was a job for Second City, and right out of tradition. Take the better aspects of the common literature, assume that the audience has intricate knowledge of it, and dissect it on every level. Take something that is being ruined when it doesn't have to be, and satirize its faults. And you might as well be daring about it. If you're going to go after television, do it *on* television. Like a bullfighter taunting a bull.

In 1976, the Toronto branch of Second City branched itself into TV. Andrew Alexander arranged a deal with Global TV, then formed a partnership with Len Stuart, who put up $35,000 for the first seven shows. As Bernie Sahlins describes the initial stages in the marriage of SC and TV, "Andrew Alexander and I were discussing it, and Toronto was much riper for television than America. It took more chances, and there was less competition. So we managed to get a commitment to do three shows for Global TV in Canada, a small network. Then we had a meeting in Toronto, with people from there and people from Chicago. We sat around for a couple of days and figured out the format. The format was a sort of impoverished TV station which did programs in slavish imitation of everybody else. In the end, the only modification from what we originally planned was that originally, we were thinking in terms of an ongoing story. But after we shot the first one, no matter how we tried to edit it, we could not make both the story and the bits form any kind of organic whole, so we threw out the story and the bits worked."

In on the ground floor and brainstorming sessions were Andrew Alexander, Bernie Sahlins, Del Close, Sheldon Patinkin, John Candy, Eugene Levy, Andrea Martin, Catherine O'Hara, Dave Thomas, Joe Flaherty, and Harold Ramis. Joe Flaherty had come in on it because Harold Ramis would be there: "Bernie said he and Andrew had a deal with Global Television to do a half-hour show, to be shown once a month on Global, over a span of six months. I said I'd do it if we got Harold Ramis up, because I love working with him. He was in Los Angeles, and he came up."

"Everyone knew," says Harold Ramis, "that if there was a new comedy, there was a new comedy television show waiting to happen. Once *Saturday Night* broke, we knew it wasn't us. We wouldn't be the first in there, and we didn't have the access, and we didn't have the sponsors, and we had no network, and we had no budget. We didn't know when we'd be broadcast so we couldn't be topical. We figured since we were a low-budget show made at a local TV station, we should look like a low-budget local show, we should parody a low-budget independent TV station. So, rather than feeling we were up against *Saturday Night,* I personally felt that we were basically turned loose in Canada, given a studio and a mandate to do whatever we wanted to do."

The Canadians may have been uniquely suited to the task of spoofing TV. They may have grown up with more of it than anybody. Much earlier than in the States, Canada was hooked up to cable, and Toronto was getting its own stations as well as Buffalo's local and network programming. Nor were the influences on Second City television limited to Toronto and Buffalo. For anything that looked like a bad local show from Pittsburgh, there was Joe Flaherty to thank.

Initially, the series was called *Second City Television.* It soon became *SCTV.* Playing station owner Guy Caballero was Joe Flaherty. Caballero was a sleazeball conniver in a wheelchair. The wheelchair was for sympathy. Caballero would stand up at strategic moments, for effect. The station covered all the local bases, from kiddie programs and the news to a combination fitness and religion program (Catherine O'Hara as a convent nun, scourging herself in the style of setting-up exercises). Staff included Andrea Martin as cleaning woman Pirini Scleroso and resident repressed sexologist Cheryl Kinsey, Joe Flaherty and Eugene Levy as newsmen Floyd Robert-son and Earl Camembert and once in a while, walk-ons as themselves by cos-tume designer Juul Haal-meyer and make-up artist Bev Schechtman. Broad-casts were from the fic-tional, now mythic, Melon-ville. Says Joe Flaherty, "I threw that on, I think, with our sign-off or sign-on. 'This is *Second City Televis-ion,* serving the Melonville, Ducksburg, someplace else —' I still remember Gene Levy looking at that and going, 'Ducksburg, huh?'

Joe Flaherty as SCTV's Guy Caballero. (Photo courtesy of Rick Alexander)

I said, 'Why not?' He said, 'Ducksburg. Donald Duck—didn't he come from there?' But we stuck with Melonville for some reason. It always came back."

In January of 1977, Jack Rhodes (Filmways Productions) bought American syndication rights to *Second City Television*. In September of the year, a series of twenty-six episodes made its debut in fifty-five markets across the U.S. In the middle of Second City's first batch of half hours for Global, Global had ordered six more. Then they ordered another thirteen. These added up to the first year, but the work hadn't been continuous. There were layoffs in between. During one, at the request of Ivan Reitman, Harold Ramis started a movie treatment based on the *Lampoon* show. A screenplay developed from the treatment. Then, says Ramis, "I sort of alternated the *Animal House* screenplay with production in Toronto. When we got picked up for a second year, I was in Los Angeles and *Animal House* was ready to break. I didn't want to go back to Toronto, so I proposed that we find a house in L.A. big enough for all the writers, then they'd all come down here. We had an old dream, much talked about, a comedy commune. Everybody living in one place and working full-time, really full-time on that show. Not everyone ended up staying in the house, but at least five people stayed—John Candy, Catherine O'Hara, Dave Thomas, Joe Flaherty, and me. In a big house in Bel Air, with a swimming pool and a pool table. In seven weeks we wrote sixteen shows."

Catherine O'Hara and Dave Thomas. (Photo courtesy of Rick Alexander)

The series ran two seasons on Global, then wasn't renewed. Cast members dispersed, some heading to Los Angeles, others stayed in Canada. John Candy did his own CTV comedy show. In 1979, Andrew Alexander and Len Stuart struck a deal with Allarco Broadcasting of Edmonton (in the province of Alberta, Canada) and the CBC (Canadian Broadcasting Company) which, explains Alexander, "was a function of keeping the show on the air. We had two years under our belts, fifty-two shows, at Global, then they didn't want to do it any more because they couldn't afford to. The American distribution that we had for the first two years was beginning to drop, so we found a partner in western Canada, in Edmonton. The terms were that if we would give up half ownership of the show, and if we produced it in their facility, there was going to be life after death. So we did twenty-six more shows out there.

"It was an interesting experience producing in Edmonton. It's a big city by Western standards but there's not much to do. I'd say our best work on *SCTV* came out of Edmonton, because we had that bunker mentality."

The Edmonton shows became a special experience. They didn't uniformly start out that way. Dave Thomas remembers, "We always thought we were L.A.-bound. And we were going to Edmonton. Where would we be going next? The Northwest Territory? Alaska? We were very depressed. We put it together, but we couldn't get commitments from everybody. John was doing *Big City Comedy*.* Catherine was taking a year off. Eugene and Andrea were in Los Angeles, but agreed to be part-time performers. They'd come back if we would block-shoot their parts in two weeks. But they didn't want to do a complete season. Harold had left halfway through the second season, and now we were faced with the problem of trying to put together a show without him, or John, Catherine, Andrea, or Gene.

Had another show surrendered so many of its actors—and writers—at once, chances are it would have folded. But on *SCTV*, talent succeeded talent, proving the Second City formula of accession as sound on the TV screen as on stage.

"We started looking around," Thomas continues. "Joe brought Tony Rosato, from Toronto's Second City stage, into the show. Andrew brought Robin Duke, also from the stage company. I found Rick Moranis."

In 1981, *SCTV* signed a deal with the NBC network, to become a weekly ninety-minute late-night show. After shooting a few more episodes in Edmonton, the operation returned to Toronto. Despite everything generally bruited about on the subject of network interference, the series remained remarkably untouched. "I think," observes Andrew Alexander, "the network

---

*Of which the head writers were Jim Fisher and Jim Staahl, with Michael Short on the writing staff and Tino Insana in the supporting cast.

perceived us as this traveling minstrel show. We were in Edmonton, then we were in Toronto, and you kind of had to look on a map. Where is Edmonton? You're really out of the hub of what's going on, so they figure you're *really* out of the hub of what's going on. It's hard to kick us around because we weren't there to kick."

The most significant concession to the network may have been the inclusion of musical guests. According to Eugene Levy, "We fought it initially because it seemed too variety-ish. It didn't seem to fit. But we said, okay, it's a ninety-minute program, it helps make up time. And we worked the music acts into the show, in an organic way, so they could do their numbers and also be involved in performing a little bit. Then we'd book guests and find, in many cases, they were big fans of the show, and they liked doing the sketches more than doing their numbers.

"But we didn't make any real concessions. For instance, they wanted all the 'A' material up front, and the more experimental material in the last half of the show. We just told them we were trying to write a ninety-minute show that had a beginning, a middle, and an end, and we couldn't do that. The great thing about being in Edmonton and Toronto was that they didn't come up all that much. Anyway, we figured the worst that could happen was they'd pull the plug, and if they pulled the plug, they pulled the plug."

A highlight of the NBC period is fondly recalled by Martin Short: "It was the first show of the '82–'83 season, which was our last season on NBC. It was based on the premise that *SCTV* went on strike and we needed to buy Canadian programming, in other words, satirizing the kind of blandness Canadian programming can be. If the show had been based in New York, I don't think we would have been allowed to go on. We would have been told that no one in the audience was going to understand it. But we were in Toronto, and we did it.

"Andrew Alexander was great in that respect. He never tried to stifle our enthusiasm. And the show was literally not written five days before we had to shoot something. I remember Joe Flaherty really pushed it through and we all got enthusiastic about it. It was great, and it was *SCTV* at its most exciting, where we all took assignments and all the offices were churning out material. It became very expensive. We went way over budget. Now, Andrew by all rights could have—and many producers would say *should* have—put a stop to us. Five days is not enough time to put a show this intense and complicated together. But Andrew didn't stop us because he knew it was a good idea. It became one of the most successful episodes. It won us our second batch of Emmys."

Slotted 12:30–2:00 A.M. on Friday nights, NBC's *SCTV* won raves and entered the so-called "Late Night Comedy Wars." New York's *Soho News* hailed it as "The Funniest Show on Earth," and *Time* magazine deemed it "the fastest, smartest ninety minutes on any television channel, anywhere." The "comedy wars"—*SCTV* vs. *Saturday Night Live* (11:30–12:30 Saturday nights on NBC) vs. *Fridays* (12:30–1:30 Friday nights on ABC)—depended less on time slot than on which show was funniest in the minds of the late-night comedy viewing audience. It's interesting that all three shows had Second City connections—*SCTV* for obvious reasons, *SNL* by way of the Second City and *SCTV* talent it periodically siphoned off (including but not limited to Gilda Radner, John Belushi, Dan Aykroyd, Bill Murray, Robin Duke, Tim Kazurinsky, Tony Rosato, Jim Belushi, Martin Short, and Brian Doyle-Murray) and *Fridays* by virtue of head writer Jack Burns.

NBC cancelled the series in 1983, for lack of ratings, at a time when the viewing audience was about as large as the entire population of metropolitan Los Angeles. Immediately, Cinemax cable picked it up, in a forty-five minute format, as their first original entertainment series. Announced HBO president Michael Fuchs, "This significant programming development represents a major coup for the pay-TV industry. By providing a home for this much-heralded series, Cinemax is extending a valuable and important part of contemporary television." Added David L. Mesiter, senior vice president of Cinemax and HBO Enterprises, "As our first original entertainment series, it helps establish the identity of the type of high-caliber programs subscribers will be able to see exclusively on Cinemax."

Through its various years and peregrinations, *SCTV* was never less than terrific TV. In all its modes and incarnations, it resembled in spirit nothing so much as the earliest days of The Second City and The Compass, with a bunch of friends doing the kind of theater they wanted to do for themselves and their friends, for fun. And when you get right down to it, in television terms, Edmonton is probably the industry's equivalent of a coffee house in Hyde Park.

In the beginning, in syndication, doing *SCTV* imparted feelings not unlike improvisation, and describable in the same language. Harold Ramis, who always found calamity liberating on stage, thought it just as stimulating on television: "There was something about the careening disaster. Terrible ratings. Stations dropping us and picking us up, it seemed almost at random.

Being on at one in the morning in some cities, three in the afternoon in others. It felt like chaos and it was sort of delightful, relieved us of all kinds of responsibility. We just did the best we could."

The best was unlimited by any of the usual considerations. Says Andrew Alexander, "We didn't know anything about syndication. We didn't know anything about producing a TV show either. It was all new. It was on-the-job training the first couple of years, and it shows. If you look at the first couple of episodes, it was minimalist television."

The best was certainly unlimited by budgetary considerations. It was minimalist budget. (Another parallel with early Compass and Second City, where a major decision in terms of "scenic design" might have meant the buying of another chair.) There even came a point when the most elaborate set the budget would allow, for *Doorway to Hell,* was a door backlit with a red light. A whole plot was constructed around it.

Patrick Whitley was brought in at Global to keep an eye on the costs. (He has stayed with the fold ever since, producing pieces as diverse as Showtime specials for Martin Short and Dave Thomas, and Catherine O'Hara and Andrea Martin's PMS film for the David Letterman film festival). But even minding the mint was interpreted through Second City–colored glasses. Says Whitley, "My function primarily was to create an atmosphere for the cast to allow them to focus on their writing and their performing, so that they could literally go it on their own and do what they wanted to do. They were fortunate in that respect. We sort of said, here's some money, here's a studio, here's three cameras. Go and do what you want.

"And what happened, because we were on such a tight budget, is that the material really had to hold up. The writing really had to be good. Because—for instance—I was watching one of the first shows the other night. There was a *Leave It to Beaver* parody and one scene was in this really gaudy kitchen. Later in the show, we did a commercial, a public service announcement parody about underage drinking, and the kid walks into the same kitchen— which was now supposed to be a bar—because it would have been expensive to build a different set."

An early piece that cost money was the parody of *Ben Hur, Second City Television*'s first epic, and show number thirteen at the end of the thirteen-show cycle. There were pressures to back out and do something they could afford. But no. They forged ahead. Recalls Harold Ramis, "Once we decided to do the piece, we spent so much money on it we couldn't afford to do any other pieces, basically. So we ended up stretching it to a full half hour, and the piece was so dull when we rehearsed it. John Candy was trying to do Charlton Heston as Ben Hur, and then he did a line as Curly from the Three Stooges, probably just to be funny, and we said, yeah, do it that way. That was the turning point.''

If you remember the movie, you also remember an emotional scene where Ben Hur is on the ground, choked with thirst, pleading for water. No one dares help him, until a compassionate man in a white robe defies the guards and gives him succor. Ben Hur, on the ground, at first sees only the hem of this man's garment. But we realize at once that the man is Jesus. In the *Ben Hur* parody, the drink is poured from a cocktail shaker and served with an olive, and what Ben Hur sees are checked houndstooth pants. "The joke was," says Harold Ramis, "we weren't going to do *Ben Hur*. We were going to do a parody of *The Robe*, but we were going to call it *The Trousers*. You had to know *The Robe* to get it. It was an obscure premise but we thought a very funny one. That's where we got the idea for the pants. We thought Jesus should be wearing some distinctive pants." Wearing the pants, his face unseen, was Sheldon Patinkin.

In another scene, Messala (Mazola) has told Ben Hur that his sister and

mother were lep—. "Did he say leopards?" "No, lepers." At last Ben Hur is reunited with his beloved sis and mom, and—uh-oh, they *are* leopards. Bad luck for Ben Hur. But they are cured, and Ben Hur lives on to be the ancestor of Davy Crockett.

From a spare-no-expense standpoint, the *Ben Hur* parody was rough around the edges. In terms of writing, no effort was spared. It was intricate, intelligent, and marvelous comedy.

The *SCTV* budget was usually balanced by trade-

Joe Flaherty as Count Floyd. (Photo courtesy of Rick Alexander)

offs —high-ticket numbers offset by economical ones. "Some of the scenes they would write," says Patrick Whitley, "would be far too expensive. I think the first thing we ever did that might be considered a high production-value piece was called "Polynesian Town." We lit up three city blocks. It was quite elaborate. A lot of people in management were fighting. 'Can't do it. Can't do it. Too expensive.' And I said, 'Let them do it, and they'll offset it with some inexpensive *Sunrise Semesters* and things like that."

"Things like that" included most pieces which could be performed— even improvised—by one or two people in front of one camera. These were extremely inexpensive to do, and were vastly helpful for picking up time. *Sunrise Semester,* for instance, might be Rick Moranis demonstrating the art of impersonating an orangutan impersonating James Stewart impersonating Ed Sullivan.

Another inexpensive piece, an utter grit-your-teeth-it's-them coup, plastered Tex and Edna Boil across the screen. Tex (Dave Thomas) played the organ. Edna (Andrea Martin) pitched sales in her best dime-store pants suit, with a sing-song voice stiff enough to split a biscuit. They were every bit as grating as the cheap local TV commercials they parodied.

Rick Moranis (left) and Dave Thomas (right) as the McKenzie Brothers. (Photo courtesy of Rick Alexander)

Along similar lines was the classic Count Floyd—an actor (Joe Flaherty) in a cheap vampire costume, crooning in a bad Transylvanian accent, pitching horror movies on the local station's kiddie-fest, *Monster Horror Chiller Theater*. Because it's such an appallingly cheap local station, it hasn't invested in many horror movies, so the Count is reduced to hyping whatever is on the shelves. When the movie is over, he makes a few feeble attempts at post-hype ("Hey, kids, wasn't that really scary where the waitress put ketchup on the French fries?") then apologizes for the choice of films, and says they'll do better next week, which of course they never do. The Count Floyd bits are excruciatingly bad—in other words, good parody of something that is bad to begin with.

The single most successful example of building a cheap set, leaving it there, and letting two oafs talk in front of it was the McKenzie Brothers. This deft stroke answered not only financial considerations, but also the problematical issue of Canadian content. Doug and Bob McKenzie (Dave Thomas and Rick Moranis) were born when Andrew Alexander came back from "yet another of those long-winded discussions I'd had with the CBC about what is Canadian content, what is Canadian comedy. One of those long, drawn-out philosophical chats that they like to have. And if you've got a Mountie in a sketch, that somehow resolves the problem. It's ridiculous. . . ."

"Andrew came into our offices on Richmond Street one day," recalls Dave Thomas. "Joe Flaherty and I were the head writers at the time. And Andrew said the CBC wanted Canadian content in the show. I said, 'What do you mean, Canadian content? We're going to Alberta to shoot it. It's going to be a complete Canadian production. There are only a couple of Americans in the cast. How much more Canadian can it get? Do you want us to put up a map of Canada and sit in front of it drinking beer, wearing tuques and parkas?' He said that would be great. And we compromised and put a Mountie beer mug on the set. Originally, we just did it as filler for the Canadian version of *SCTV*, which was two minutes longer than the American version. Then it caught on."

It caught on as a perfect spoof of community access television and therefore, another type of programming *SCTV* could satirize. The McKenzie Brothers delved deep into issues of the day. "Like, how come there's only eight parking spaces at takeout doughnut places?" "Today, we're gonna show you how to stuff a mouse in a beer bottle because, like, we heard of this guy who got a free case for finding a mouse in a bottle."

Bob and Doug spoke Canadian by ending sentences with *eh?* "What do you think of that? Beauty, eh?" They invented a word, *hoser,* because they had to be able to insult each other with something permissible on TV. Says Thomas, "We found ourselves in a situation, being guided by standards and practices, and needing some sort of expletives to deal with each other the way these brothers would in real life but couldn't on the air. This was sort of our alternate language. I had heard the verb, *to hose*, which had various connotations as all those obscure words do. *Hoser* we came up with specifically for the show."

Each McKenzie Brothers scene was totally improvised. When the rest of the cast had left for the day, they'd go down to minimal crew, with Rick Moranis and Dave Thomas sitting in front of the map, extemporizing. "Rick and I would do maybe twenty to thirty of these in a row, until we couldn't do any more. Each one was two minutes long. At the end of one, we'd go into another right away, with no idea what we were going to say or what we were going to deal with. Either one of us would just go with what the other guy said and try to make it go somewhere. If it didn't go anywhere, it became one of the lost Bob and Dougs. Out of the twenty or thirty that we would tape maybe five or six of them would be usable and the rest thrown out." It was a very economical way of shooting.

When *SCTV* went to NBC, the network at first didn't want the brothers, thinking them too regional to have a broad appeal. Then the McKenzie Brothers album hit—*The Great White North*, a top-selling LP, and also a single, "Take Off," with Geddy Lee from Rush on vocals. The album sold over one million copies and earned the Juno Award (Canada's equivalent of the Grammy Award) for Best Comedy Album. Then NBC wanted them enough to build an episode around the lads. Next the brothers appeared in a feature film, *Strange Brew*, co-written and co-directed by Dave Thomas. The movie won Canada's Golden Reel Award as the highest grossing theatrical film of 1983.

The McKenzie Brothers finally went the way of the buffalo because, explains Thomas, "It was operating on such a moronic, low level. It really became insulting to the intelligence to keep it up, and difficult to snap into that sub-cretinous mold. The costumes were very hot and uncomfortable too, particularly for making publicity visits to Los Angeles in the summer. But they were good to us, those characters. We both were able to buy houses on the money we saw from them."

It is remarkable that any *SCTV* material was improvised. Even more remarkable is the fact that in the beginning, the cast of the television show was simultaneously the resident company on the Toronto Second City stage. They had this idea that perhaps they could work out material for the TV program during the improv sets. It was physically harrowing rather than efficient. But they did it because, explains Andrew Alexander, "We never thought the TV show would go much beyond what we were doing. They were done for a local market. Nobody was getting paid very much. It was, 'After these six or seven shows, what will I be doing?' It was not, 'I'm a big TV star. I'm going to quit my other job.' "

In November of 1976, the stage show was called *The Wizard of Ossington*. John Candy and Peter Aykroyd (Dan's brother) were two hockey players, one English-speaking, one French-speaking, brought together to make a TV commercial. Dave Thomas was the deadpan director. Catherine O'Hara and Brenda Donohue were women truck drivers trying to keep awake on a long-haul run. And Jimmy Carter was saying prayers at the White House: "Oh, Lord . . . you're working for me now."

After something like thirteen segments for television, senior cast members gave up their stage duties. Catherine O'Hara and Dave Thomas, the most junior members, did not. For Dave Thomas, this was not exactly fun: "Both Catherine and I were in the stage show when we started the television show. We were getting up at 6:00 A.M. for a 7:00 A.M. makeup call, shooting right up until the last possible minute, put in a car, and driven downtown to do the stage show. You'd get home around 1:00, get about five hours of sleep, then have to go through the whole thing again. Really horrible.

"Once, I was doing this sort of Captain Kangaroo character, called Captain Combat, for the television show. I was trying to get some sleep and I nodded off behind some set dividers. The makeup was really thick, and I had eyebrow glue on my eyes. The eyebrow glue fell on my eyes and sealed them shut while I was asleep. Then someone woke me up, and I couldn't get my eyes open. I was so disoriented and overtired that I got on the set and just started screaming at Andrew and Bernie. I was swearing at them that I was going to quit the TV show and the stage show. And Bernie was very funny. When I finished my tirade, he looked at me, and said, 'Are you talking to me or Andrew?' It was evident that I was talking to both of them. So they pulled me out of the stage show, which was a tremendous relief."

After thirty shows, Bernie Sahlins gave up his coproducer status. "I swore I would never sit in studios for a series again and have faithfully kept that vow. The problems is, after the second or third show, you're just doing what you know, you're not learning anything. You might as well be a claims adjuster for an insurance company. I'm convinced if it didn't pay so well, nobody would do it. It's boring." When Sahlins left, he insisted on taking the name

"Second City" with him. *Second City Television* became *SCTV*, and entered its years of greatest success. Those remaining on the show were involved at every level, and were anything but bored.

The TV show was produced, in true Second City fashion, with the players writing their own material. Even when writers were added (Paul and Dave Flaherty, Mike Short, Brian Doyle-Murray, Bob Dolman, Dick Blasucci, Judith Kahan, Valri Bromfield, Jim Staahl, Jim Fisher, a long list of others) the cast never ceased to write. It was much like the green room—everyone kicking around ideas, critiquing them, and going for broke.

Martin Short, who would join *SCTV* and from *SCTV* move on to *Saturday Night Live*, felt the difference was night and day. On *SNL*, people jumped when they got a memo from some executive on high. Everyone, from network to sponsors, could chip away at an idea. But on *SCTV*, "The only onus we had was to make each other laugh. A lot of the very bizarre things we were doing were because we as a group thought they were funny and we were hoping someone else would buy our taste. In that respect, it was pure art. It wasn't watered down by 'What do we think the audience will think of us?'

Left to right: Joe Flaherty, Martin Short, and Eugene Levy spoof the German movie Das Boot *for Cinemax.*

"The situation was unique in television. The creative aspect of what went into the show was determined by the cast. Everything had to go through cast approval. You got to see pieces through. You got involved in the editing. You'd write a piece, and it would go to a read-through. If it was accepted, it would go on one color card, and if it was rejected, on another card, or more often than not, it would go into a rewrite. You'd take suggestions from other cast members, and you would then rewrite it. I often found,

Andrea Martin as Barbra Streisand and Valri Bromfield as Ruth Gordon. (Photo courtesy of Rick Alexander)

with my pieces for example, that they were improved through this process because I would take suggestions like a sponge. You didn't have to utilize every one because often your vision wasn't shared. Out of eighteen, maybe you'd use twelve. But certainly, the thing is with notes, the good ones stay and the bad ones go away."

The parallel, clearly, is with improv sets on stage. After an improvisation, the director gives notes. If a piece is worth keeping, they're incorporated or not, and if the piece is thereby improved, it stays.

Another aspect of writing that compared with Second City stage—the difference between having a terrific idea in your head and trotting it out for an audience—is expressed by Paul Flaherty: "The best moment is when you're writing a scene and you laugh and you're out on the floor in the office, and you haven't told anybody. And then you go to read it to them, and no one laughs. That's the worst. That's the one inscrutable thing I'll never understand. Why is it funny in the office and then it bombs in the read-through?"

When Harold Ramis was head writer, he drew on his experience directing for the Second City stage: "The mark of a good director, and I felt this very strongly at *SCTV* as head writer, is that you nurture every idea no matter how small, how fragmentary. If you could get something useful out of it, it was worthwhile. In the Second City format, if you got a good blackout out of something, it was worthwhile."

In the *SCTV* format, if you got a good commercial parody from something, it was worthwhile. Ramis continues: "One piece I loved, *Man Who Would Be King of the Popes,* was a good impression piece. We were trying to parody all the big sort of pseudo-Shakespearean epics that were coming out. *Lion in Winter, Becket,* all those. Joe knew *Becket* by heart. And *Lion in Winter.* He did a great Peter O'Toole. Dave Thomas did a great Richard Harris. John Candy did Richard Burton and Catherine O'Hara did Katharine Hepburn. The piece started out to be a big piece and ended up being a promo. It was much better as a promo, just doing highlights of the supposed movie."

Also as on Second City's stage, the women were outnumbered and the humor was guy-pokes-guy. Says Joe Flaherty, "The guys would tend to write Abbott and Costello things, Three Stooges kinds of things. No matter how lofty the concept was, it would generally always come down to, 'And then I slap your face, and you—.' We would, in fact, almost leave a void for the women. 'This is basically the idea for the scene. What do you want to do with it?' It was better that way, because they could add what they wanted and make the scene better." Catherine O'Hara became increasingly involved in writing the sorts of things guys wouldn't think of, from "Pre-Teen World" to "I'm Getting My Head Together and Screwing It on Right and Going on the Road."

For Robin Duke, the writers bloc was another of life's little challenges: "When I started, I don't think it was taken for granted that I would be writing too. I think they thought maybe I would fit into some scenes, but I wanted to write. I came from the Second City stage, where it was the natural thing to do to create your own material. And it was a case of, if you wanted to be in the show, you had to write. All the guys are going to write for guys, and then a woman comes in, but not a really developed character. If you want to be fulfilled in your performing, you have to create something for yourself. I guess anybody would want to have these wonderful characters written for them, but that isn't the reality of it so you have to do it yourself. Which was perfectly okay. Everyone was happy if you wrote a good piece."

Andrea Martin would have been just as happy not to write. "I did one character, Libby Wolfson, who happened like this. For years on *SCTV,* I played a variety of characters, all of whom looked nothing like me. Either I had glasses or a twitch or an accent, and I was very happy to do it, and Rick Moranis came aboard. Rick and I became very friendly, and he said one day, as we were improvising a scene and he was laughing hysterically, 'Why don't you just do a character that's close to you?' I said, 'Oh, Rick, I can't. I can't.' He took out a pen and said, 'You just talk. Don't even think about it. I'll write it down.' That's how Libby Wolfson got started. Very concerned about her weight, her breath, her underarms, and we made her into a talk show hostess. I made her more neurotic than I am, but really, she came out of my own idiosyncracies.

"I had no desire to write. I really didn't know if I *could* write. But, once, people just sort of got fed up with me and said, 'Listen, you can do it. Everybody else does it.' I went home and wrote the 'Libby Wolfson Exercise Show,' which is actually one of the best I ever did. I love the piece, and I guess Libby was the most rewarding character I played. But the process of writing was so excruciating. The doubting, the second-guessing, there was so much of that. I just don't enjoy it. It's not something I'd choose to do."

SCTV's production schedule was several weeks of writing, followed by several weeks of shooting. "Which," says Martin Short, "was a great way to do it. It was less stressful than *Saturday Night Live* was because it meant that if you didn't have anything, you could walk around for a week dead, with no ideas, but then the second week you could make up for it. Often you would go into the shooting with four shows written, and you'd have to make up two while you were shooting. The writing was grueling, but the hours weren't as bad as the shooting. Those hours could be very long. They could go from seven in the morning until one in the morning."

One time, they shot twenty-three hours straight because they were shooting on location in a church and only had the church for the day. To Harold Ramis, "there's something about production that always struck me as something like being in the army. You just suspend all your expectations about sleep or waking time and you're on duty."

Rehearsal was essentially the read-through. And, as Ramis explains, "There was very little read-through. When things are written by the company, the writing is the rehearsal. You don't write it until you know you can perform it. The things you write down are the things you worked out. So rehearsal was not necessary. Camera blocking is really what the rehearsal was."

A goal during the shooting phase was not to be the last one to leave at the end of the day. Early on, Dave Thomas was the announcer: "Which meant that everyone else got to go home, and I had to go into this little stinking recording booth and stay for an extra three or four hours doing the announcements. So when I was recording the cast crawl at the opening, I thought

I'd just give my name a little extra push since I was doing the extra work. I improvised the line and it stuck. 'Dave Thomas as the Beaver.' "

Harold Ramis, not a fan of overtime, "was doing the 'Sunrise Semester' format. It occurred to me to do do-it-yourself dentistry with Mort Finkel. The backstage story to that one is that I had gone with the device of, since you won't be licensed to give yourself shots of Novocain, use shots of rum instead. Someone always got stuck with doing the last piece of the day. Everyone would leave when their pieces were done. So I was the last one this time, and it was late. In the scene, I drank three shots of rum, then swigged from the bottle at the end. And the crew had put real rum in the shot glasses. I actually got really drunk. When I see that piece now, I can see myself sort of gagging on the straight rum, and then sort of finishing the piece with really glassy eyes. I actually got through the piece. I did not make a mistake. Because I just wanted to get home."

Sketch ideas came from everywhere, provided they could be contained within the premise of cruddy TV station. "Muley's Roundhouse" was suggested by Brian Doyle-Murray. Says Harold Ramis, "Brian had been a trainman, he'd worked on the railroad as a summer job during college. And he said, 'Remember those train shows when we were kids?' I remember watching a show in Chicago, 'Lunchtime Little Theater' with Uncle Johnny Coons, that was exactly the same kind of show. He would say, 'Bring your lunch down in front of the TV. Be sure to ask your mom. Let's see what we have for lunch today.' We did that as 'Muley's Roundhouse.' And in the middle of 'Muley's Roundhouse,' we'd have a Three Stooges parody called The Three Dummies, with Candy, Flaherty, and Eugene. Each one does a great stooge. And Catherine O'Hara did Margaret Dumont." Muley's most intriguing feature was his perennial whine. "Look at this stupid toy you sent Ol' Muley. You don't send junk like this to other children's shows." Ol' Muley was a bitter man, very depressed.

One *SCTV* scene was derived from the sixteenth-century English comedy *Ralph Roister Doister**, with the premise that the moguls of Melonville would stoop to anything that was cheap to shoot. A two-album record set of *Shakespeare's Greatest Jokes* resulted from Dave Thomas visiting the Stratford Festival in Canada: "This stuffy audience in the 1970s was laughing at classical references to bread-leavening jokes. Give us a break. There comes the point when even Shakespeare would go out and say, 'Stop this. I wrote this stuff

*SCTV's equivalent of early Second City stage references to Wittgenstein. It's hard to say which is more obscure.

for the ordinary Joe. It isn't reaching you. You people are idiots for laughing at this.' "

A sketch about Francis Bacon (Rick Moranis) and William Shakespeare (Dave Thomas) was called "Shake and Bake." In it, the pair frantically dash off lines backstage and throw them to the actors. The actors return after saying the lines and being pelted with vegetables. It came from Dave Thomas's perception of the personality of Shakespeare "as a guy saying, 'Yeah, I can write that play,' and just being a sweating weasel trying to get the job done, and having Francis Bacon as a friend he could bounce ideas off of."

When Dave Thomas lost interest in being Tex Boil at the organ, his departure was worked into a Tex-and-Edna spot. He stormed off on camera. "Then," recounts Andrea Martin, "Edna did it with other people. I think right after him I used a dog, a little trained dog at the organ. Then Joe Flaherty did it as my new husband, a count. Then John Candy. I seem to remember Edna being driven to auditioning people on the air. 'Tex has left.

Boil Boy (Martin Short) and Edna Boil (Andrea Martin) in a commercial for Boil World. (Photo courtesy of Rick Alexander)

Who would like to be my new partner? Come on down.' We got a lot of mileage from that. Finally, toward the Cinemax days, we wanted to use the same characters, but how far could you go with them? We had Marty do the guy from *Deliverance*." This character took the form of Boil Boy—Martin Short in longjohns, a living warning of the dangers of inbreeding. By then, Edna was touting Boil World: "Come see Mother Nature's greatest mistakes at Boil World. There's Lung Lady, nothing but a head and a pair of lungs—come watch her breath. . . ."

When Harold Ramis left *SCTV* to do *Animal House*, his character of station manager Moe Green departed the airwaves in the guise of being kidnapped by Leutonians. The station never did get him back. The kidnapping was reported with ill-disguised glee by the station's news team, Earl Camembert (Eugene Levy) and Floyd Robertson (Joe Flaherty). Notice that Floyd Robertson and Count Floyd had the same first name, and were both played by Joe Flaherty. This is because both Floyds were the same man. On this cheap station, the saner of its two news anchormen was doubling as Melonville's resident Monster Horror Chiller ghoul.

The news team had grown out of a stage piece, "Big News Little News." Floyd got all the big items. Earl got all the little items. The two were generally infighting more than they were reporting current events.

When Moe Green left, he was replaced as station manager by Edna Boil's sister, Edith Prickley (Andrea Martin), a bodacious broad in a leopardskin jacket and hat and rhinestone-studded glasses. She told bad jokes loud, with a snorting laugh, and totally shook things up. The character of Edith Prickley had also come from a stage piece, "Parent-Teacher," in which Martin was already wearing her leopard togs.

Says Andrea Martin, recalling

Andrea Martin as Edith Prickley. (Photo courtesy of Rick Alexander)

Ms. Prickley's creation on Toronto's Second City stage, "Catherine's mother had that leopard jacket and hat, and Catherine, as we all did, brought costumes that we kept backstage in this makeshift cupboard, and we pulled things out from this assortment of costumes when characters indicated it.

"So I just happened to put on this leopard jacket, and this hat, which I'd never used before. Playing the parent of a delinquent boy, I knocked on the door, walked in, and Catherine said, 'You must be—' and I said, 'Edith' and she said 'Prickley?' I said, 'Yes, Edith Prickley.' As soon as she said the name, the costume sort of worked with the name, and the character evolved."

The Sammy Maudlin concept and crew came from a stage piece developed when Second City played Pasadena. Host Sammy Maudlin (Joe Flaherty) and lackey William B (John Candy) drooled over their shallow guests, favorites being Mr. Comedy himself, Bobby Bittman (Eugene Levy), and Catherine O'Hara's Lola Heatherton (who conveys affection of the mildest sort with, "I want to bear your children. WAAhahahaha"). The scene begins with a talk show of turgid reciprocal fawning. Then Lola comes out, and blasts everyone for being so phony. With this, she wins their applause for her forthrightness. On another Maudlin show, there were outtakes. Bobby Bittman showing outtakes from his special. Harold Ramis as Kenneth Clarke, showing outtakes from his history of art series for the public broadcasting system. William B, squirming while everyone laughs at clip in which Chingachgook (Lon Chaney, Jr., portrayed by Eugene Levy) heaves a rock that catches William B in the groin. Quips Sammy, "Ho! Boy! Hit him right in the schnutz! What is this—Frontier Nutcracker?"

Sammy and William B reveled in Vegas jargon:

William: Sammy, may I toast you and say something before
we start this whole . . .

Sammy: Shloibin.

William: I was going to say "schlamucka."

Sammy: Shloibin, schlamucka. I love those showbiz words.

Lin Ye Tang (Dave Thomas) began as a series of improv sets on stage.

Thomas would take questions from the audience, answering them as the prime minister of Vietnam and a string of other Oriental aliases. *SCTV*'s Lin Ye Tang was a master of Oriental wisdom and martial arts. Thomas as Lin never appeared the same way twice: "The joke in the cast was that they never found a way to make me look Oriental. Each time I did it, I'd try another look. I never did get it." Joe Flaherty called it The Many Faces of Lin Ye Tang. Harold Ramis thought of it as "an ongoing evolution that never evolved."

The polka band boys, Yosh (John Candy) and Stan (Eugene Levy) Schmenge, came from Leutonia, and from Candy and Levy sitting around a hotel room. Says Levy, "I think the third or fourth show in our first season, we had a piece with an ethnic theme to it, 'The Leutonian Hour.' Then when Harold was leaving the show, we figured, let's have him kidnapped, and we relied on Leutonia for the agents of the deed. *Schmenge* was a word we'd been using right along, as in the sentence, 'He is a real schmenge.' We were thinking of having a Schmenge Olympics or something. We talked about, for a scene, running a pole-vaulting film backwards and calling it the pole-catching event. It was going to be the Schmenge Olympics, but we never did it.

"Sometime later, in Edmonton, John and I one Sunday afternoon were up in his hotel room, watching television, trying to come up with a scene. We were watching these two horrible guys and said, 'Wow, there's a couple

Left: Catherine O'Hara as Lola Heatherton (photo courtesy of Rick Alexander). Right: The Schmenge Brothers, Yosh (John Candy) and Stan (Eugene Levy).

of schmenges.' The light bulbs kind of went on at the same time, and we looked at each other. 'The Schmenge Brothers? What do you think? Is there something there? A polka band?' We talked about it, but we never did it that season. It wasn't until halfway through the next season that we remembered the idea and decided to do it.''

The Schmenge Brothers not only appeared on *SCTV*, but also made a "Power to the Punk People (Polka)" video, which *Time* magazine rated as one of the top twenty music videos of 1984. *Time* described them as "a couple of accordion yankers whose attempts to go current have the impact of Lawrence Welk playing a guest set with the Grateful Dead." In 1985, Yosh and Stan spun off an HBO special, *The Schmenge Brothers: The Last Polka*, which traced their roots through Rick Moranis, Robin Duke, Catherine O'Hara, and Mary Margaret O'Hara (Catherine's sister), playing those closest to the Schmenges during their career.

Sid Dithers (Eugene Levy) began with a parody of the Sunday morning religious program *Lamp Unto My Feet*. In *SCTV*'s "Match Unto My Feet," Joe Flaherty played the priest who shared his insights with the audience. This segment revolved around a Passover meal on which the priest paid a visit. Morris Dithers as patriarch and granddad sat at the head of the table, with Andrea Martin as his wife. Harold Ramis was his Jewish son who had married a gentile, Catherine O'Hara. Dave Thomas was the son who did not want to go into poppa Dithers' family business, shoelace lips. At the table, off-camera, sat the children, hurling food.

Says Levy, "The scene took four or five hours to do. When I watched the playbacks, I found myself more and more reclined in my seat, so by the end of the scene, I seemed to be lower than when I started. The look was kind of funny. When we'd bring Morris back, as Sid Dithers, he'd just get shorter and shorter as the shows went on." Dithers, in a constant state of perplexity so complete that he all but had garbanzos for eyeballs, went on to appear in such gripping roles as the drill sergeant in "An Officer and a Gentile."

John Candy, as Johnny LaRue, played a dissipated, out-of-shape fitness show host who smoked while doing the workouts. One exercise consisted of opening and closing the refrigerator. The exertion sent his heart into overdrive. The onstage Johnny LaRue expanded to include the backstage Johnny LaRue, an obnoxious pawn in station politics who one minute figured to call the shots, and the next was whimpering to save his job.

This layering of character involvements became a hallmark of *SCTV*. For Harold Ramis, it was the best part: "I loved the texture of the show when it was working on all those levels, when one piece would go into another piece, or contain another piece. It began with the very first show, with Johnny LaRue finding out that he was broke, that his accountant had squandered all this money, and a tragic love affair. LaRue goes berserk, and the last piece of the show is a Sigmund Freud parody, which ends with Johnny LaRue bursting into Sigmund Freud's study saying, 'Doc, I need help.' "

Multilayering could extend from a Chekhov play (Chekov from *Star Trek* in an Anton Chekhov play, and the cast being beamed aboard the Enterprise) to "The Grapes of Mud," which interwove *The Grapes of Wrath* with a kiddie show. Ol' Muley moped around, bringing the same dejection to the Great Depression that he regularly brought to his miserable lunchtime snacks on "Roundhouse."

There was a Christmas show parodying three Neil Simon plays rolled into one and called *Nutcracker Suite*. There was a combination *Casablanca*/Rogers-Astaire/*Wizard of Oz*/Hope-Crosby/*Fantasy Island* that was completely mindboggling in its intricacy and impressions and included a favorite *SCTV* ploy, the beating up of a dummy (supposedly Tattoo). In the hands of the *SCTV* specialists, flinging stuffed people into the air was always good for a laugh.

Dr. Tongue (John Candy) and Bruno (Eugene Levy) evolved from a stage piece combined with the fact that John Candy wasn't in town. In "The Uncle Silvio Show" on the Chicago stage, Tino Insana was Silvio, the kid's show host. Dr. Tongue (Candy) was the special guest, accompanied by his pantomimed snakes. "Well, what have we here, Dr. Tongue?" Then Dr. Tongue would expound on the snake and skip rope with it. In Toronto, on the Old Firehall stage, Candy was still Tongue, and Eugene Levy was Silvio.

On *SCTV*, Dr. Tongue had the kid's show and hosted cheap-o 3-D movies—obtaining the effect by leaning toward the camera and back, vainly attempting to menace the lens with some totally innocuous object. He'd host "Dr. Tongue's House of Cats," "Dr. Tongue's House of Stewardesses." By his side, as his silent hunchback flunky, was Bruno (played by backstage, fictitious Woody Tobias, Jr., played by Eugene Levy).

"When we did the early ones," says Eugene Levy, "before Bruno could talk, it was kind of fun. The chemistry with John was a nice little duo, even though it was all visual on my part. I just grunted. We did a few of those, and we always looked forward to doing them. Then I think it was one season we were in Edmonton, that John did not do, and we did a piece in which Count Floyd hosted "Death Motel." That was Woody on his own, without

Dr. Tongue, acting in a piece. I did the whole piece just grunting and grunting and grunting. Then I suggested that it might be funny to have the actor playing Bruno coming out on the show. So when the piece was over, Count Floyd told the kiddies, 'We have Woody Tobias, Jr., the man who plays Bruno, in the studio today.'

"Here was Bruno, who happened to be ugly and a hunchback, talking about wanting to be a serious actor. He was trying to make it in the business and didn't quite understand why he was only cast as a hunchback. Then, when John came back the next season, the hunchback was able to talk. Then this on-camera banter started up between the two of them. 'You did so.' 'I did not.' 'Did so.' 'Did not.' 'Did.' 'Didn't.' 'You're a liar.' 'You're a liar.' 'Liar, liar, pants on fire.' The Dr. Tongue and Woody segments were always fun, and effortless to do."

When John Candy left to do his series for CTV, Rick Moranis—whose background included writing and acting for CBS radio and television while still attending high school, and who had appeared nationally on the network's *Alan Hamel Show* and *90 Minutes Live*—was added to the *SCTV* cast. He distinguished himself as Gerry Todd, special effects disc jockey (Crosby, Stills, Nash, and Young are Stills, Nash, and Young backing Bing Crosby's "White Christmas"), and in some of the finest impressions ever done on TV.

True, impressions as mimicry had not previously been a Second City device. The emphasis had not been "do Lyndon Johnson" so much as "do a Lyndon Johnson type." But previously, Second City hadn't the luxury of time and makeup, enough to make the audience believe they were seeing Jerry Lewis, Bob Hope, or Woody Allen.

At the beginning, *SCTV* didn't either. Eugene Levy did Lou Jaffee (an announcer with a particularly jarring, unmodulated vocal quality that caused one to question why anyone would pay him to talk) and Rockin' Mel Slurp (terminally unhip host of "Mel's Rock Pile," a teen music show). Says Levy, "We didn't have a lot of wigs and things like that. The budget was too low. So I was using my own hair, which was long then, and it was basically how many looks can I get from this mop? Lou Jaffee was parted hair but straightened, and it kind of went up, and Mel Slurp was more or less the same but not straightened."

In the later years of *SCTV*, hair, costuming, and makeup were exquisite arts. Hair stylist Judi Cooper-Sealy could do anything with a human head, contributing to the building of a character, rather than simply waiting for a hair to go out of place: "We went through wigs like crazy, chopping them up and so on. We'd have about two hundred wigs on hand, and keep buying them up as we needed them." Costume designer Juul Haalmeyer would "recut, remake, and re-edge everything. We went through a thousand dollars' worth of dye every cycle, and a dozen bottles of bleach a week. You had to be ready for anything. You'd get a script and they'd say something like, 'We're doing Vikings and beekeepers in a boat."

Bev Schechtman brought twenty years of background in makeup, sculpting, and commercial art to the ears, teeth, and noses of the *SCTV* cast. In so doing, she provided the key to any number of impressions, among them Dave Thomas's Bob Hope. He recalls, "I was doing a very bad impersonation of Bob Hope. I was doing Bob in Vietnam, doing monologues for the troops. And Brian Doyle-Murray thought it was an hysterical thing. I told him I thought Bob's career had gotten down to golf and war, and it would be great if we could find a way to combine them. The two of us sat down and came up with "Bob Hope's Desert Classic."

"Brian helped me write it, and the two of us handed it in and got an enthusiastic response from the rest of the cast so we slugged it in for pre-

Eugene Levy as Lou Jaffee and Dave Thomas as Bob Hope in the "Bob Hope Desert Classic." (Photo courtesy of Rick Alexander)

production. But I wasn't sure I could do Bob Hope. I was in the chair, with my hair done and the fake nose on. I was looking at a picture of Bob, and I said to Bev, 'You know, this still isn't right. There's something wrong.' She said, 'Well, his jaw sticks out more than you do. Stick out your jaw.' I stuck out my jaw, and the minute I did that, I found the center for the impression and for how I would be able to do Bob."

After that, this Bob Hope could do anything, including appear in "Play It Again, Bob" opposite

Rick Moranis's Woody Allen—a take-off on Woody Allen's *Play It Again, Sam.* The scene was culled from Moranis's and Thomas's improvisations into a tape recorder, transcribed, cut, and transformed into a script.

During the mid- to late-seventies in New York, Second City alumni were steadily replenishing the cast of *Saturday Night Live.* The work suited their talents well, since live was their medium, and ensemble their métier. Bill Murray made the move to *SNL* for the 1977–78 season, and functioned primarily in

Catherine O'Hara and John Candy in Yellowbelly. *(Photo courtesy of Rick Alexander)*

sketches with Dan Aykroyd until he wrote his own sketch. Suddenly he was Richard Herkiman in the shower. His soap was a "shower mike." Murray went into his repellent lounge singer character. Wife (Gilda Radner) stepped in for a quick shower. Herkiman sang a few bars introducing her, then announced the surprise guest, the man she'd been seeing behind his back for the last two years, Richard Cularsky. "Come on in, Richard. Good to have you aboard!" Cularsky (Buck Henry) stepped into the shower, fully clothed. The scene was Murray's first *SNL* hit, and a turning point in his career.

In the late seventies and early eighties, with Bernie Sahlins pretty much tied to Chicago, Toronto's Second City sought other means to tap into its roots. Alumni—Catherine O'Hara, John Candy, and Eugene Levy, to name a few—were brought in to guest-direct, taking the cast in new directions and imparting their own imprint to the personality of the company. Sketches included a people scene in the boy-meets-girl tradition (spermatozoon meets ovum in a piece with a happy ending); instant opera (containing the immortal outburst, "Forgive me for being into bestiality"); a middle-aged man coming face-to-face with his sixties hippie self; Jean-Paul Sartre arriving in heaven and telling God He doesn't exist (Sartre: "It's not what I expected." God: "What did you expect?" Sartre: "Nothing"); a "rhapsody for the deaf" with the lyrics of "Swing Low, Sweet Chariot" conveyed in absurd sign language; a revivalist preacher addressing a wealthy congregation ("If God had not meant there to be poor people He wouldn't have given you all their money"); and the kidnapping of Conservative party leader Joe Clark ("We want five hundred dollars." "I'm sorry, we can't come up with that kind of money." "What shall we do with Joe Clark, then?" "Well, there's no rush on it, really. Put him in a small paper bag").

Among new faces were Cathy Gallant, Robin Duke, Deborah Kimmett, Mary Charlotte Wilcox, Don Dickinson, John Hemphill, Ken Innes, Steven Kampmann,* Derek McGrath, Tony Rosato, Martin Short, and Peter Torokvei. Most of this assemblage were soon on *SCTV*, and three of them—Duke, Rosato, Short—on both *SCTV* and *Saturday Night Live*. (A few years later, in some NBC quarters, the whole of *SCTV* would be groomed to replace *SNL* should it be cancelled.)

Robin Duke followed pal Catherine O'Hara to the Second City stage: "We'd always done plays in school. Catherine would say she wanted to be an actress and I'd say, yeah, I wanted to be an actress too. I went to university and she went to Second City, and I'd go watch her in the show and just be hanging around. Then I started going to workshops and got involved."

Duke took a liking to social humor and character comedy, with an all-time master of character as her model: "My mother told me when I was very young, I would just insist on staying up to see Jack Benny. I was too young to really understand any of his jokes, but he made me laugh. I didn't know what he was saying, so I guess it was his manner." One onstage character she created was peculiar Molly Earl, who became peculiar craftswoman Molly Earl on *SCTV*.

Martin Short joined The Second City ranks in 1977, to portray a gossip-hungry hairdresser (on Liz Taylor: "If they ever remake *Cleopatra*, she'll have to play Rome"); a straight son whose wired father wants to turn him on to

*Kampmann made the move from Chicago to Toronto because the cast always seemed to be smaller there than in the Windy City. With seven people in a team, you can be brilliant in a scene, then not be onstage again for twenty minutes. With five people, you can be in almost every piece.

pot; a rabbi lecturing on why you have to be Jewish to be funny; Frank Sinatra and the prototype for Ed Grimley:

"The first piece that Catherine O'Hara and I did, we wrote together. It was called "My Way." I would come on as Frank Sinatra performing, and Catherine was a woman ringside, very drunk. I'm singing. She's heckling through the whole thing. At one point she screams, dead drunk, 'Ava Gardner, you let her go, Frank, why?' Sinatra keeps acknowledging but going on, and the audience keeps wondering when he's going to do something. Finally, at the end, he takes a bow, turns around, and kicks her in the face. Catherine does this great flip over the back seat, and the lights go out. She would go back in that chair, in the dark, and not worry about it. Fantastic.

"Ed Grimley came from the revue that was in progress when I joined, called *The Wizard of Ossington*. There was a piece called "Sexist," and the premise was two people applying for one job. The guy I played, a role originally done by John Candy, is a moron. The woman is very, very qualified, overly qualified. The employer goes through education, employment history, and at the end says, 'I can't choose, you people are so evenly qualified.' She says, 'This is outrageous.' The guy says, 'Of course, maybe if you arm wrestle.' We arm wrestle. I win. She storms out with a diatribe against male chauvinism. The guy says, 'What's her problem?' I say, 'Maybe she's having her period.'

"I started to call this character Ed Grimley. I based him on a few people I knew. Things happen over the course of doing a piece in a run. I was doing the piece with Robin Duke and Peter Aykroyd. I remember one time I looked at Robin and she was downstage. I kind of bared my teeth by accident. The audience laughed. My tendency when they laugh is to freeze and figure out what I've done later. So that teeth-baring became part of the character.

"Then I used to grease my hair a little bit to give a bad look. I remember Peter laughing one night and saying, 'It keeps getting higher every time you do this.' So as a joke I came out with it completely up and I felt, well, that got a laugh, okay, I'll keep it in. And Ed Grimley just kind of evolved."

When a famous female impersonator was appearing at Toronto's Royal Alexandra, Don DePollo happened to be up from Chicago, working next door to Second City: "We wanted to go, but you had to wear a suit to get in. We didn't have our own suits with us and we didn't have time to go home. So we took the prop coats and prop ties from the green room, none of which fit, and went to the Royal Alex looking like an Italian street gang without any money. We looked like hit men who couldn't do anything right, but the people in charge at the Royal Alex knew who Martin Short was and who Steve Kampmann

Martin Short as, top to bottom, Ed Grimley, Jackie Rogers, Jr., and Jerry Lewis. (Photo courtesy of Rick Alexander)

was, so we got the best tables in the place. They sent over champagne.

"When it was over, Short and I were out front. He's saying, 'So you're the famous American, eh? I understand you can make all kinds of mugs and faces.' I said, 'Yeah, well, how's this?' and made a face. He said, 'Oh, that's easy, have you ever done one of these?' and he did one. They got bigger and broader and sillier, and we were with four other people who were getting fed up. We didn't stop until Steve Kampmann and Peter Torokvci picked me up, and I forget who picked up Short, but they carried us away, facing each other, in sort of prone positions, 'You haven't seen the last of me.' Making faces, into the night, grown men."

In 1979, Lorne Michaels approached Martin Short with a holding deal guaranteeing a spot on *Saturday Night Live* in the event that either Dan Aykroyd or John Belushi departed the program. In December 1979, both men left, together, to make the picture *The Blues Brothers*. By then, however, Short was starring in the TV situation comedy *The Associates* (as Tucker Kerwin), followed by *I'm a Big Girl Now* (Neal Stryker). Before long, New York critic Marvin Kitman would proclaim him "The best thing we've gotten from Canada since the hockey puck."

When Dave Thomas and Rick Moranis left *SCTV* to make *Strange Brew*, a movie featuring Bob and Doug McKenzie, Andrew Alexander asked Martin Short to fill in. He joined the cast in 1982, having already worked with Second City cast members on stage, and in the supporting cast of David Steinberg's CTV comedy program. Thomas, who had also been on Steinberg's show, remembers the gang with little to do on the show, and, out of boredom, constantly getting into mischief. "Originally, we each had our own dressing rooms. Then, to punish us for fooling around, they put Marty and me in one dressing room and John Candy and Joe Flaherty in the other." Ultimately, the four shared one dressing room, but still, they treated the place like a playground. When they demolished an expensive lighting column in an impromptu game of tag football, "We ran out of the studio like the Bowery Boys and hid in our dressing rooms," Thomas confesses. "They never found out that we did it."

Martin Short brought favorite stage characters to *SCTV*—among them Ed Grimley, whose slacks hiked up to his armpits, whose overlarge plaid shirt buttoned up to the throat, whose hair rose in a monstrous point, and whose earnest personality made him the king of the nerds. Short's Jackie Rogers, Jr., cross-eyed albino nightclub singer with a mane of long white hair, laughed "fff-fffff-ffff," and wrote a book about his father called *Damn You, Daddy, Sir:* "It's a love letter really, I suppose, with a dash of hatred in an almost mocha kind of swirl, if you'll have it." The character's name came straight from Short's childhood. "I always put on TV shows in the attic and, when I was nine, picked out a stage name, which was Jackie Rogers."

Brock Linahan, Short's officious, unblinking TV interviewer, was based on Canadian interview whiz Brian Linahan, who is famous for knowing *everything* about his subjects. The real Linahan asks questions tacked to background trivia such as "When you took the subway in 1952, there was a bearded Ukrainian sitting next to you." Stunned subjects can only reply, "How in the world did you know that?" But *SCTV*'s Brock Linahan would ask the same question and get, "What in the world are you talking about? I wasn't even born in 1952 and I've never been on a subway. Doesn't anyone research these questions?"

Short's Rusty Van Reddick, a former child star, continued into his forties with a TV show about a prankster tot in kneepants. On screen, he portrayed the little scamp precisely as he'd been playing him for decades. Off screen, he smoke, drank, and abused his writers with the furor of an aging, fading star.

Short's impressions, complete with makeup, hair, costume, and voice, have included Pierre Trudeau, Gore Vidal, Robin Williams, Martina Navratilova, Norman Mailer, Jerry Lewis, David Steinberg, Tom Hayden, and Mr. Rogers (as when he entered the ring, boxing with John Candy's Julia Child, in "Battle of the PBS Stars").

As makeup, hair, and costume evolved, so did an item called "Farm Report." In the beginning, it was simply an early, early morning show. "Good morning, farmers. It's six A.M. I call you farmers because who the hell else is up at this hour?" The hot news was the price of pork bellies and hog lips. It progressed to a "Farm Film Report," in which the farmers review current films and liked them, or not, depending on whether anything got blowed up, blowed up real good. In later years, farmers John Candy and Joe Flaherty invited guests on the show, who sang, or twittered, or did whatever they did, and then got blowed up real, real good. These guests ranged from Brooke Shields (Catherine O'Hara) to Bernadette Peters (Andrea Martin) to Dustin Hoffman (Martin Short) as Tootsie, simpering about how sensitive he became once he was cast in a woman's role. Each guest was a faithful impression of the real-life counterpart.

Nor was *SCTV* without its occasional real-life guest star. Robin Williams, an improv addict who'll go a distance out of his way to join in the sets of Toronto's Second City stage, took a turn on *SCTV* as Bowery Boy Slip Mahoney.

Another time, Sir Ralph Richardson and Sir John Gielgud were in To-

Sir Ralph Richardson (seated, left) and Sir John Gielgud (seated, right) on the set of SCTV. (*Photo courtesy of The Second City*)

ronto performing in *No Man's Land*. Andrew Alexander, Sheldon Patinkin, and Harold Ramis stopped by their dressing room and invited them on the show. They agreed, and pieces were whipped up for them—for example, Harold Ramis's "Stonehenge Estates," in which all the rocks from Stonehenge were moved to Arizona and assembled into condominiums for senior citizens. This idea bit the dust when Sir John and Sir Ralph vetoed the script and provided a thought of their own, "something based on the two of us backstage, with Sir John's hobby, which is crossword puzzles, and something based on Sir Ralph's hobby, which is motorbike racing. Why not take these subjects and craft them into a little scene?"

When *SCTV* went to NBC, there was talk that it might be nice to create something easy to shoot, with sets that could be reused, and the chance to log several scenes in one taping session. Eugene Levy developed and wrote the soap opera, "Days of the Week," in which he revealed his considerable and much appreciated talent for writing female parts as deftly as those for male cast members. Real guest stars wandered in from time to time. Carol Burnett, in Toronto doing an HBO picture with Elizabeth Taylor, came to the set because she was a diehard fan. They sat her down in a courtroom scene. She didn't say a word. She added a voice-over later. Bill Murray also came by as a guest. Eugene Levy remembers, "By the last episode of the first season of 'Days of the Week,' the wedding sequence, we were really burned out. I mean, really, really, really tired. Bill came up and we all felt kind of bad for him because we weren't really prepared. We didn't have a lot written for him. As a result, he did a lot of improvising on that show, and I worked him into 'Days of the Week' with a little touch of *The Graduate*."

It's been said that *SCTV* began as a satire of TV, then switched its emphasis to sophisticated impression. But the fact is that it never swapped the one for the other. Over the years, it blended the two to add a new level to the satire. At the same time, it leaned increasingly toward character comedy, placing the emphasis not on someone making a joke, but on humor coming out of character. Then, whenever Ed Grimley said "I'm going mental, I must say," or Johnny LaRue mopped his brow, a joke in the nature of a knowing wink was shared with the viewer. Once again, *SCTV* followed Second City tradition, finding humor in the character, in the relationship, not in the ha-ha joke.

It also steered clear of the shock-value joke—straight Second City. When the *SCTV* team went from NBC to Cinemax cable, they were free to throw rules out the window. Yet the closest they came to a topless woman was Lung

John Candy as Divine. (Photo courtesy of Rick Alexander)

Lady of Boil World. "I think," says Martin Short, "the cast had a shared sensibility of what was acceptable comedically. It would have been like saying 'shit' on stage. It wasn't encouraged, not for any puritanical reason, but because it was just too simple to do. When we went to Cinemax, the shows never changed, simply because no one was particularly into writing material for shock as much as to get the laughs."

Above all—how Second City can you get?— *SCTV* was a dynamite group of team players, concentrating on looking good by striving to make the other guy look better. "If I had a talent creatively on that show," says Andrew Alexander, "I think it was picking the right cast and production people that would work together." It is, indeed, a talent. It's difficult to imagine a more ideally matched team.

All told, there were seventy-two half-hour *SCTV* shows, forty-two ninety-minute shows, and eighteen forty-five-minute shows, winning 13 Emmy award nominations, two Emmy awards for best writing, three Actra nominations and two Actra awards. These were remixed and cut into half-hour shows for current syndication, enabling viewers to continue enjoying what the *Los Angeles Times* proclaimed to be the "best comedy show on TV—maybe the best one in TV *history*."

CHICAGO

The late seventies brought Shelley Long to Chicago's Second City stage. The daughter of schoolteachers from Fort Wayne, Indiana, she originally planned to follow in their footsteps. But, after two years at Northwestern University, she dropped out to become an actress and a model. At twenty-one, she became involved in writing children's films for Encyclopædia Britannica, then wrote for, associate-produced, and co-hosted "Sorting It Out," a Chicago TV magazine show. An experience during one program segment revealed Long's knack for improvisation.

Says she, "One of the cameramen filmed some beautiful footage of fall foliage, and my boss, the head producer of the television show, said to me, 'Shelley, why don't you find a poem, that we can read while the footage is showing?' " Staring into a deadline, with no time to stop by the library or a bookstore, she ad-libbed. "I sat down and wrote a poem myself—I had written quite a bit of poetry in college." Long took the poem to her producer. He asked, "Who is it by?" She answered, "Shelley." Thinking she meant English poet Percy Bysshe Shelley, he went ahead with the poem. Later, when he caught on, Long smiled. "Well, I didn't lie to you." He agreed, "Yes, it is by Shelley, isn't it?"

Long enrolled in Second City workshops essentially to relax and to keep her hand in acting, but workshop director Jo Forsberg felt strongly that she belonged in the company. She auditioned and was hired, proving herself indefatigable. Already a Chicago celebrity by virtue of her TV show, she entered an established cast under more than the usual pressure to measure up. She fit in quickly—as a young woman meeting a young man (Steve Kampmann) at a reunion, having a fabulous time with him, then learning he's a transsexual; as mother to daughter Miriam Flynn in a getting-ready-for-a-date scene, with the twist being that the mother has the date; and as a daughter having to tell parents (Miriam Flynn and Eric Boardman) that she's moving in with her boyfriend (Will Porter)—at a time when such scenes were deemed highly shocking.

Shelley Long at The Second City. (Photo courtesy of The Second City)

While still performing at The Second City, Long received a stream of additional offers—TV and other acting jobs—and accepted every one. Says Joyce Sloane, "Shelley is one of the hardest workers I've ever known. She's a total professional. She researches everything she does. She is an absolute workaholic."

One of Long's stage partners was Jim Belushi, John Belushi's younger brother. John had told him to charge the stage like a bull. Jim answered that he'd never been to Mexico. He didn't know what a bull charged like. Replied John, "Don't let that stop you."

Like older brother John, Jim attempted to shatter the language taboos on stage: "One night Bernie said, 'I'm sick and tired of you impoverishing these sets with your language.' So there was a kind of challenge there. Would I be able to succeed at Second City if I couldn't use any bad language? I took the challenge and I stuttered for two weeks."

Recalls Joyce Sloane, "John was not the pillar of taste, but he came back once and said, 'What kind of language is that to use on stage?' He really let Jim have it, which is interesting."

Two stand-out scenes of this period Chicago vintage are "Whitehorse Tavern" and "Walnut Room." The former was based on a real encounter between Jim and John Belushi in New York. In this scene, Jim was John and Will Porter was Jim—two brothers hitting the hooch while honoring literary greats who committed suicide. Says Jim Belushi, "One night I was doing it when John walked onstage. It was a complete surprise. John put some money in the juke box and said, 'Is this a gay bar?' We said, 'No.' John said, 'Oh, I thought it was a gay bar.' And he walked off. He let us die out there. He finally came back and said, 'I know where the gay bar is.' He took us out, which at least ended the scene."

In "Walnut Room," a mother (Mary Gross) and her small son (Lance Kerwin) are lunching at a restaurant. The mother is picking on the child. A lone wolf (Jim Belushi) moves in for the kill, advising the waitress (Meagan Fay), "A chocolate milkshake for the young man, and a double martini for the lady." Anticipating a nooner, the mother gets rid of her son by giving him enough change to see a bargain movie downtown. The wolf takes the lad aside, gives him fifty dollars and suggests he run away from home. He returns to the mother long enough to wish her good day, stick her with the check, and depart.

The scene had been inspired by something Mary Gross saw at Water Tower Place—a well-dressed mother ignoring and abusing her two daughters.

When the daughters said they wanted to see a movie, the mother asked, "Well, do you have your money with you?" When her daughter said she only had two dollars, the mother answered, "Then you can't go to a movie, can you?" Says Mary Gross, "This incident really bothered me. I guess because I didn't get up and smack her. I couldn't get it out of my craw. So either that night or the next night I was talking about it backstage and Fred Kaz said, 'I had a nephew whose mother was really cruel to him, and once I took him aside and said, here's ten bucks. Run away from home.' So we just put those elements together and came up with the scene that night."

1979 brought some four hundred representatives of five generations of Second City players back to Old Town to celebrate the company's 20th anniversary. What began as an unstructured cocktail party blossomed into an impromptu revue. Scenes included Shelley Long as a sexologist describing the finer points of faked orgasm, Avery Schreiber as a machine, and Jim Staahl as the Reverend Billy Graham. ("This isn't my money. This is God's money. I'm just spending it for Him.") In a show-stopping rendition of the song "Chicago," Nancy McCabe-Kelly fell to her knees, inadvertently grinding them into broken glass. She asked for fresh pantyhose and forged on.

The Second City lunged into the eighties with its customary élan. In Chicago, Jim Belushi, Danny Breen, Dan Castellaneta, James Fay, Meagan Fay, Mary Gross, Mike Hagerty, Isabella Hoffmann, Bonnie Hunt, John Kapelos, Tim Kazurinsky, Maureen Kelly, Richard Kind, Lance Kinsey, Bruce Jarchow, Nancy McCabe-Kelly, Harry Murphy, Rob Riley, George Wendt, and cohorts lit into such popular concerns as the Me Generation, Mayor Jane Byrne, the Cook County Hospital emergency room, a trip to Mr. Rogers' neighborhood on Chicago's Halstead Street, and the demise of Morris the Cat. In one scene, a Chicago cop first pumped bullets into a fleeing crook, then ordered, "Freeze." Another took the form of a political ballet entitled "Sleezy Beauty." More recently, an embittered veteran looked for a friend's name on the Vietnam Wall while a young one enthused over the grandeur of the monument, two old ladies confronted the lack of respect for the elderly in America today, Renaissance players harmonized about nuclear energy, cast mingled with audience in a parody of Phil Donahue's TV show, and two gals done up as Marlene Dietrich and Mae West sang the bawdy nuclear weapons put-down "What Do You Do When Your Weapons Don't Work?"

A unique offering in Toronto in August 1979 was *The Girls Show*, a special week of reunion in which women—Maggie Butterfield, Robin Duke, Catherine O'Hara, Andrea Martin, and Mary Charlotte Wilcox—played all

Top: Bruce Pirrie (left) and Dana Andersen (right) (photo courtesy of Hugh Wesley Photojournal); center, left to right: Linda Kash, Dana Andersen, Bruce Pirrie, Bob Bainborough (photo courtesy of Hugh Wesley Photojournal); bottom: Don Castellaneta as Jack Nicholson taking the oath of office for the U.S. Presidency, and Harry Murphy swearing him in (photo courtesy of Jennifer Girard).

the parts. As Toronto entered the eighties, Dana Andersen, Bob Bainborough, Sandra Balcovske, John Hemphill, David Huband, Ron James, Linda Kash, Don Lake, Kathleen Laskey, Debra McGrath, Mike Myers, Bruce Pirrie, Deborah Theaker, Mark Wilson, and friends portrayed everyone from postal clerks and politicians to Marcel Marceau Cousteau. A young Sigmund Freud and his mother undertook a train ride laced with Freudian sexual symbolism; army veterans who somehow missed the action nonetheless relived the horrors of war ("The Tet Offensive was hell, man. They kept coming and coming, all those forms. I was typing for eight straight days"); folk singers Joni Bitchin, Buffy St. Elsewhere, and Neil Diamond paid tribute to William Shatner as "Canada's greatest star"; Emily Brontë did stand-up comedy; in *Mein Giffer*, Ronald Reagan visited Rudolph Hess at Spandau ("They elected an actor as President twice? How did they beat us?"); and a leaf raker mused, "If Bruce Springsteen is so popular with the working class, why do they call him 'The Boss' and not 'The Union Steward'?" In a musical send-up of a family moving into a new neighborhood, two parents encountered a Frank Sinatra-like real estate man and a Christopher Cross-like neighbor. The parents' two offspring could have passed for David Byrne and Cyndi Lauper, while grandma tore into song as Ethel Merman.

Elsewhere in the eighties, Second City continued to involve itself in television specials starring Bill Murray and Avery Schreiber for PKO Productions (1980); an Edmonton Second City company, which produced four revues over two frantic years (1980–1982); Second City Chicago's E.T.C. (Experimental Touring Company—or sometimes, Experimental Training Center) next-door to 1616 N. Wells, established in 1982 to provide a home stage for each of the two U.S. touring companies on alternate weeks; Second City Productions' *The Life and Times of Nicholas Nickleby* presented as part of the Great Lakes Shakespeare Festival (1982); Second City Toronto's own National Touring Company, and a permanent Second City company in London, Ontario, Canada (both begun in 1983); a New York engagement called *Orwell That Ends Well*, at the Village Gate (1984).

The time-honored tradition of comparing early Second City to its present form continues, unabated. Recent cast members staunchly stand their ground. Jim Fay finds it "pretty interesting that people have a perception that Second City has somewhat drastically changed in the last twenty-five or twenty-six years. I think it changes any time you put somebody new in the cast." Richard Kind suggests that "we're dealing with a different set of cards in terms of the audience and their interests." As Mike Myers sees things, "There's a real shift in satire worldwide if only because, after twenty-five years of it, people certainly need a break and really, the quintessential political sketches have all been done, or at least there's a feeling of that. With television, everybody's seen the quintessential sketches, and there's no point in mouthing what's already been done. So we don't."

For Dan Castellaneta, who has taken workshops with David Shepherd, "The focus may be more attitudes than politics, but we're responding to audience interests. From the beginning, David Shepherd wanted to do a theater about the people who came to see the show. In some ways, that exists at Second City today. What's on the minds of the audience is the main thing, and what is most important about the theater. This is what we reflect."

Throughout, Second City has kept its homey feel. Says Joyce Sloane, "For a long time, it was really a ma-and-pa business. Most of our office space in Chicago is just about seven years old. Before that, we worked in the little room where the managers work now. My office was a desk, Bernie's office was a desk, and there were shelves all around us with things ready to fall on our heads. We didn't even have a window. The space we have now belonged to the man who managed the building. I told him we had to have these offices. I finally convinced him. We got them when he retired."

In 1984, when Second City was a quarter-century old, ma and pa sold the homestead. Or, properly speaking, pa sold it to Andrew Alexander and Len Stuart, and ma bought in. Andrew Alexander took over as executive producer of Second City's Chicago operation, with an option to buy the theater. The terms of the sale were reported at $2.5 million, though Sahlins and Alexander both declared that number "a little high."

With the sale, Sahlins became artistic director in Chicago, not to mention, a happy man. Said he, "Andrew knows the operation, and he's the logical one to carry it on."

Joyce Sloane came in as a partner, while remaining producer for Chicago. Commented Andrew Alexander, "This was an idea I had been considering all along, because she knows this operation better than anybody. I was very surprised when I bought Second City that Joyce had not in fact gotten a piece of the action prior to that. From my own observation, she was obviously an important key to its success in Chicago. I really do wonder if there would be a Second City there today if it weren't for her."

The same week that the sale was completed, Toronto opened a "best of" show—*It Came From Chicago*—a tribute to twenty-five years of talent and Second City tradition. The cast included Bob Bainborough, Kevin Frankoff,

Debra McGrath, Bruce Pirrie, Jane Schoettle, and Adrian Truss, with a special appearance, on tape, of Barbara Harris and Alan Arkin in "Museum Piece." As the footage ran behind them, the scene blended into a live remake starring Debra McGrath and Adrian Truss.

In December 1984, Second City threw its big bash—the twenty-fifth anniversary reunion—to which graduates past and present thronged. "We flew everyone in," said Joyce Sloane. "It was such a love-in. Cheryl coordinated it. The plane from L.A. was called Jet Set Second City." The weekend-long celebration combined a public and a private show. For the public, alumni all-stars threw a fifty-dollar-a-seat gala at Chicago's 1250-seat Vic Theater. Proceeds went to the Second City John Belushi Scholarship Fund, created to aid theater students of Chicago. The revue was a "best of" bonanza, with some twenty-five scenes, selected by Joe Flaherty and Bernie Sahlins, that ran the gamut from football at the University of Chicago to Einstein in Marilyn Monroe's boudoir. A highlight was the ever-popular "Funeral," in which a family struggled valiantly to keep straight faces in mourning the departed, who stuck his head—and lost his life—in a can of baked beans. "I remember his last words. He said, 'I think there's some beans. I'll go take a look.' I tried to get him over to the can opener." When Betty Thomas spoke these words in rehearsal, she got as far as proclaiming she'd never forget the last words—then did. The blooper drew such laughs that a decision was made to keep it in for the show.

Among the celebrity performers at the anniversary bash—Ed Asner, Jim Belushi, Shelley Berman, Danny Breen, Severn Darden, Joe Flaherty, Mary Gross, Tim Kazurinsky, Robert Klein, Eugene Levy, Shelley Long, Andrea Martin, Harold Ramis, Martin Short, David Steinberg, Betty Thomas, Dave Thomas, George Wendt, Fred Willard, and ringer Joe Piscopo. The show was cohosted by Gene Siskel and Roger Ebert. The two-

SCTV winning the 1981–82 Emmy Award for best writing for a variety, musical, or comedy show. Back row, left to right: Milton Berle (presenter), Bob Dolman, John McAndrew, Doug Steckler, Mert Rich, Jeffrey Barron, Chris Cluess, Stu Kreisman, Mike Short, Paul Flaherty, Brian McConnachie, Martha Raye (presenter). Front row, left to right: John Candy, Joe Flaherty, Eugene Levy, Andrea Martin, Catherine O'Hara, Dave Thomas, Dick Blasucci. (Photo courtesy of The Second City)

hour special was taped by, and later aired on, HBO.

The private show, on Saturday night, was for friends and grads only. Four hours at 1616 N. Wells. Proclamations from the mayor, the governor, the president. Accolades for Bernie Sahlins, Paul Sills, David Shepherd, Viola Spolin, and Joyce Sloane. Among highlights were Shelley Berman and Severn Darden in a dazzling improvisation, and an impression—by Robert Klein—of Bernie Sahlins, recalling his days as Equity deputy, in a labor-management dispute: "As far as I can remember, I was the first one to do an impression of Bernie. Now everyone does it.

" 'Look, you're all working. You're a family.'

"I said, 'Bernie, we are going to strike, because this isn't fair.'

" 'What are you talking about? I'm your father. This is a family.'

" 'We're going to strike. Pop—we're going to strike . . .' "

To Klein, the effect of the weekend was "really something. Our gang. There's Spanky. There's Darla. There were a lot of people known to be highstrung, all having a remarkably good time. The funny thing was, I'm checking into the hotel. I come up the stairs. I see Paul Sills, and I give him a big hello. I say, 'You know, you were so tough on me, and so easy on Steinberg. I guess there was a method to your madness. Now, if Steinberg were here'—and I started to do Steinberg. In walks Steinberg, 'Are you imitating me?' I busted out laughing and we gave each other, spontaneously, a big hug."

Family reunions can be like that. They're like family albums come to life. Says Ben Gordon, "You go to a reunion in Chicago and you see people performing a sketch that you learned or you've done or even improvised on, performed by the people who originated it twenty years before and it's like seeing a picture of your grandmother for the first time and realizing you have the same nose. That's when you know you're part of the family."

9

The Second City Connection

Without substantially changing, The Second City has come a very long way, though the world around it can hardly be recognized as the same place.

Thirty years ago, technology made promises of menacing portent. The conquest of space. Mastery over the atom. In 1986, the Challenger space shuttle and the Soviet nuclear plant at Chernobyl exploded.

In 1950, the computer loomed as the heartless, humorless symbol of technology's power to dehumanize. In the 1980s, Joan Rivers, for one, computerizes her comedy material. "I have a filing system, a *major* filing system. All the jokes are on cards, and I back that up with computers, which I hate because if the power goes off, they can lose things. I don't like computers and I don't trust computers and I think they're the devil's tool. I have three of them in my house. Damien I, Damien II, and Damien III."

Once, college intellectuals fought the swapping of names for numbers. Now, colleges turn out computer scientists who learn, through the binary system, to reduce all names and numbers to either 0 or 1. Once, the big exam was graduation final. Now it's an employer-mandated drug test. Students used to worry about existentialism. But we're still here, and though we still don't know why we're here, students no longer care. What "is" is has no bearing on getting an MBA. As Dan Castellaneta observes, "The parallel between the late fifties and the mid eighties would be Kierkegaard, sheltered income and Camus, IRAs."

College, the fifties' ivory tower, became in the seventies a haven from the draft. Political satire became political nostalgia—Vaughn Meader's *First Family* Kennedy spoof is a top-selling re-released LP. Dada used to be a nihilistic movement, not Idi Amin's last name.

Alienation was a horrible thought. Then we got to know each other too well. "There was a time," laments Shelley Berman, "when people could argue. I mean, really argue. They could really disagree. They didn't kill each other. Or beat each other up. There was a time when motorists could really yell at each other, and there was no idea that one would go into his car and get a gun and kill you. And there was a time when you went to the movies and saw movies without people having sex. Why show me these two people in slow motion? For basketball, I'll buy a ticket. Basketball I'll watch. Football I'll watch. But if it's a sport I can play, why make me a spectator? Why?"

The sixties promised the dawning of the Age of Aquarius, when men and women would put aside all racial and national differences, united at last by humanity and love. Astrology teaches that the age preceding it, the Age of Pisces, began when Christ walked the earth; that the signs of the Piscean age are authority, militancy, fanatic dedication; that the Piscean age will be with us for several dozen more years. The Aquarian age continues to dawn, and dawn, and dawn. The eighties have lost patience. Astrological ages are vague and unreal in a decade that pesters, "Is it soup yet?"

Today, a Burger King stands where Playwrights Theatre Club used to be, and a high-rise residence where the first Second City stood. But Second City is stronger than ever, a Chicago landmark as well as a thriving enterprise. "Her very soul," wrote Sam Lesner in the *Chicago Daily News*, "has become an integral part of the home in which it was born. We cherish it, pamper it and only reluctantly criticize it." Alan Myerson considers it "as a functional movement, with the possible exception of the Group Theater–Actors Studio movement, the single most important event of the American theater of the twentieth century."

In a changing society, The Second City is a constant, no less committed to quality theater than in 1959. Joyce Sloane, actively interested in or on the boards of most of the theaters in town, continues to support the art in all its forms, though as ever, she places The Second City above all: "I've built my life around Second City, and it's been a very good life." For Bernie Sahlins—

who views it in the context of a tradition going back to the commedia dell'arte, Roman mime, and Greek comedy—the obligation to the world of performing arts is paramount. The Second City twenty-fifth anniversary reunion supported the John Belushi Scholarship Fund, and in 1985, Bernie Sahlins, wife Jane Sahlins, and partner Bill Conner together created the first annual Chicago International Theatre Festival—bringing major companies from all over the world to perform in Chicago over a period of two weeks. Sahlins described the electrifying venture not as a break from Second City, but rather, as an extension of it—"realizing the full scope of what theater can be."

David Shepherd has added a long-awaited dimension to the full scope of what it can be with far-reaching successes in theater of the people, by the people, and for the people. "I did not conceive my work to be a springboard to stardom, but as a way of serving the community. I didn't hit it with The Compass. I did hit it with ImprovOlympix." ImprovOlympix—improvisation with teams and the element of scoring—has proved itself popular and effective in settings from senior citizens' homes and high schools to the Brooklyn House of Detention. In recent years, Shepherd has also pioneered a new form of improvisation, VideoImprov Parties, and taught Second City workshops in both Chicago and Toronto. Paul Sills, who left Second City to develop the Game Theatre in the sixties and Story Theatre in 1969 and 1970, has pursued—with Sills & Company in Los Angeles, and briefly also in New York—his work with improvisational games. Viola Spolin conducts the workshops. Begun in 1980 when some West Coast Second City graduates wanted to "get back to basics," Sills & Company offers the rare opportunity to see Spolin's techniques realized in their purest form. Recalls Avery Schreiber, one of the founders, "Paul was in town. We all said 'Let's get a theater together. Let's get a workshop. Let's start performing. Hey, Mickey. Hey, Judy. Let's put on a show.' " Explains Valerie Harper, another ardent supporter of the group, "A number of us got together and chipped in about fifteen hundred dollars each to start a nest egg. When we began, there were nights when only six people showed up to watch. But we refused to feel discouraged. Then attendance picked up, and we were meeting our budget, and things fell into place."

Players at Sills & Company have included John Brent, Hamilton Camp, Severn Darden, Melinda Dillon, Macintyre Dixon, Paul Dooley, Murphy Dunne, Garry Goodrow, Valerie Harper, Tino Insana, Bruce Jarchow, Mina Kolb, Dick Libertini, Nancy McCabe-Kelly, Derek McGrath, Ann Ryerson, Dick Schaal, Avery Schreiber, with occasional guest improvisations by visitors such as Robin Williams. Says Avery Schreiber, "He was kind of coming regularly for a while, and playing with us. His background is another sort of improvisation, so at the beginning he wasn't actually playing the games. Finally, we put him on the spot, told him he couldn't just stand up there and go cuckoo. We said, 'You've *got* to follow the form.' So he did. During the break, very exhausted, he said, 'Wow, this stuff is work!' "

Says Valerie Harper, who has improvised such scenes with Williams as an anteater (Harper) and a butterfly (Williams) which gradually transform into people in an immigration office, "His presence may be disruptive, but it's not destructive. He has a great and fast and fabulous mind."

Sills & Company works on the barest of bare stages—the sparser the stage, the purer the space. In the New York show, Severn Darden took to wearing a different necktie for every scene because "It's the only touch of spectacle we have." In 1986, Paul Sills moved East to work more closely with New York theater. Sills & Company in Los Angeles is now known as the Spolin Theatre Game Center, and operates as the joint venture of Viola Spolin and Hamilton Camp.

Just as Viola Spolin, in Los Angeles, continues to give workshops in connection with The Spolin Theatre Game Center, Jo Forsberg conducts the Players Workshop in Chicago and maintains an affiliation with Second City. Her son Eric, her daughter Linnea, and Second City graduates Judy Morgan and Jeff Michalski assist as writers, teachers and mentors to the growing legions—from actors to doctors—interested in what improvisation can teach. In Los Angeles, Sandy Holt leads workshops which combine Spolin and Forsberg techniques with many of her own. As she sees it, "Second City is like a basic form for writing, for acting, for editing, for directing. It's something like the way that one of the basic forms of music is jazz. I teach that, and I teach that humor comes out of human frailty, out of the awkwardness between people." In the Westwood Village section of Los Angeles, Dick Schaal has spearheaded *The Village*, a combination of story and game approaches and the revue format. In Chicago, Del Close is active with a workshop, the ImprovOlympics, CrossCurrents, and an extended improvisational form known as The Harold; former Second City director Michael Gellman has mounted experimental one-acts at CrossCurrents; Dan Castellaneta explores a Compass-like long-form improvisation as director of Instant Theater; and Don DePollo spearheads the improvisational Event Game.

The Second City has increased *its* emphasis on workshops by introducing an innovative multileveled system. As Andrew Alexander explains it, "Sheldon

Patinkin has refined it and now there are five levels, each level based on experience. At level five, students earn the right to put on their own hour show. We've really put a lot of emphasis on the workshop program lately, and it's really starting to pay dividends."

The workshops, vital to the life of Second City, are just as essential to the entertainment industry at large, a fact of which the industry is well aware. "These days," says Richard Libertini, "this whole idea of Second City improvisation is widely accepted. They do it on television almost. You say you worked in Second City and people want to use you. But back then, it was a handicap in some cases. They'd say, 'Oh, he's not going to use the script. He's going to make up his own lines.' I used to hide it sometimes, because I sensed in some places that they were a little resistant to it."

"A big part of becoming a successful, working actor," explains Peter Boyle, "is getting your chops. Becoming fearless. Becoming a lion tamer. Realizing that if you keep doing it, don't worry if it doesn't work once. The next one might. For instance, by the time John Belushi hit *Saturday Night Live*, he'd been working every night for something like five years. You get your chops at Second City and take that attitude with you to auditions. It applies to commercials, which are really little scenes, just as much as it applies to motion pictures." When Boyle heard that a movie company would be making a low-budget film about a right-wing World War II veteran, he tried out for a role that echoed a scene he'd done at Second City with J. J. Barry. Asked to read from the script, he suggested that he could improvise faster, then proceeded to lose himself in a character he already knew intimately. Boyle got the part, and the movie, *Joe*, made him a major star. "And there's no way I would have that chutzpah in the audition had it not been for my Second City training."

Even actors who never belonged to The Second City company recognize their debt to it through workshops. Robert Townsend, who studied under Jo Forsberg, credits improvisation as "the key to good acting. If you can stay in character and do your job, that is what it's all about. I did a lot of improvising in the movies *Soldier's Story* and *Ratboy* because it was in character. It worked. This applies to body movement as much as to what the character says. I've found this equally true when I've done commercials. The techniques teach you to work with what you have. If you don't have anything, just work with space."

While improvisational skills are a definite plus, they represent just a part of the package. Improvisation at Second City is, after all, a function of ensemble work. The "cast chemistry" so valuable on screen today is frequently rooted in Second City training. David Steinberg, as a director, has been "called into situation comedies to help families be like families. It's a Second City skill. Many directors wouldn't know how to do that. I personally have not done anything as a director or a producer in which I haven't surrounded myself by as many Second City people as I can. Not because of old school ties, but because they're the best."

"Whenever I work with Second City actors," explains actor/director Alan Arkin, "and I try to do it as much as I can, they invariably know what their role is within the entity. Most actors work on their parts. Second City actors will work on their parts in conjunction with what service it plays to the whole. And I tell you, the time it saves a director, and the time it ends up saving a particular actor, is nothing short of phenomenal."

"Guys like Bill Murray and Dan Aykroyd didn't do stand-up so much as ensemble comedy," notes *Ghostbusters* producer/director Ivan Reitman. "They learned to listen and work in unison in character. That's comedic acting. Some of the present-day stand-up comics may not have that skill."

Comedic actors, not comics, emerge from Second City, not only able to act but caring about wanting to. Bill Murray, who earns a reported five million dollars a picture, recently appeared for dramatically less in a New Hyde Park Festival Theatre ("live from a cow barn in New York's Hudson River Valley") production of Bertolt Brecht's *A Man's A Man.*

"I'm not making a derogatory remark about stand-up comedians," asserts Martin Short, "but it seems that people like Bill Murray don't do jokes. John Belushi never did jokes. It's a matter of projecting an attitude." "We are actors," confirms Robin Duke. "I've always felt you acted and then you add the comedy onto it. It's got to be realistic, and then you add a twist." "Do the character first," concludes John Candy, "and then the comedy comes."

Moreover, the value of the training extends beyond performance. Second City has produced many of the most successful screen and TV writers around. For instance, Dan Aykroyd and John Belushi wrote as well as appeared in *Saturday Night Live* sketches. "Just structuring, setting up something, climax, plot points, characters," says Robin Duke, "all those things we learned to do on stage, on our feet, in two minutes, are the things you do when you write."

Steve Kampmann and Peter Torokvei left Toronto for Tinseltown. They became writers for *WKRP in Cincinnati.* "We were very lucky," allows Kampmann, "that Second City gave us the flexibility to be able to write. Trying to get acting work down there is next to impossible." "It was a very natural transition," agrees Torokvei. "All the rules we learned still apply, so it was easy to go from sketch writing to doing twenty-four-minute scripts. Also, we were so underpaid in theater that we went for the highest paying jobs we could find."

Linda Kash has determined, "If you come out of Second City being a writer, you have a different perspective in writing for women. I know when I get out, I would certainly hope to write something that would help women in comedy."

Ann Elder, who has written hundreds of TV programs from Lily Tomlin and Neil Diamond specials to Disneyland extravaganzas, has further disseminated the Second City connection through creative writing classes she's taught.

The Second City influence is at work in myriad unexpected ways, on everything from police dramas to talk shows. Of the former, Betty Thomas (Officer Lucille Bates on *Hill Street Blues*), feels that "the assertiveness I learned in the green room at Second City has helped me in general working with men. Once again, I've found myself in an all-male environment, on *Hill Street Blues*. Second City taught me to work with men and make my point without being a shrew, and to have a good time."

"When I go on Johnny Carson's show," says Arlene Golonka, "they give you an outline, and then you improvise, moment to moment. That free-form improvisation hits and misses all the time. But if you have the techniques, you really can be good. Sometimes you don't even need an outline, because it all pours out." David Steinberg agrees. "On *The Tonight Show*, Carson and I improvise very much like Jack Burns and I used to do. He just takes a word, or an idea, and we improvise. Provided that you've read and informed yourself, it's how much you can *not* prepare, that's how successful you'll be."

On the big screen, Second City players have seemingly banded together to dominate the motion picture industry—Dan Aykroyd, Bill Murray, Harold Ramis, and Rick Moranis in *Ghostbusters;* Bill Murray, John Candy, and Harold Ramis in *Stripes* (cowritten by Harold Ramis); Dan Aykroyd and John Belushi in *The Blues Brothers* and *Neighbors;* John Candy and Eugene Levy in *Armed and Dangerous* (originally begun as a Dan Aykroyd–John Belushi project; screenplay by Harold Ramis and Peter Torokvei); Rick Moranis, Eugene Levy, Andrea Martin, Brian Doyle-Murray, Joe Flaherty, Steven Kampmann, Robin Duke, and Mary Gross in *Club Paradise* (directed by Harold Ramis; screenplay by Brian Doyle-Murray and Harold Ramis); Jim Belushi in *About Last Night . . .* (loosely based on David Mamet's Obie-winning *Sexual Perversity in Chicago*, screenplay cowritten by Tim Kazur-

James Belushi (left) and Rick Moranis (right) in Little Shop of Horrors. *(Photo copyright 1986 The Geffen Film Company)*

insky); Rick Moranis, Jim Belushi, John Candy, and Bill Murray in *Little Shop of Horrors;* John Candy, Joe Flaherty, Eugene Levy, Paul Dooley, Murphy Dunne and Richard Libertini in *Going Berserk* (directed and co-written by David Steinberg); Severn Darden as a learned scientist questioning dolphins in *Day of the Dolphin* (directed by Mike Nichols); and Bill Murray, J. J. Barry, Murphy Dunne, Roberta Maguire, Avery Schreiber, Doug Steckler, and Betty Thomas in *Loose Shoes* (directed by Ira Miller) merely highlight a list of joint endeavors that cannot but grow.

Along with the players themselves, the Second City connection has drawn Chicago into the cinematic fold. When John Belushi made *Continental Divide*, he modeled his character on Chicago columnist and family friend Mike Royko. Aykroyd and Belushi's *The Blues Brothers*, filmed on location in Chicago, wrought havoc on the city. As the result of one car chase, the Bluesmobile crashed through the window of the Richard J. Daley Center. Mayor Jane Byrne was unperturbed. "Let them be. They want to make Chicago a film center." By the time outdoor shooting was over, *The Blues Brothers* had brought Chicago ten million dollars in revenue. Chicago had come a long way since the days when Mayor Daley discouraged the making of movies in his town for fear that Chicago would only inspire gangster flicks. Even though Jim Belushi and Dan Aykroyd are slated for a comic remake of *Dragnet*, David Mamet recently wrote the screenplay for a new version of *The Untouchables* as well as an episode for *Hill Street Blues*, and Dan Aykroyd's name is bandied about as someone who might play Eliot Ness. . . .

Second City players make movies together for the same reasons they do everything else together. They like each other. Says Harold Ramis, "It's more than liking their work. I like *them*. I would rather be involved in a failed enterprise with people I really like than succeed with people I don't. So I treasure those experiences, and when I'm given the opportunity, I do work with these people. Also because they're great. In *Club Paradise*, which did not get very good reviews, the real strengths of the movie are the Second City performances. There's no time wasted with those people." To one reviewer, the movie "seemed like a kind of summit meeting of the best and brightest comic/satiric talents of a generation."

Dan Aykroyd and John Belushi meet with Chicago's Mayor Jane Byrne while in town to make the movie The Blues Brothers. *(Photo courtesy of Paul Natkin/ Photo Reserve, Inc.)*

Second City players bypass endless hours of preliminaries because they speak the same language and work with the same tools. Ramis first directed Bill Murray in *Meatballs* and *Caddyshack,* and found that "What it comes to very often when you're working with Bill is just pitching the script, at the very last minute, and starting from scratch. Building complete scenes through our technique. Setting up the beats, setting certain key lines that you work to, and then just trying. So instead of doing the same script six takes, you do six versions on six takes and edit the high points of each. Or you get one great take. Sometimes, he will do a flawless improv, just flawless."

These days, when movie people come to shoot in Chicago, they make a beeline to Second City to recruit for the cast. In Toronto, says producer Sally Cochrane, "because Toronto is the New York and Los Angeles of Canada, just by getting into the touring company, a player will be approached by an agent. A player who gets on the main stage has his or her pick of agents. Sometimes, within days of joining the resident company, Second City performers get auditions for small parts, voice-overs, and commercials, and can be very busy."

The success of the Second City connection is no secret. In fact, says Bernie Sahlins, "We're so successful, it has almost become a standing joke

To date, Ed Asner is the only Second City graduate to be represented twice at Movieland Wax Museum—once as the slavemaster in Roots, *and once as his Emmy Award–winning character Lou Grant, with whom he is shown posing here. (Photo courtesy of the Movieland Wax Museum)*

around here. There's hardly anybody nowadays about whom we're not asked, 'Didn't he start at Second City?' I've gotten to the point where I just say yes to everyone. 'Sure, Steve Allen started here. Of course, Will Rogers was here.' " He's even kidded about renaming the place the Ratzioni Handbag Company "in order to regain some privacy."

THE SECOND CITY
(1987–?)

Not much more than twenty-five years ago, an experimental art form called The Second City began visibly, significantly, and increasingly over time to alter the face of Chicago theater. Like ripples in a pool, its influence spread. Today, The Second City qualifies as one of the longest-running creators of comedy in the history of English-language theater. As The Second City enters its second quarter-century, nothing seems more likely than that history will repeat itself.

"The present speaks for itself and so does the past," says Andrew Alexander, whose affection for the entertainment arts—from large screen to small screen to stage—bears a striking resemblance to the fervor that inspired Second City's theater-loving founding fathers in the fifties.

Accordingly, he's set his sights on new horizons. "So far, beyond our immediate stages, we haven't controlled our future at all, which hasn't been the ideal arrangement for either our graduates or for Second City. I've wanted to do something about it for a long time, and made an in-depth survey about opening up an operation in Los Angeles because I feel that if we had a full-time operation there, it would be advantageous for everyone concerned. The people we send there would be from the Toronto and Chicago stages, and Los Angeles is the logical place for our graduates to showcase themselves, which will be a huge improvement over just going the audition route. Some really great actors don't always give really great auditions, particularly when they're new in town. But this way, instead of sitting at home waiting for the phone to ring, they'll be making their mark and getting valuable exposure night after night. Moreover, we hope to move into the television production business and generate some of our own projects with these people and the Second City people who are already out there.

"We'll be taking the philosophy of the stage and transferring it to film and television. I think we have established certain standards that we shoot for, and I think that we can be part of the industry, and be in closer contact with the studios and the networks, without sacrificing our working attitude. The fruits of this will become obvious from the projects that will emerge and somehow cut a new edge. For instance, *SCTV* was such a rewarding experience in this regard that I don't see why we can't continue to break new ground.

"In the grand scheme of things—it might take ten years, it might take five—I'd like to view us as a kind of mini-MTM, maybe a major MTM. That type of nurturing production company. It espoused the kind of standards that I appreciate in production, and the people we turn out have consistently flourished in that kind of climate.

"Chicago and Toronto will still exist and the body of the work is not going to change, although I'm sure that what we do will have an enormous impact on both companies. But we're going to go into the nineties controlling our future a little better. Rather than seeing where the medium will take us, we'd like to see where we can take the medium."

If only with the evidence of history behind it, The Second City's future can hardly be in doubt. All in all, it's good to know that whatever world crises the nineties may bring, The Second City will be around to help us maintain a sense of humor.

The Second City Family
(as of December 1986)

Alan Alda
Andrew Alexander
Jane Alexander
Howard Alk
Bill Alton
Dana Andersen
Bill Applebaum
Alan Arkin
Larry Arrick
Rose Arrick
Ed Asner
Steve Assad
Dan Aykroyd
Peter Aykroyd
Bob Bainborough
Tom Baker
Sandra Balcovske
Sandy Baron
J. J. Barry
Barbara Barsky
Joan Bassie
Lloyd Battista
Walter Beakel
Mindy Bell
Jim Belushi
John Belushi
Robert Benedetti
Shelley Berman
Haym Bernson
Dick Blasucci
Joel Bloom
David Blum
Eric Boardman
Roger Bowen
Peter Boyle
Danny Breen
Nonie Newton-Breen
John Brent
Valri Bromfield
Rob Bronstein
Hildy Brooks
R. Victor Brown
Susan Bugg
Jack Burns
Mona Burr
Lucy Butler
Maggie Butterfield

Hamilton Camp
Alex Canaan
John Candy
Sandra Caron
Carol Cassis
Dan Castellaneta
Cindy Cavalenes
Loretta Chiljian
Del Close
Sally Cochrane
Gabe Cohen
Stephanie Cotsirilos
Robert Coughlan
Suzette Couture
Larry Coven
Kevin Crowley
Dennis Cunningham
Bob Curry
Barbara Dana
Dawn Daniel
Cassandra Danz
Severn Darden
Ian Davidson
Don Depollo
Bob Derkach
Don Dickinson
Melinda Dillon
Bob Dishy
Macintyre Dixon
Nancy Dolman
Brenda Donohue
Paul Dooley
Robin Duke
Andrew Duncan
Murphy Dunne
Jayne Eastwood
Bekka Eaton
Steven Ehrlick
Peter Elbling
Ann Elder
Jeff Ellis
Melissa Ellis
Robert Elman
Tom Erhart
June Ericson
Jim Fay
Meagen Fay

Jim Fisher
Joe Flaherty
Ted Flicker
Miriam Flynn
Josephine Raciti Forsberg
Martin Harvey Friedburg
Cathy Gallant
Gail Garnett
Susan Gauthier
Brian George
Michael Gellman
Piers Gilson
Carey Goldenberg
Ben Gordon
Bobbi Gordon
Mark Gordon
June Graham
Judy Graubart
Ed Greenberg
Joel Greenberg
Mary Gross
Sid Grossfeld
Allan Guttman
Mike Hagerty
Philip Baker Hall
Rick Hall
Larry Hankin
Deborah Harmon
Valerie Harper
Barbara Harris
Judy Harris
Melissa Hart
John Hemphill
Jo Henderson
Nate Herman
Burt Heyman
Mo Hirsch
Pam Hoffman
Isabella Hoffman
Anthony Holland
Sandy Holt
David Huband
Bonnie Hunt
Kenna Hunt
Ken Innes
Tino Insana
Henry Jaglom

Ron James
Bruce Jarchow
Gene Kadish
Lee Kalcheim
Steven Kampmann
Irene Kane
John Kapelos
Jerrold Karch
Linda Kash
Fred Kaz
Tim Kazurinsky
Maureen Kelly
Gail Kerbel
Richard Kind
Lance Kinsey
Deborah Kimmet
Robert Klein
Keith Knight
Mina Kolb
Richard Kurtzman
Don Lake
Don Lamont
Zohra Lampert
Kathleen Lasky
Linda Lavin
Martin Lavut
Sid Lazard
Mickey LeClaire
Eugene Levy
Charles Lewson
Richard Libertini
Ron Liebman
Lynn Lipton
Shelley Long
Roberta Maguire
Freya Manston
Andrea Martin
Sandy Martin
Erin Martin
Bill Mathieu
Elaine May
Paul Mazursky
Nancy McCabe-Kelly
Robin McCullough
Debra McGrath
Derek McGrath
Anne Meara
Jeff Michalski
Ira Miller
Mike Miller

Lucy Minnerle
Raul Moncada
John Monteith
Judy Morgan
Jane Morris
George Morrison
Harry Murphy
Brian Doyle-Murray
Bill Murray
Mike Myers
Allen Myerson
Jessica Myerson
Audrie Neenan
Mike Nichols
Catherine O'Hara
Tom O'Horgan
Sheldon Patinkin
Robert Patton
David Paulsen
Lawrence Perkins
Denise Pidgeon
Bruce Pirrie
Nancy Ponder
Will Porter
Rosemary Radcliffe
Gilda Radner
Harold Ramis
Suzanne Rand
David Rasche
Fiona Reid
Mert Rich
Maria Ricossa
Rob Riley
Joan Rivers
Harv Robbin
Carol Robinson
Tony Rosato
Eric Ross
Eugenie Ross-Leming
Lee Ryan
Ann Ryerson
Bernard Sahlins
Gerry Salsberg
Albert Salzer
Paul Sand
Diana Sands
Reni Santoni
Dick Schaal
Larry Schanker
Harvey Schaps

Avery Schreiber
Jeanette Schwaba
Lynda Segal
Omar Shapli
John Shank
David Shepherd
Suzanne Shepherd
George Sherman
Jim Sherman
Peg Shirley
Martin Short
Paul Sills
Cyril Simon
Kim Sisson
Joyce Sloane
Jon Smet
Viola Spolin
Jim Staahl
Leslie J. Stark
Doug Steckler
David Stein
David Steinberg
Jerry Stiller
Janice St. John
Ruby Streak
Maggie Sullivan
Craig Taylor
Paul Taylor
Dorthy Tenute
Deb Theaker
Betty Thomas
Dave Thomas
Richard Thomas
Dave Thompson
Peter Torokvei
Eugene Troobnick
Adrian Truss
Larry Tucker
Tom Virtue
George Wendt
Ron Weyand
Penny White
Collin Wilcox
Mary Charlotte Wilcox
Fred Willard
Mark Wilson
Mary Louise Wilson
Victor Wong
Paul Zegler
Dan Ziskie

Index